D0275301

Responsibility Accounting and Performance Evaluations

Responsibility Accounting and Performance Evaluations

Elwood L. Miller, Ph.D., C.P.A.

Saint Louis University

 VAN NOSTRAND REINHOLD COMPANY
NEW YORK CINCINNATI TORONTO LONDON MELBOURNE

Van Nostrand Reinhold Company Regional Offices:
New York   Cincinnati

Van Nostrand Reinhold Company International Offices:
London   Toronto   Melbourne

Library of Congress Catalog Card Number: 81-10326
ISBN: 0-442-28818-2

Manufactured in the United States of America

Published by Van Nostrand Reinhold Company
135 West 50th Street, New York, N.Y. 10020

Published simultaneously in Canada by Van Nostrand Reinhold Ltd.

15 14 13 12 11 10 9 8 7 6 5 4 3 2 1

Library of Congress Cataloging in Publication Data

Miller, Elwood L.
    Responsibility accounting and performance
evaluations.

    Bibliography: p.
    Includes index.
    1. International business enterprises—Accounting.
2. Executives, Rating of. I. Title.
HF5686.I56M55   658.3'125   81-10326
ISBN 0-442-28818-2   AACR2

To my teammate,
Virginia

Preface

Complex industrial companies are in various stages of metamorphosis from domestic corporations to multinational enterprises to transnational networks. A few are about to step (or be pushed) across the final threshold.

Multinational enterprises represented the first organizations that attempted to marshal and manage resources on a global basis. Overseas operations have now completed their evolution from stepchildren to strategic links. Today, overseas activities are accounting for more than half the volumes and earnings of a growing number of U.S.-based corporations. Wittingly or not, multinational enterprises have assumed responsibility for the efficient and effective employment of the world's economic and human resources entrusted to their care.

Growth has been accompanied by growing pains. Stockholders have been transformed into stakeholders—employees, trade unions, managers, investors, communities, governments, and other influential groups—with a variety of interests and concerns. Decentralization has given way to an uncomfortable (if not alien) form of coordinative management. Familiar unidimensional measures of performance (suspect even in simpler times) have been rendered obsolete. Multiplicities of environments, situations, objectives, roles, and participants —as well as the ever present conflicts and tradeoffs—have created a maze of interdependencies that often seem to defy solution.

This book attempts to provide help in recognizing the problem and its significance, identifying the issues involved, examining the issues in context, and suggesting *approaches* to more realistic evaluations of activities and their managers. Solutions cannot be offered because few, if any, exist. Realistic performance evaluations are situational. Moreover, they are attitudinal. Very sensitive, personal aspects are involved. Since situations and attitudes change, the best that can be achieved here is an attempt to paint a still picture of a moving scene.

Executives at all levels—those who evaluate others and those who are evaluated in turn—may find something of value in this book. Also, young people who aspire to become executives may benefit from the experiences and opinions presented. (It may, however, prove to be that the greatest benefits will accrue to those who—unlike the author —have yet to reach the age at which their attitudes and opinions are no longer malleable.) In any event, an effort has been made to organize the book to enable the reader to peruse information presented for recall and reconsideration, as well as to examine topics of particular interest.

Realistic performance evaluations represent a collaborative enterprise. All participants, including the chief executives of the entities concerned, should be afforded the opportunity to exercise effective influence over the manner in which their performances will be judged. Desire, ingenuity, and common sense can produce tangible benefits for all concerned.

Acknowledgments

All works are built upon the ideas of others. This book is no exception.

The studies, opinions, and suggestions of many pioneers, contemporary writers, and practitioners concerning the dilemmas of performance evaluations have been appropriately acknowledged. However, the seeds of ideas implanted by countless teachers and business associates—many whose names have fallen victims to a poor memory—have been woven into the weft and warp of this book, unacknowledged but not unappreciated.

Particular gratitude is owed to many. Among the executives who contributed valuable time and ideas were: Mr. H.B. Klenk, Controller, 3M Company; Mr. Robert Staley, Chief Financial Officer, Emerson Electric Company; Mr. James J. Kerley, Chief Financial Officer, and Mr. William W. Teeple, Assistant Treasurer-International Financial Planning and Analysis, Monsanto Company. Systems and approaches that fit the particular circumstances of their respective companies have been summarized in Appendixes to this book.

Gratitude and special appreciation was earned by my wife, Virginia, who typed each word many times, provided constructive criticism, and served as a considerate (but demanding) taskmaster.

Special thanks should also go to the several publishers that granted permissions to reproduce selected materials, and to the editors at Van Nostrand Reinhold for their interest and efficiency.

Books, much like children, can only be nurtured up to a point at which they must be ushered into the world on their own. Both events seem to occur prematurely, often leaving important things undone.

Errors of omission and commission are mine.

Suggestions and comments are invited and would be appreciated.

Contents

9. REALISTIC EVALUATIONS 168

10. FUTURE CHANGE 192

Responsibility Accounting and Performance Evaluations

1
The Problems in Perspective

Most issues in business can be placed into context without a great deal of difficulty. Reasonable solutions may not be all that easy to develop, to be sure, but at least the problems can be defined, if not structured. The issues concerning performance evaluations seem to be exceptions.

Inasmuch as business endeavors are social arts, the attitudes, traits, and practices of people are involved. At any given time there will be individual and collective differences. Just as certainly, these same characteristics will change with time and circumstance. Beyond these relatively safe generalizations, few others will hold true where performance evaluations are concerned. That's simply the nature of the topic.

What follows in this chapter represents an abbreviated overview of the many-faceted problems confronting performance evaluations. All will be examined in depth within the appropriate sections of this book that follow. Those that appear to remain as barriers to realistic evaluations will be addressed in the final chapters, along with some conjectures regarding future change.

THE CURRENT DILEMMAS

Performance evaluations actually concern people evaluating people. Of course, business units (or responsibility centers) are also evaluated, but these impersonal things do not function unless people make them go. Consequently, people assessing the efforts of others represent the crux of the matter—and perhaps the most important dilemma as well.

Many executives—and just one would be too many—fail to recognize (or have permitted the pressures of time to obscure) the fact that the focus of performance evaluation is upon people. In some cases, assessments of operating units and their managers have become confused. In other instances, evaluations of activities have assumed primacy. The contributions of managers have been relegated to lesser importance—not unlike the position taken by Frederick W. Taylor in the early 1900s that man was an adjunct to a machine.

All sorts of factors have contributed to the problem. Decentralization made complex enterprises manageable, therefore possible. The delegations of authority necessary to create the shared-management structures, however, also created a host of attendant problems.

Attempts to classify the problems proved to be rather frustrating. From the standpoint of origin, broad classifications of external and internal issues were possible. Such classifications, however, were so broad that they were vague and not very useful. Furthermore, solution to a problem in one area often created one or more in another.

Classification by type of problem suggested quite a few groupings: attitudinal, conceptual, situational, mechanical, and implementational. Such segmentation held promise. Significant problems persist in each of the categories today. Also, classification by type of problem would be useful. Although the ordering was not hierarchial, it was somewhat functional or procedural, at least. In other words, solutions to attitudinal or conceptual issues would also help point out logical choices in action concerning problems in subsequent areas. Some very fine lines separated the classes of problems, however, and the problems themselves required examination before choices in action could be identified. Consequently, that approach was reserved for summary treatment of the issues in the latter part of this book.

The above efforts did point out the importance of situational factors. Evaluation problems increased as decentralized domestic firms found it desirable to have some of their units perform significant work for others. The problems increased geometrically as these firms evolved into multinational enterprises. Today, performance evaluations of domestic and foreign operations (as well as their respective managers) represent two different activities entirely. Consequently, it seemed appropriate to begin by examining the issues within the context of the domestic environment initially, then within the international domain.

Domestic Issues

The invention of responsibility accounting provided a basic conceptual and structural framework. A variety of responsibility centers were devised, each differing in scope and purpose. Managers of the centers were presumed to have control over certain input and output relationships which, in turn, suggested reasonable methods to evaluate activities and their managers.

In short, responsibility accounting helped supply options, as well as some solutions, to the following questions:

- How many and what kinds of responsibility centers are needed?
- What should be the objectives of the units?
- What are the roles of the units and their managers?
- What criteria should be used to measure the performance of units and managers?
- What standards should be employed to evaluate the measurements produced?
- How often should the evaluations be performed?
- How should the results be communicated?

Over time, trial and error produced successes and refinements. Lessons were learned from experience. Some questions were answered while others were raised. Today, executives of few multinational enterprises are entirely satisfied with the evaluations of their *domestic* operations and managers, much less their foreign counterparts.

At the outset, domestic companies had to decide whether or not the management reins should be loosened and, if so, how much. (Emerging companies face the same problems today.) Growing pains usually solved the first problem, but not the second.

The structural peculiarities of the industries and the companies themselves helped to determine the types and numbers of centers, as well as the authorities to be delegated to their managers. The remaining problem involved how to influence the decisions of subordinate managers so that actions taken would be compatible with the best interests of the company. Conflicts arose between autonomy and control, as well as between short- and long-term objectives. These conflicts have yet to be resolved satisfactorily.

As more and more domestic units began to furnish goods and services to related units, the resultant maze of interdependencies blurred the roles of individual units. Original concepts of autonomy, control, and purpose no longer fit as neatly as before. Organizational structures were examined, revised, then changed again.

Control and reporting systems were revamped to accommodate and respond to changing needs. Electronic data processing brought mixed blessings and reactions. Some firms chose to employ EDP to get better information to line managers faster, thereby enabling a greater degree of decentralization—or at least helping it to work better. Other companies saw in EDP the opportunity to recentralize authority for certain "big decisions." Roles changed in nearly all firms.

Evaluations of the contributions of individual units and managers were also subjected to closer scrutiny. Interdependencies raised questions of controllability, traceability, and equity. Should evaluations of the contributions of activities and managers differ and, if so, how? Should the expenses associated with support services and shared assets be allocated, or, are all such arbitrary apportionments self-serving and self-defeating? Should goal congruence or equity prevail where transfer prices are concerned? Who should be responsible for the effects of those big decisions made by the headquarters? Finally, substantial changes in the trends of domestic price-levels, both general and specific, raised the question of separating the results of circumstance (good as well as bad) from those of accomplishment.

Measurement systems were challenged as some became blunt and others obsolete. Different means were necessary to measure efficiency and effectiveness. Standard-cost and flexible-budget methods—once virtually limited to production activities—were found to be appropriate and useful for application to all sorts of service and support activities by many progressive organizations.

(In fact, there is considerable evidence to support the opinion that there have been more innovative applications of flexible budgeting by not-for-profit organizations, companies engaged in services, and the support activities of industrial firms than by units producing and marketing products. A service or expense activity that remains a conspicuous exception is the EDP center. Many companies continue attempts to "control" EDP costs by allocating them away, in whole or in part, to other units, rather than making the internal quantitative and qualitative evaluations applicable to any other expense center.)

The validity of the normative measures that many managements had grown accustomed to, and comfortable with, became subject to more frequent and serious doubts. Had interdependencies also obscured the identifications of profits with activities, as well as the relationships of profits with assets employed by those activities? Could it be that profit—never really considered to be a reasonable measure of effectiveness—had also become suspect, due to circumstances, as a realistic measure of accomplishment or contribution? Similarly, had the familiar macro measure, return on investment—flawed even in simpler times—become misleading when applied to micro units? If so, had not the more flexible residual income measure been invalidated as well where contributions of individual units and managers were concerned? Finally, did all these profit-based measures, standing alone, emphasize short-term results that might not be compatible with the best long-run interests of companies?

As measures became questionnable, so did the standards or benchmarks with which they were compared. However, the variability of one national standard—the dollar—served to emphasize the defects peculiar to all the normative, monetary measures. Instability of the dollar finally motivated many chief executives to ask difficult questions that were long overdue. What alternatives for money measures exist? Which are appropriate for our company? Since monetary measures will remain necessary for many other purposes, how can the effects of changing price-levels be separated from those of operations?

Are multiple measures and standards needed? If so, how can we avoid "paralysis of analysis"? What measurements will trigger correct responses from managers—from other stakeholders? Should situational, rather than normative, approaches be considered? What relationships exist, or should exist, between managerial and financial reporting systems? What are other companies doing? What are the costs connected with changing our approaches, with maintaining the status quo?

International Complications

For some companies, excursions into international operations are relatively new. Others have become experienced multinational enterprises (MNEs). All are faced with the same (or similar) complicating factors of multiple environments, distortions, and considerations.

The established MNEs had to contend with the domestic challenges mentioned previously, as well as those encountered in foreign environments, and at the same time. However, concurrent attention enabled many seemingly different problems to be assimilated and re-solved, albeit with varying degrees of interest and success.

Some of the relative newcomers in international business can be said to have recognized domestic problems only as the result of attempts to address those new-found ones encountered overseas. A minority, however, have yet to become aware of the problems or their possible consequences.

All the domestic problems cited previously were the products of a single, relatively uniform environment that American companies had taken for granted. Foreign operations must contend with a myriad of different, often alien, environments. Means must be devised to understand, neutralize, and/or eliminate the distortions introduced by the multiplicity of different: languages, laws, government regulations, political expediencies, social customs, foreign currencies, banking regulations, inflation factors, interest rates, tax bases and rates, accounting requirements, and reporting practices. Add to the above the complicating factors of distance and communication, and some idea of the external distortions (or cultural shocks) can be gleaned.

Exportations of domestic practices encountered a variety of barriers. People-intensive environments frowned upon and/or prohibited machine-intensive operations. Attitudes toward work, policies regarding overtime, packages of wages and benefits, and hosts of other variables affected productivity, efficiency, and effectiveness. All sorts of tradeoffs and changes in thinking were necessary. After a while, some American expatriate managers assimilated their adopted cultures so well that they too became indigenous. The resulting communication and attitudinal problems led many MNEs to adopt policies requiring rotational tours of duty for expatriate managers.

External variables involving economic, legal, tax, and political environments presented profitable opportunities as well as significant risks. Internal changes were employed to enhance opportunities, circumvent barriers, and ameliorate risks.

Foreign operations were assigned various strategic roles, thereby enabling MNEs to purchase, produce, assemble, distribute, market, and accumulate profits wherever conditions were the most desirable. Organizational structures and reporting systems were not only flexible, but often subject to what seemed to be continuous change.

Most U.S.-based MNEs learned, early on, that they could use "managed" transfer prices to circumvent nearly every barrier imposed by local regulations. However, all too few recognized that, if transfer prices were to be used in pursuit of strategic objectives, the domestic objective—pursuit of equity among interdependent units— had to be abandoned. Perhaps even fewer really considered how the resulting inequities were to be addressed.

Some MNEs not only used, but blatantly abused transfer pricing mechanisms. Protests of developing countries motivated the indus- trialized nations to promulgate—through the Organization for Eco- nomic Cooperation and Development (OECD)—a code of international business conduct in June, 1976. A prominent feature of the OECD guidelines required disclosures of various consolidated and disag- gregated information, including "intragroup" pricing-policies. (See Appendix 1A.)

The United States also became concerned over receiving its proper share of taxes on the earnings of controlled foreign operations. Sev- eral methods of surveillance and increased authorities were furnished the U.S. Internal Revenue Service, particularly:[1]

- *Subpart F*—concurrent U.S. taxation of covert distributions of earnings.
- *Section 482*—monitoring of transfer prices, and IRS authority to reallocate incomes/deductions in foreign transactions between related taxpayers.
- *Section 367*—prevention of tax evasion on gains from transfer/ sale of appreciated assets, or from reorganizations of foreign affiliates.
- *Section 861*—establishment of geographic source-of-income rules to identify and apportion foreign-source incomes and expenses.

In addition to the multiplicities of the normal business variables cited, two unique problems were encountered overseas—different accounting methods and foreign currencies.

In the final analysis, restatements of operating results in accordance with U.S. accounting practices for consolidation purposes represented only mechanical, nuisance problems. Nonetheless, the process created two different operating-income numbers and someone had to decide which one was real.

Foreign currencies presented a variety of mechanical, conceptual, and real problems. The mechanics of translating statements and budgets were also nuisance factors, yet, unlike those relating to accounting methods, a variety of approaches were available until *FASB-8* was issued in 1975.[2] Here again, multiple income numbers were produced. Which were real—those in foreign currencies or U.S. dollars? Translations of balance sheets also produced differences for parent companies to assess. Were these differences real or imaginary? How should they be reflected? Budget submissions required decisions on rates to be used and, if different rates were applied to actual results, what did the differences represent and who was responsible for them? Ongoing transactions involved risks of real (conversion) losses. How could these risks be minimized? Who was in the best position to manage the risks? What were the associated costs?

Finally, most MNEs learned that decentralization was the *antithesis* of multinational enterprise. The true potentials of global operations could only be pursued if their inherent flexibilities were centrally coordinated. Functions considered to be vital were recentralized and orchestrated by the parents. Then, the final straw was added to the burdens of unit identities—expenses of providing common services were allocated to the units by parent companies.

VIOLATIONS IN PRACTICE

Economic reality is a much used, little understood, phrase. Perhaps "common sense" would be more appropriate. Where performance evaluations are concerned, violations of common sense must be placed squarely upon executive attitudes and accounting practices. Taken together, the effects might be termed "management myopia."

Management Attitudes

Changes in a relatively few management attitudes would not solve the problems that exist, but such changes would surely initiate efforts in the right direction. Just as surely, improvements will not be forthcoming without direction from the top.

Some executives are determined to evaluate others as they perceive themselves to be judged. Boardroom attitudes override all other considerations. Usually such attitudes manifest themselves in applications of profit and return-on-investment measures to others who are really not responsible for profitability in any reasonable sense. If return-on-investment and similar accomplishments are essentially *cooperative* results, who or what is really being evaluated? A more inane extension of this attitude is typified by the practice of assigning foreign subsidiaries ROI target-rates that are admittedly beyond achievement by any stretch of the imagination. Such practices can become expensive games.

Ethnocentrism might be an appropriate label for the malady afflicting executives who cannot think beyond domestic frameworks. (On second thought, the malady may even be more pervasive since domestic evaluation practices, suspect in themselves, have been applied—with or without adjustment—to overseas operations.) MNEs are not decentralized companies. The organizational and environmental complexities of international operations cannot be ignored. Neither can the strategic roles and multiple objectives of units continue to be relegated to secondary or tertiary importance behind profit generations that have become more circumstantial than anything else.

Realities are confused, if not ignored. Interdependencies have obscured the traceability of contributions to subsidiaries, as well as the controllability of many important variables by managers. Consequently, the sin of sins is committed whenever the duality that exists is ignored, and evaluations of units and managers are made without any distinctions whatsoever.

Many senior executives stipulate that they simply do not have adequate time. That is probably true. Also, at annual compensation levels of half a million dollars or more, that time is certainly expensive. However, they can inform subordinate officials that normative measures may be expedient, but are no longer relevant. Simplex approaches to complex issues need not be tolerated—nor would they continue if the word would be issued that more realistic methods were required.

Other executives agree that the measures used are faulty, but they are the best available. Such comments, if accepted literally, represent myopic preferences for expediency over common sense. Few senior executives achieved their positions suffering from myopia. More likely than not, such statements really acknowledge the multiplicity of interdependencies, objectives, and trade-offs that compound problems of evaluation. What seems to be necessary is acceptance of the fact that, although an ideal system may be impossible, existing systems can be made more realistic. (Symptomatic of real problems, however, would be fears that multiple measurements might enable a manager to be rewarded for achieving important strategic objectives although the profit goal assigned was not met.)

Accounting Follies

As an accountant, the author at one time believed that accountants could measure and report economic events in almost any manner desired, so long as someone was willing to pay the attendant costs. Experience transformed that belief into a concern that consolidation practices and taxation (as well as other forms of politicization) had removed financial reportings from the realm of reality. The well-intentioned but misdirected pronouncements of the FASB have further transformed that original belief into a suspicion that financial accounting attempts to do the impossible with unsound theory ill-applied. A related apprehension is that the myths woven into financial accounting will spill over and contaminate managerial accountings—and managerial decisions.

Even if the different objectives of financial and managerial accountings are recognized, it should also be *realized* that not all relevant dimensions of performance can be included in *any* accounting data. Strategic objectives and monetary instabilities call for the prudent use of a variety of nonaccounting measures. If not, accounting data may commingle the results of accomplishment and circumstance or, worse yet, provide misleading indicators.

Perhaps the greatest accounting folly surrounds the unidimensional emphasis placed upon profitability measures. That statement does not argue that profits are unimportant. To the contrary, profits must continue to be recognized as "the business of business." Without profits, businesses and their other related objectives would cease to exist. The point to be made is that, if interdependencies destroy realistic identifications of profits with the activities generating them, then applications of macro measures to micro units may only produce misleading results.

All too many methods of performance evaluations violate the precepts of financial and responsibility accounting. There are no realistic, comprehensive accounting measures of performance. Where autonomous units are concerned, accounting data can be designed to furnish reasonable measures of the outcome of operations, at least in nominal dollars. To the extent that managers of those units have control over operations, accounting data can also provide insights into managerial efficiency. The reasonableness of accounting measures of *efficiency* varies inversely with increases in uncontrollable variables and interdependencies. Of course, accounting profits should always be considered suspect as measures of *effectiveness.*

As insinuated earlier, the FASB can claim the dubious distinction of contributing much toward transforming accounting information from sense to nonsense.

Undoubtedly, the now infamous *FASB-8* represented the furthest departure from reality. Based upon the manner in which the objectives were defined, *FASB-8* required that foreign operations be reported as if they had been conducted in the United States *and* in U.S. dollars. The analysis within *FASB-8* was structurally sound. The objectives were faulty. Even greater fault must be attached to the fact that the majority of the FASB (there was one sterling dissent) recognized that the results would be unreal, yet purposely decided *not* "to produce an exchange gain or loss that [was] compatible with the expected economic effect of a rate change. . . ."[3]

Since consolidated financial reports are myths, perhaps the addition of another myth would not have been all that important. However, *FASB-8* served to *sanctify* emphases upon measurements of foreign operations in U.S. dollars, both in internal and external reports.

(The impending revision—or renunciation—of *FASB-8* will probably be along the lines argued by the lone dissenter to the original pronouncement. The use of current rates—those existing at the date of the statements—for all items will retain the "essence" of foreign-currency statements. Also, the reportings of unrealized translation differences in temporary equity accounts will recapture some economic sense. Although revision is appropriate and overdue, the FASB will have, in the end, suffered a net loss of stature.)

Not many good marks can be awarded the FASB for its efforts over the last six years to identify the effects of changing price levels either. Here again, the FASB defined away most of the problem in its 1974 exposure draft that addressed only changes in general price levels.[4] In its latest experiment, *FASB-33*, the board decided not to decide.[5] Instead, selected summary data regarding general and specific price changes were to be disclosed as supplementary information. Although the information may not be realistic or useful, at least the FASB elected not to further devalue the primary financial reports.

Although additional examples could be cited here, those mentioned should serve to illustrate that searches for simplex, normative measures to apply to complex situations—and to expect to produce economic sense—are pursuits of the Holy Grail.

SIGNIFICANCE OF THE ISSUES

From the standpoint of interested outsiders, there is an increasing awareness that realistic performance evaluations represent one of the most significant, yet unresolved, issues confronting executives. Some insiders as well, particularly those being evaluated, realize that some very real problems exist.

Concerns of Outsiders

Performance evaluations of firms, segments, and managers create a variety of concerns among interested outsiders.

Academic curiosity is perhaps the least important, yet it will be mentioned first. There is no comprehensive collection of information that can provide insights into the state-of-the-art of performance evaluations insofar as multinational companies are concerned. This absence becomes increasingly relevant as more and more of the gross world product becomes the output of MNEs.

The majority of other outsider concerns would tend to fall in one or more of three categories: those of realism, time span, and economics.

Realism.   Decision making involves *rational* choices among alternatives. Choices can hardly be considered rational if they are not based upon realistic information.

Numerous outsider organizations are interested in assuring that realistic performance measures of companies are made available to them and to interested stakeholders. Common examples include: the Federal Trade Commission, the Securities and Exchange Commission, the FASB, the OECD, and the European Economic Community.

A variety of profit and non-accounting data, in macro as well as micro terms, are specified. Since the nature of companies has blunted consolidated and other macro information, greater emphasis has recently been placed upon disaggregated and non-accounting data. There is also some evidence of attempts to structure information so that future performances in some areas (such as cash flows) may be projected as well.

(It would appear, however, that efforts to obtain realistic future-oriented information are ill-advised until reportings of past events are considered to be reasonable.)

Time Span. Recurring criticism has been focused upon the perceived overemphasis—if not dependence—upon short-term financial measures such as return-on-investment.

Critics argue that decentralization, and the spawning of profit and investment centers, increased the structural distances between managers and those who evaluate their contributions. Those distances all but guaranteed dependence upon objective, short-term, profitability criteria.[6]

Some European observers believe that many American firms have, wittingly or not, gravitated toward the *rentier* philosophy common to French companies. Others hold that American firms tend to behave more like investment banks than businesses:

> The U.S. companies in my industry act like banks. All they are interested in is return on investment and getting their money back. Sometimes they act as though they are more interested in buying other companies than they are in selling products to consumers.[7]

In the international realm, abject reliance upon profitability and ethnocentric (one-way flow-of-funds) concepts have caused the demise of many successful foreign operations. Coca Cola in India is one example. Given the lack of emphasis, over time, upon value-added and similar contributions to the local economy, the Indian government used the company's profit data to advantage when the time was ripe. Profits earned and repatriated over time were compared with the firm's investment. When the former was found to exceed the latter several times, the American parent was asked, first to sell part of its ownership to indigenous investors, and eventually to sell out altogether. Certainly, many political considerations were involved as well, but the parent company's emphasis upon profits only served to exacerbate (and serve the purposes of) those considerations.

There is much to support the belief that today's multinational enterprise will either contract, or grow to become a "transnational network."[8] The global orientation inherent in the latter option calls for breadth of vision rather than tunnel vision.

Economic Consequences. There is a growing number of well informed, concerned outsiders who are converging upon a common opinion from different avenues. Collectively, the concern is growing that managements of American firms are suffering from *competitive myopia*.

In the Japanese view, the competitive myopia afflicting many American firms is the direct result of obsessions with short-term earnings:

> . . .American business is losing confidence in itself and especially confidence in its future. Instead of meeting the challenge of the changing world, American business today is making small, short-term adjustments by cutting costs and by turning to the government for temporary relief. . . .Success in trade is the result of patient and meticulous preparations, with a long period of market preparation. . . .hardly in the interest of a manager who is concerned with his or her next quarterly earnings report.[9]

Professor Raymond Vernon of Harvard University has probably studied MNEs longer than anyone else—and has proven to be one of their staunchest supporters. His criticisms (as well as those in this book) have been intended to serve constructive purposes. In Vernon's opinion, American MNEs are beginning to feel the effects of complacency and parochialism. A few decades ago, American technologies and resources precluded any real foreign competition in domestic or international markets. Instead of building upon that lead position, all too many "American companies were contentedly herding and milking their cash cows, convinced that they were the most innovative and efficient producers on the face of the earth."[10] One-way flows of funds, reluctance to seek out and invest in improved technologies, turning deaf ears toward advances and innovations in foreign markets, and the fallacious early demise of international divisions all lead to the diminution, if not surrender, of many foreign *and* domestic markets. The costs of such parochialism are evident in the steel, auto, chemical, and drug industries, among others, in which U.S. firms have now been forced to play catch up.

American firms can rebound and "stay out in front," Vernon argues, given some healthy, overdue changes in attitude.

Another management mentor, Peter Drucker, has expressed his concern that all too many companies have grown fat and complacent.[11] Both characteristics will lead to the demise of firms, both large and small, in the "turbulent times" that Drucker sees ahead. During long periods of relatively good times, organizations become complacent and tend to allocate resources by "inertia and tradition" rather than future promise.

Drucker contends that organizations need to *develop scorecards that assess the performances of management* in addressing the needs of the future. His "scorecard" would appraise management performance in four areas: appropriating capital, people decisions, innovation, and strategy. All areas suffer a common fault: elaborate analyses are made prior to making decisions, but only cursory evaluations, if any, are made of the actual results. Also, where subsequent evaluations are made, managements are often hesitant to admit making the wrong decisions and to take the corrective actions necessary.

In periods of turbulence, Drucker argues that the continued existence of many companies will depend upon their abilities to identify and know their "performing and productive resources—and especially [their] performing and productive people."[12]

Many of the evaluation components will be intangible, and most will not be quantifiable, yet all can be judged—"and fairly easily," in Drucker's opinion. Top managements *understand* the peculiarities and qualitative aspects of their markets, companies, and industries. This experience provides the "temperamental empathy" needed to *complement* blunt, short-term, unidimensional financial analyses.

In a broader vein, MNEs appear to be destined to manage the allocations, directly or through operating concessions, of increasing portions of the world's material and human resources. The potential costs of unsound decisions will have international economic impact.

Concerns of Insiders

Managers at all levels try to make what they consider to be "right" decisions. Yet, even right decisions, based upon certain assumptions of the future, may be invalidated by unforeseen circumstances. Consequently, as judgments of their judgments are subsequently made by others, managers are naturally concerned that expectations and circumstances will be considered fairly.

While all managers are accountable to others, the probabilities of receiving fair evaluations will depend in large measure upon the insights and attitudes of thier evaluators. Different echelons tend to pose different problems, although some concerns are shared.

Concerns of Local Managers. Naturally, if local managers are to be in position to make "right" decisions, they must know what is expected of them. What are their roles and objectives? Where conflicts exist, what weights are available to enable discriminations?

Since local managers engage in interdependent activities that impact operations of sister units and the parent, how will those contributions to other operations be identified and appraised?

Where lines of authority and responsibility are blurred, focus upon the wrong variables can not only distort accountability, but can result in misleading and unfair evaluations.

Mutual Concerns. Both local and top managers share common dilemmas.

How can distinctions be made between evaluations of activity and managerial performance? How can such systems be made operational? Will they work?

Should every product and activity "be put on trial for its life every few years" as some have suggested?[13] If adequate attention is given to the segments, will the whole take care of itself? Or, if the focus is placed upon the trees, will sight of the forest be lost?

Can new approaches to evaluation and motivation enhance competitive positions in world markets? Are the new approaches worth their increased costs in time and money?

Concerns of Top Management. As mentioned earlier, few top managers are completely satisfied with their evaluations of domestic operations, much less those in foreign countries. When taken together, some very thorny issues surface.

If alien forms of coordinative management facilitate the shiftings of global resources to manage growth and change, how can the interdependencies that result be considered in performance evaluations?

Would organization by world-product lines solve most of the problems of interdependency? On the other hand, would the rapport of international divisions with local markets be lost? Would a hybrid form of matrix organization be best?

How can the results of accomplishment be separated from those of circumstance? How can the effects of different foreign and domestic rates of inflation be isolated? Do strategic and environmental factors render the results of foreign operations noncomparable? If so, how can initial resource allocations be made on a rational basis, let alone subsequent assessments of those decisions?

Should financial evaluations be made in terms of foreign currencies or U.S. dollars; local or parent accounting and tax systems? If multiple measures are to be used, how can paralysis of analysis be avoided?

If internal dilemmas are resolved, will outside stakeholders understand and appreciate the new measures, or will they continue to focus upon traditional ROI and EPS evaluations? Would new, alternative methods of reporting earnings, resource evaluations, and accomplishments help outsiders make more realistic evaluations? If reporting practices are considered suspect until they become generally accepted, how can new methods be introduced?

Within all multinational enterprises, every manager worth his or her salt contends with most of the above issues, whether consciously or not.

PROBLEM RECOGNITION

As is the case with most issues, the first step toward resolution requires recognition that problems exist. Solutions (or at least progress toward them) will depend upon the attitudes and efforts of those in position to bring them about—the top executives who make the evaluations. Changes in attitudes will come about only when these executives believe it to be in their own best interests to do so.

More likely than not, top managements would admit that the national and international issues developed previously must be subordinated to those affecting themselves and their companies. It would be unnatural if it were otherwise. The point to be recognized, however, is that changing times and growing interdependencies have obscured, if not done away with, many former abilities to consider issues in isolation.

The former clean-cut demarcations between and among many of the roles of companies and countries have become indistinct. Companies have outgrown many of the countries in which they operate. Decisions to invest and disinvest can have traumatic effects upon national and regional economies. The effects (whether benefits or repercussions) reverberate and, much like echoes, return to those who generated them. Even the goliaths, such as the United States, would experience aftershocks from the failures of certain companies (such as Chrysler) and the flounderings of vital sectors (such as the steel, auto, and chemical industries). However, while many chief executives may attach some validity to slogans, such as, "What affects General Motors, affects the nation," they tend to ignore the corollary, "What affects the nation, affects General Motors." All too many national and multinational firms act as if they do not believe that consumers must be in position to *buy* the goods and services produced. To an ever increasing extent, the vitalities of local and national economies—particularly the average consumers within them —will do more to determine the good and bad times for businesses than all the pleas for additional tax concessions, protective quotas, and similar special-interest lobbyings. Companies can no longer espouse capitalism and free enterprise, on the one hand, yet seek to enlist the government as a partner on the other. Instead, interdependencies seem to call for an increase in genuine concern for raising the real standards of living of all customers.

Similarly, the internal demarcations between and among the roles of companies, segments, and managers have become obscured. Assessments of the *real* efficiency, effectiveness, and contributions of interdependent activities have become much more difficult, just at the time that the potential costs associated with unsound decisions have increased.

It would appear that most multinational systems of performance evaluations are inadequate. Continued obsessions with short-term unidimensional measures, ignorings of multiple objectives, and insensibilities toward situations and circumstances can only encourage misleading results and unsound decisions.

Recognition of the *need* for *realistic* performance evaluations is the pivotal step. Once that threshold is passed, it will also be recognized that fair assessments of the efficiency, effectiveness, and contributions of interdependent activities represent rather personal, subjective endeavors. The entire process will be recognized for what it really has become—a *collaborative enterprise*!

What will bring about these changes in attitudes? Perhaps a bit more maturation of the relatively young U.S.-based MNEs will be necessary. As multinational enterprises evolve into transnational networks, the diversity of stakeholders and their various interests should generate the necessary change in attitude from parochialism to internationalism.

NOTES

1. For further information, see: George C. Watt, Richard M. Hammer, and Marianne Burge, *Accounting for the Multinational Corporation* (New York: Financial Executives Research Foundation, 1977), chapters 27, 31, 32, and 33. (The title of this reference is broader than the contents. Principal topics are consolidated statements and taxation.)

2. Financial Accounting Standards Board, *Statement of Financial Accounting Standards No. 8:* "Accounting for the Translation of Foreign Currency Transactions and Foreign Currency Financial Statements" (Stamford, Conn: FASB, October 1975).

3. Ibid., p. 38.

4. Financial Accounting Standards Board, *Financial Reporting in Units of General Purchasing Power,* Exposure Draft, December 31, 1974.

5. Financial Accounting Standards Board, *Statement of Financial Accounting Standards No. 33:* "Financial Reporting and Changing Prices" (Stamford, Conn.: FASB, September 1979).

6. Robert H. Hayes and William J. Abernathy, "Managing Our Way to Economic Decline," *Harvard Business Review,* July-August 1980, p. 70.

7. Ibid., p. 68.

8. See Perlmutter in: Chapter 4.

9. Ryohei Suzuki, "Worldwide Expansion of U.S. Exports—A Japanese View," *Sloan Management Review,* Spring 1979, p. 1.

10. Raymond Vernon, "Gone are the Cash Cows of Yesteryear," *Harvard Business Review,* November-December 1980, p. 151.

11. Peter F. Drucker, "Managing for Tomorrow," *Industry Week,* April 14, 1980, pp. 54–57, 59, 63–64. This article was one of a series of prepublication excerpts by Drucker from his *Managing In Turbulent Times* (New York: Harper & Row, 1980), 239 pp.

12. Ibid., p. 55.

13. Ibid., p. 56.

OECD Guidelines for Disclosure of Information

Annex to the Declaration of 21st June 1976 by Governments of OECD Member Countries on International Investment and Multinational Enterprises

GUIDELINES FOR MULTINATIONAL ENTERPRISES

Disclosure of Information

Enterprises should, having due regard to their nature and relative size in the economic context of their operations and to requirements of business confidentiality and to cost, publish in a form suited to improve public understanding a sufficient body of factual information on the structure, activities and policies of the enterprise as a whole, as a supplement, insofar as necessary for this purpose, to information to be disclosed under the national law of the individual countries in which they operate. To this end, they should publish within reasonable time limits, on a regular basis, but at least annually, financial statements, and other pertinent information relating to the enterprise as a whole, comprising in particular:

i) the structure of the enterprise, showing the name and location of the parent company, its main affiliates, its percentage ownership, direct and indirect, in these affiliates, including shareholdings between them;

ii) the geographical areas* where operations are carried out and the principal activities carried on therein by the parent company and the main affiliates;

iii) the operating results and sales by geographical area and the sales in the major lines of business for the enterprise as a whole;

iv) significant new capital investment by geographical area and, as far as practicable, by major lines of business for the enterprise as a whole;

v) a statement of the sources and uses of funds by the enterprise as a whole;

vi) the average number of employees in each geographical area;

vii) research and development expenditure for the enterprise as a whole;

viii) the policies followed in respect of intra-group pricing;

ix) the accounting policies, including those on consolidation, observed in compiling the published information.

---

*For the purposes of the guideline on disclosure of information the term "geographical area" means groups of countries or individual countries as each enterprise determines is appropriate in its particular circumstances.

2
Decentralization and Accounting

Responsibility accounting and performance evaluation are the logical products of decentralization. None of these practices are new. The origins of each can be traced, at least conceptually, to the earliest divisions of labor.

An overview of the decentralization process and its supportive assumptions is given since it provides the basic framework upon which contemporary practices of responsibility accounting and performance evaluation have been constructed.

The components of the accounting information system are also examined briefly in order to differentiate between the natures of their outputs and their intended uses.

CONCEPTS OF DECENTRALIZATION

As with many concepts, decentralization has several meanings. Activities, operations, physical facilities, and management structures are all often referred to as decentralized. The first three references pose few barriers to understanding since they represent tangible things that are separated and often dispersed widely. Management structures or organizations, however, do pose problems since an intangible—authority — is the frame of reference.

Delegation of Authority

In the formal sense, authority is the power to make decisions, to give orders, and to exact obedience.[1] Authority is the essential ingredient of the management process. In fact, the *delegation* of authority makes organization possible.

An organization is usually defined as a group of people collectively pursuing some common objectives or purposes. Stripped to the barest essentials, management of an organization involves three functions:

- Planning—establishing the organization's objectives and devising the strategies to achieve them.
- Organizing—acquiring and putting together the human and other resources necessary to implement the plans.
- Controlling—directing employment of the resources to promote efficiency (doing something right) and effectiveness (doing the right something).

Consequently, organizations and their segments should be both efficient and effective if growth is to be achieved in a free enterprise economy.

An essential component of each of the management functions cited above is decision making—making rational choices among alternatives. Management organizations are considered as centralized or decentralized based upon the levels in which the authority to make decisions vests. A centralized management structure reserves decisions regarding all important matters for top management. Decentralization refers to delegation of decision-making authority to the lower echelons of the management hierarchy.

Absolute centralization of authority in one person represents the antithesis of an organized management structure. Naturally, little could be accomplished and, while the company might be effective, it could hardly be considered efficient. At the other extreme, delegation of all authority to others also signifies the absence of management organization. The several autonomous parts of the company might well achieve efficiency but, for the company as a whole, effectiveness would be happenstance without some coordination of effort. Consequently, centralization and decentralization represent opposite ends of the management continuum. Some degree of decentralization of authority characterizes all corporate organizations.

The Delegation Process. Since one cannot give what one does not have, formal authority flows from the top down in corporate organizations by means of a *process* called "delegation."[2] The process consists of four parts that are inseparable:

- Determining the goals or results expected—authority to act without knowing why is pointless.
- Assigning tasks—relating the things to be done with those who are to do them.
- Delegating authority—granting the power to make decisions to those subordinates who are to accomplish the tasks.
- Exacting responsibility for results from those subordinates delegated authority.

The last item above is of crucial importance. Responsbility cannot be delegated—only authority can. Neither can the delegant avoid his responsibility to expect an accounting of the results of authority vested in subordinates. Therefore, the concepts of decentralization, responsibility accounting, and performance evaluation are interwoven and cannot be considered in isolation.

Principles of Delegation.   The delegation of authority also involves some logical implications (sometimes called "principles") that are often ignored or forgotten.

The *scalar principle* refers to the dynamics of delegation through which authority flows in a pattern of decreasing scope (similar to links in a scalar chain) from the board of directors to the lowest ranks.

The *principle of functional definition* calls for clear specifications of the tasks to be performed, who will perform them, and the results expected. In practice, this requirement is reflected in the lines on organization charts, amplified by position descriptions.

From the above, the *adequacy of authority principle* stipulates that the authority delegated to subordinates must be adequate to accomplish the results expected.

Since biblical times, the difficulty of serving two masters has been reiterated. Management theorists have recognized this problem by means of the *unity of command principle.* Authority is delegated on a one-to-one basis, or, a subordinate reports to a single superior. In circumstances where this rule must be bent in the short run, management must be ready to cope with, and allow for, the confusion that will occur.

The principle stipulating that *responsibility is absolute* has a two-fold implication. First, where authority to make a decision vests at a certain level, the problem should not be "bucked up" to a superior. Second, since responsibility is an obligation growing out of authority, responsibility can neither be delegated nor escaped.

Last, but most important, the *parity principle* mandates that the responsibility exacted from a subordinate cannot exceed the extent of the authority delegated—nor can it be less!

The process of delegation and the underlying assumptions have been presented for recall and consideration since, together, they serve as the framework upon which responsibility accounting and performance evaluation are constructed.

GENESIS IN THE UNITED STATES

Since decentralization of authority is more of an art than a science, it has varied between and among firms as well as over time. It may be useful to recount briefly its genesis in the United States and some reasons for different applications by various firms and industries.

Although the United States is used as the locale of reference, it should not be inferred that decentralization was a U.S. invention. Church and military organizations were among the earliest adherents. Business applications were probably first addressed by Henri Fayol, a Frenchman, around 1900.

A Conducive Environment

Although its origin may be moot, decentralization did not gain wide acceptance in the United States until 1920. The period of prosperity and economic growth following World War I not only provided the impetus for management reorganizations but the ability to cope with the new complexities as well. Prior to and during World War I most large-scale industries engaged in the manufacture and distribution of a single line of related products. Where business combinations arose, management's prime concern usually involved the control of price and production rather than serving the needs of the marketplace. The

1920s ushered in new materials and sources, dramatic changes in manufacturing and marketing technologies, eager demands from expanding markets, and auras of confidence in the future.

Pressures for more flexible, responsive management structures came in several forms. For some firms (in the auto, metals, and oil industries), reorganization was necessary due to the increase in the sheer size of their operations. Others (notably in the chemical, electrical, and rubber industries) found they could not centrally manage the complexities resulting from product diversifications within their domestic markets. Still others (primarily in the oil, food, paper, and machinery industries) reorganized to cope with the maze of problems associated with the establishment of operations in foreign countries.

Early Applications

While the pressures for change were divergent, the process of decentralization was strikingly similar across most companies.

Two conjectures seem to be plausible. First, the majority of the large industrial firms circa 1920 were organized along functional lines with all integrative management decisions vesting in the chief executive officer. In short, most large firms had quite similar forms. Second, chief executives of that era were relatively few in number and, while their relationships could not be described as fraternal, the news of successful reorganizations traveled rather fast. The timing of significant decentralizations of authority in some cases was delayed, however, pending the turnover of those chief executives who were unwilling to relinquish any of their authority.

The DuPont Contribution. The E. I. duPont de Nemours Company is credited with implementing the first integrated form of decentralized industrial structure in 1921.[3] In order to diversify, the president, Irenee duPont, reorganized the company into five product departments (explosives, cellulose, paint, Pyralin, and dyes). Each department was headed by a manager with: his own staff, authority over all operations of his department, and the responsibility for the financial performance of his department. Policy-making and coordinative supervision vested in an executive committee that, along with the department managers, was supported by various specialized service or staff functions—such as research and development, and accounting.

Within the chemical industry, the DuPont model was implemented by Union Carbon and Carbide (by 1930) and by Allied Chemical (in 1945).

The General Motors Experience. Another well known progenitor of decentralized management is General Motors. What may not be as well known is the fact that the DuPont and General Motors reorganizations were performed at the same time and orchestrated by two brothers. Pierre duPont succeeded William Durant as president of General Motors in 1920 and inherited a melange of uncoordinated yet related operations. The components were restructured much the same as at DuPont, but by market segments (e.g., prices for autos) as well as product divisions. Each division was considered autonomous and headed by a manager with full authority and financial responsibility. Also as at DuPont, centralized support services were established to assist division managers and the executive committee, with the latter performing the broad policy, coordinative, and evaluation functions.

The GM model was copied, with minor parings here and there, by Ford Motor Company—but not until after Henry Ford stepped down in 1946. The Chrysler Corporation retained centralized control over its functional segments until the early 1950s. Subsequently, decentralization was approached in a somewhat piecemeal fashion. Hindsight suggests that, among other causes, Chrysler's present difficulties may well be the result of attempting to function competitively with an ill-defined management structure.

Single-Industry Examples. The innovators among multi-industry firms, mentioned above, had their counterparts within single-industry companies. Space permits only the recognition of decentralization within vertically integrated firms—pioneered by Standard Oil of New Jersey (in 1927)—and the concept of regional decentralization introduced in the mercantile industry by Sears, Roebuck (in 1929). It should also be mentioned that the organizational structures of many of today's large financial and insurance firms parallel closely the decentralized model developed by Sears, Roebuck.

A Philosophy of Balance

Decentralization represented a philosophy of organization adopted by influential U.S. firms in the 1920s as the best means to manage growth.

Firms that grew internally (by constructing additional operations more than by acquiring smaller companies) sought more autonomy for their operating units. Companies that had grown externally by means of mergers sought an effective method of coordinating the directions and policies of their component parts. Although the purposes differed, the results represented movements from the opposite ends of the centralized-decentralized continuum toward a more common ground.

Decentralization is by no means a static philosophy of management. It is a matter of degree that, for most companies, has fluctuated over time dependent upon the natures of chief executives and their perceptions of the best ways for their companies to respond to (if not anticipate) changing business environments. In some instances, decentralization was carried to an extreme that approached disintegration—the near disasters of General Electric (in 1954) and General Dynamics (in 1958) are classic examples of loosening the reins over integrated operations too much. Consequently, the key to successful decentralization has been recognized as the maintenance of reasonable *balance* between complete autonomy and effective control.

The large majority of modern organizations attempt to achieve and maintain balance by retaining centralized authority over those functions considered to be vital to the company as a whole. Common vital concerns are found in the financial areas: dealing with comprehensive budgets, profit goals, and capital sourcings as well as major capital deployments. Policies are often used to guide the decisions made below the top-management level regarding product, marketing, personnel, and similar operating matters.

Naturally, what functions are considered to be vital will vary between and among companies. Also, as the business environments change, the relative importance of the functions also change. In the latter cases, management must often recentralize authority over certain business activities. In other cases, technological change—such as computerized systems—has enabled centralized management of important functions previously impossible. It is also highly probable that computerized networks will continue to cause many shifts in authority structures, but, on the whole, should result in a net movement toward greater centralization.

Benefits and Costs

Decentralization signifies the voluntary surrender of authority by persons in positions of power—not an obvious facet of human character. Normally, management will adopt decentralization if the perceived benefits exceed their related costs.

Most benefits that accrue are rather obvious yet deserve mention. As cited earlier, decentralization makes organization possible. It also is a time-proven approach to managing the problems of size and complexity. The economic and other benefits associated with large enterprises are retained along with many of the advantages inherent in small organizations. Shared decision-making distributes the work: top managements are freed to address broad issues, such as policies and coordinative actions; subordinates have the authority to respond to day-to-day operating problems without seeking higher approval. In the latter case, local managers are usually better informed regarding local problems and better decisions often result. The independence granted local managers tends to increase their status, enthusiasm, and motivation. Also, the operating echelons provide excellent training grounds for the top managers of tomorrow.

Many of the potential costs (or risks) associated with decentralization are also apparent. Decentralization often yields the best results when operating units are independent, yet, the coordination required is no small feat—an appropriate balance is necessary. Without coordinative oversight, local managers may reach dysfunctional decisions that appear to be in the best interest of local management yet are counter-productive to the firm as a whole. Compatible or congruent decisions are often functions of the efficiency of managerial accounting and information systems. Where such systems are inadequate, local managers will establish their own support services—the total costs of information increase while the overall usefulness generally does not. Perhaps the most difficult "cost" attaches to the willingness of top management to let go and to expect (and accept) some minor diseconomies in return for the larger, synergistic benefits. A final and important cost involves exacting responsibility for results from subordinates—or performance evaluations of activities and their managers. Real top management support can transform the costs of evaluations into tangible benefits for all concerned. The purpose of this book is to assist in the realization of those benefits.

THE ACCOUNTING INFORMATION SYSTEM

The materials in this section are presented at the risk of compounding the cardinal fallacy of looking at the business information system as a collection of separate systems. Not only are the segments interrelated, but the accounting information system serves as the basic core of the larger information systems of modern enterprises (Figure 2-1).

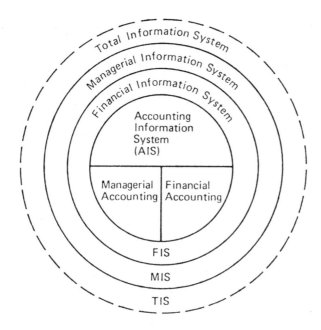

Notes:

(1) The total information system (TIS) is circumscribed by a broken line to represent the infinite nature of the environmental data involved.

(2) The MIS includes all essential internal data plus some information regarding the external environment; for example, industry, competitor, and GNP data, as well as projections.

(3) The FIS represents the conventional accounting information system augmented by internal and external data peculiar to the financial-management function of the treasurer.

Source: Reprinted by permission of the publisher from: *Accounting Problems of Multinational Enterprises* by Elwood L. Miller (Lexington, Mass.: Lexington Books, D. C. Heath and Company, © 1979, D. C. Heath and Company).

Figure 2-1. The Scope of Information Systems.

For centuries, accounting represented *the* business information system and became known as "the language of business." Today, the accounting information system is often viewed as consisting of two segments.

Financial Accounting

In its earliest recorded form, accounting (or double-entry bookkeeping) possessed the basic elements of all information systems: recording, classifying, summarizing, and reporting. As businesses evolved from single proprietorships to corporate forms, financial accounting and reporting changed from an internal focus (serving owners and managers) to an external orientation (geared to the needs of creditors and stockholders). Costs and expenses were reported by functional areas, such as, production, selling, and administrative activities.

Over time, financial accounting and reporting conventions (often called "principles" or "standards") were promulgated to protect the interests of external parties. Many of these well-intended conventions either subsumed or violated the economic realities of complex enterprises.

The total reliance upon consolidated financial reportings—a fault peculiar to the United States and Canada—virtually ignored the existence and contributions of segments of an enterprise, even though such segments may have been diversified subsidiaries and/or separate legal entities operating within different national boundaries. Interunit transfers were eliminated; only transactions with outsiders were reflected. The obsession with consolidated reportings transformed financial accounting into a *macro information system* that treated a complex organization as a single economic entity. In effect, financial reporting regressed from a system of general-purpose reports (useful to a wide variety of users) to one of single-purpose, consolidated statements useful primarily to parent-company stockholders to *evaluate the performance of the entire economic entity.* While the latter purpose is necessary, the users of financial statements need disaggregated data as well. (This lack of relevant, segmented information is finally being addressed, albeit belatedly, by the Financial Accounting Standards Board[4] in response to pressures from domestic agencies and international organizations.)

Other conflicts between financial accounting and user needs deserve mention here. Strict adherence to *absorption costing* (in which the full costs of manufacturing a product are inventoriable) causes flip-flops of fixed manufacturing overhead between periods. Although sales volume, cost, and expense relationships may remain constant, the profits reported on conventional income statements tend to rise or fall with changes in inventory levels. Paper profits produced by inventory build-ups can often lull the complacent into problems of insolvency. Conversely, reported profits may fall because of inventory reductions, even though sales volume increases. (Direct costing methods of managerial accounting were devised to understand and explain the profit fluctuations mentioned.)

Other financial accounting practices (aided and abetted by tax laws) can prostitute reported profits, discourage beneficial ventures, and encourage uneconomic actions. For example, depreciation methods that lack reasonable correlation with the economic lives of tangible assets make mockeries of reported profits. Also, intangible assets with potential future benefits (such as research and development costs) are usually written off in the period incurred. Both cases cited tend to deflate reported profits and discourage otherwise desirable investments. Finally, immediate recognition of the paper "gains and losses" resulting from translations of the statements of foreign subsidiaries encourage many managers to incur the real costs associated with hedging foreign-currency exposures.

Internally, most managers can (and do) make adjustments to compensate for the effects of the above items, among others, prior to making decisions. However, managements have been afforded little or no relief insofar as profits in annual reports are concerned.[5]

Managerial Accounting

Since few systems can serve two masters equally well, the more that financial accounting focused upon the needs of external parties, the less useful it became to those charged with managing the enterprises. Management responded by devising other accounting and reporting practices for internal purposes. These devices, often operated in parallel with financial accounting procedures, have been collectively called "managerial" or "management" accounting. The essence of managerial accounting is the organization of costs and expenses by *behavior,* as well as by function, and the tracing of them to specific activities.

Lacking external compulsions or constraints, a managerial accounting system can be as simple or complex as management wishes. A good system is generally considered to be one that furnishes the right information, to the right people, at the right time—and at the lowest possible cost.

Managerial accounting is a *micro information system* that focuses primarily upon the various parts or segments of an enterprise. The information usually includes both monetary and nonmonetary data to assist managers in making decisions regarding the planning, controlling, and evaluating of operations. Consequently, the ultimate purpose of managerial accounting concerns *evaluating the performance of segments of an economic entity.*

Managerial accounting is not new. Owner-managers recorded and used information for internal purposes long before financial accounting was invented. Just as computers and communications technologies made the coordination of decentralized and multinational operations possible, those same technological advances enabled managerial accounting to come of age. Indeed, a good case can be made to support the argument that, today, *all* accounting is managerial accounting.[6] Subject to conformance with some general minimum standards, managements decide what information is to be disclosed in annual reports and shared with outsiders.

SUMMARY

Decentralization is an accepted management invention. It is based upon some unchanging logical assumptions, yet a decentralized management structure is a temporal idea. Top management must respond to change. Good top managers anticipate change, innovate, and adapt their organizational structures.

The dynamics of changing environments require ongoing attention be given to maintaining an appropriate balance between control and autonomy—a process of fine tuning.

Managerial accounting and information systems can provide valuable assistance in the processes of decision-making, performance evaluation, and fine tuning.

NOTES

1. Several proponents of the behavioral theory of management have argued that authority does not merely vest, but must be accepted by subordinates. While it is true that an individual can defy authority, thereby running the associated risks, acceptance theory has now been equated more with leadership or influence rather than authority. See: Theo Haimann and William G. Scott, *Management in the Modern Organization,* 2d ed., (Boston: Houghton Mifflin Company, 1974), pp. 158–162.

2. For an excellent treatise on the delegation process, see Alvin Brown, *Organization of Industry* (Englewood Cliffs, N.J.:   Prentice-Hall, 1947), chapters 2–12.

3. An extensive analysis of early decentralizations appears in: Alfred D. Chandler, Jr., "Management Decentralization: An Historical Analysis," *Business History Review,* Vol. XXX, June 1956, pp. 111–174.

4. *Statement of Financial Accounting Standards No. 14,* "Financial Reporting for Segments of a Business Enterprise" (Stamford, Conn.: FASB, December 1976). Earlier needs for segmented information were cited by the FTC and SEC (in the U.S.) and by the UN, OECD, and EEC (internationally).

5. On August 28, 1980, the FASB issued an *Exposure Draft,* "Foreign Currency Translation," that, if adopted, would replace *FASB Statement No. 8.* Paragraph 12 of the *Exposure Draft* would exclude from current income the differences arising from the translation of foreign statements and accumulate the amounts in a component of equity pending liquidation.

6. I. Wayne Keller, "All Accounting is Management Accounting," *Management Accounting,* November 1976, pp. 13–15.

3
Domestic Frameworks

Although welcome exceptions exist, most methods of responsibility accounting and performance evaluation used by U.S.-based multinational enterprises (MNEs) represent outgrowths of domestic practices.

In this chapter, the invention of responsibility accounting will be depicted in the context of the familiar domestic environment. The various forms of responsibility centers and their supporting assumptions will be presented. The common methods of performance evaluations and their relative advantages and shortcomings will then be reviewed, along with the relevant unresolved issues.

Upon the above foundation—and it is an important one—applications of these practices to transnational operations will be examined in the chapter that follows.

RESPONSIBILITY ACCOUNTING

The delegations of authority spawned by decentralization required the concurrent development of methods to assess the *efficiency* and *effectiveness* of operations *(activities)* and the decisions of their managers *(individuals)*. The dualities, stressed above, cannot be overemphasized.

Responsibility accounting conceptualized the roles of the various subunits (spheres of reference or responsibility centers) to which inputs (resources) and outputs (revenues, products, or services) could be traced. The methods were devised to serve multiple purposes: to assist the managers of subunits to plan and operate their activities and, ultimately, to serve as the basis for *equitable* evaluations of the subunits and their managers.

For a variety of reasons, the basic premises of responsibility accounting have been violated in making evaluations of the performances of domestic operations and their managers. These inequities have been carried over and multiplied where transnational operations, the topic of the next chapter, are concerned. Consequently, the premises supporting responsibility accounting are presented for recall and reconsideration.

Premises and Assumptions

Responsibility accounting is constructed upon a framework of basic ideas:

- Resources used (inputs) and results produced (outputs) are measureable.
- Inputs and outputs are traceable to specific activities and can be related to particular management levels having effective control (authority) over their use and creation.
- Effective standards can be developed with which actual performance can be compared and evaluated.

Responsibility accounting focuses upon people and the bounds of their authority, as well as the activities in which they are engaged. (The personalization of accounting is not new—the Romans and Feudal Britons personified accounts to relate accountability with individuals.) It can work well, since management accomplishes things through people.

Several assumptions follow the premises cited above.

Controllability defines responsibility. That simple statement represents the essence of responsibility accounting as well as the cause of some of its problems. Controllable inputs and outputs have been defined as those ". . .subject to the influence of a given *manager* of a given *responsibility center* for a given *time span.*"[1] The term "influence" recognizes that degrees of authority and controllability often exist when activities or functions are interdependent. However, influence cannot be substituted for authority according to the premises cited earlier. Interdependencies that are created within organizations act to nullify the logic of responsibility accounting and usually result in illusory evaluations of managers and segments. Where significant interdependencies are present, the organizational structure should be examined and restructured with the purpose of either centralizing interdependent segments or redefining their controllable inputs and outputs. Liberal use of common sense will prevent the compartmentalization of activities sometimes feared.

Enterprise and individual goals can be harmonized. Conflicts often exist between and among the multiple goals of a company, those of an individual manager, and those of a company and its managers. Managerial accounting can serve to minimize these conflicts. The objectives of top management should be stated clearly and assigned priorities or weights, rather than have them implied by subordinates.

Objectives can be translated into reasonably attainable standards. Managers must participate in the standard-setting process if they are expected to internalize the goals (accept them as their own) and regard them as reasonably attainable. Such a process generates intrinsic motivation.[2] The standards can be established by analytical or judgmental means and can be in monetary or nonmonetary terms. (The latter basis is finally receiving the attention deserved.) All standards or goals should stipulate the given set of future expectations upon which they are based.

Activity reports can be designed to evaluate progress toward the objectives agreed upon. Budgets or plans, by themselves, are usually not motivational. Reports comparing objectives and achievements can provide positive reinforcement if awards are made for meeting goals. If management emphasizes only the problem areas, the system will be regarded as punitive. Even given the proper attitudinal atmosphere, real problems surround separating the results of achievement from those of circumstance. Here, the set of expectations supporting the plans is particularly useful.

Responsibility Centers

Responsibility accounting was made manageable by the definition of spheres of reference, often called responsibility centers, to which inputs and outputs could be traced. Unfortunately, common usage of responsibility centers as reference points has: (1) obscured the roles of the managers of the centers, or, more often, (2) treated the units and their managers synonymously. Both can lead to poor decisions and inequities.

In this section, responsibility centers are categorized by their roles as operating units or segments of an enterprise.

Expense Centers. Among the less-complex spheres of reference are expense centers. Typically, these are the staff and support activities of the selling and administrative functions. As the expenses of warehousing and shipping some finished products began to rival their production costs, distribution activities joined the ranks of expense centers to facilitate control. A center or point of reference may vary from a single clerk or piece of equipment, to an entire activity or department. The degree of refinement will depend upon such factors as the importance of the activities, the significance of the expenses, and the relative difficulty (and cost) associated with tracing inputs and outputs to each center.

In the context of this book, expense centers are defined as those units that furnish goods and services that are not components of manufactured products. Traceable expenditures (inputs) of expense centers are treated as *period costs*; that is, they are expensed as they are incurred and are not inventoriable.

Control is presumed over expenditures and the quantity and quality of services provided. Normally, expense centers are expected to produce outputs (services of acceptable quantity and quality) within the levels of expenses (inputs) in predetermined and approved budgets.

Cost Centers. Also among the simpler spheres of reference, at least conceptually, are cost centers. To avoid confusion, cost centers will be defined as those manufacturing units whose inputs become part of the costs of products manufactured.

Two forms are common. *Service centers* are those manufacturing activities that provide support services such as: raw material storerooms, maintenance and repair departments, plant cafeterias, and power plants. *Production centers* are those units that create intermediate and finished products.

In terms of macro-comparisons with expense centers, cost centers usually are broader in scope and complexity—such as an entire manufacturing division. (Some expense centers, such as the distribution system of Ralston Purina Company, rival their manufacturing counterparts, however.) To make them manageable, large cost centers are typically subdivided into the smallest segments to which inputs and outputs can be traced and accumulated economically. Also, the large majority of inputs traceable to cost centers are engineered costs (as opposed to the managed "costs" peculiar to most expense centers) and are more amenable to estimation, if not control.

Control is presumed over the costs incurred (inputs) and the quantity and quality of the services or goods produced (outputs). Ordinarily, cost centers are expected to maximize outputs within the constraints on inputs specified by time-and-effort, standard cost, flexible budget, and similar systems which will be discussed later.

Revenue Centers. Activities that can affect the levels of revenues (outputs) and the expenses of their generation (inputs), but have no direct control over the costs of the products or services sold, are known as revenue centers. Sales offices are excellent examples of revenue centers and are often further divided into territories, product lines, salespersons, and similar segments in order to facilitate management and evaluation.

Some revenue centers have nearly complete control over revenues. Others can affect only the quantities of items sold, with selling prices established by regional or headquarters offices. The twin objectives of revenue centers are to maximize revenues while spending within the levels of approved budgets.

Profit Centers. Units or divisions that provide goods and services (by production or procurement) and market them are profit centers.

Some crucial conditions regarding independence are shrouded in the above definition:

- The unit must have the freedom to produce or purchase its inputs—the goods and services it requires—when and where it chooses. Decisions concerning capital expenditures, usually over a modest, specified amount, are reserved for higher headquarters.
- The unit must be free to market its outputs externally (to outside customers) where it chooses, or within specific regions or territories. In order to respond to the marketplace, the unit must also control selling price and other marketing decisions.

Based upon the above, true profit centers represent miniature, independent businesses financed by a parent organization. Operating profits (revenues minus operating expenses) are convenient methods of relating inputs and outputs. Units and their managers are held accountable for the levels of operating profits generated.

Most complex organizations today create significant interdependencies among their operating units. Consequently, few true profit centers exist.

Investment Centers. In theory, at least, investment centers are extensions of profit centers. Control is considered to exist over profits and the levels of resources employed in their generation. All the freedoms essential to profit centers apply plus the authority to acquire, and determine the levels of, capital assets. Controls over the sources and methods of financing the acquisitions of capital assets are not requisites, however.

Investment centers represent autonomous businesses. Therefore, the more that constraints are imposed upon the independence of an operating unit, the less the unit can be regarded as a valid investment center.

Hybrid Forms. Among the newest concepts of responsibility centers are the variant forms of project or matrix organizations. Although introduced by firms catering to large military contracts in aeronautical and space technologies, project-oriented organization is adaptable to many complex activites. Surveillance over a given project to satisfactory completion is the central purpose. An admixture of relationships usually exists: the traditional, vertical line authority (over those personnel and activities employed solely in the project); lateral or cooperative relationships (with other functional or project units on the same level regarding interdependent activities); and diagonal or crisscross relationships (with lower-level support and service units).

In the sense that the project is the objective for cost accumulations, it could be considered as a giant cost center. However, effective control usually does not exist over the costs of significant, related, interdependent activities. Consequently, the high degree of interdependencies dictates that coordination of the project as a whole should be the focal point rather than the matrix of segments.

Cost accumulations and allocations peculiar to projects involving government contracts are subject to the detailed pronouncements of the Cost Accounting Standards Board established for that purpose. These matters are outside the scope of this book. However, the significant interdependencies existing in project organizations are also prevalent among the various segments of multinational enterprises— and those pose much the same problems.

Not-For-Profit Units. Some brief comments are warranted here concerning organizations that do not pursue profit as an objective. All aspects of responsibility accounting and performance evaluation, except those relating to profitability, apply and can be used effectively. Input-output relationships are the essentials required. They do not need to be expressed in monetary or profit terms. In fact, so long as money remains an unreliable common denominator, nonmonetary measures are of increasing importance.

Activity Reports

Discussions of terminology often are indications that a topic has come of age. That observation seems to hold true in the case of responsibility accounting.

Initially, accountings of the results of operations and the authorities delegated were known as control reports. This nomenclature was short-lived due to the negative connotations of the word "control." Subsequently, the periodic accountings were called "responsibility" or "performance" reports, and these titles are in wide use today. Both can present problems. As mentioned in the previous chapter, responsibility is the result of, and in parity with, the delegation of authority to a subordinate. However, responsibility reports commonly include activities or items outside the authority (control) of the management levels to which addressed. Similarly, performance reports become ambiguous since managements apply them, often without modification, to assess the progress of both units and their managers. Activity or progress reports seem to be preferable terms. Each has a neutral frame of reference or, if anything, leans toward addressing the operating unit or activity. Those reports focusing upon individual managers should be labeled "authority" reports, but this is not likely to happen.

In this book, the term "activity reports" will be adopted and will refer to the progress reports of units and their managers.

Commonalities. To minimize redundancies, some aspects or features common to all activity reports will be mentioned here.

The end purpose of all activity reports is the assessment of accomplishment in one form or another. However, many activity reports are used to manage day-to-day operations. Therefore, the data contained in activity reports should be: readily obtainable, relevant, controllable, and measurable. The latter item is complex enough that it merits, and lends itself well to, separate examination in Chapter 5.

The potential input and output data to be included in activity reports should be examined from three aspects: traceability, controllability, and behavior.

Traceability. Preferably, only data that are *directly traceable* to the activity concerned should be included. Unfortunately, this is not always possible. For example, the costs of operating service centers in manufacturing operations must be assigned to the producing departments. Intercenter cost allocations cannot be avoided since they are part of the step-down method used to attach all manufacturing costs to the products. Allocation bases vary from nearly direct (such as work orders for maintenance) to reasonable but nonetheless arbitrary bases. Producing departments generate similar problems in that general manufacturing costs (overhead) must be allocated to the direct material and labor components of products.

All inputs not directly traceable to responsibility centers should be classified as *indirect*—regardless of the interdependencies that exist between and among the various centers—in order to recognize the less than total cause-effect relationships.

Controllability. Many problems of controllability parallel those of traceability. In general, all indirect expenses should be considered noncontrollable by the activities concerned. As mentioned earlier, allocations of factory service-center and other overhead costs are required by financial reporting and tax systems. However, some companies have devised various methods of allocating the expenditures of non-factory expense centers to users. (Central computer and engineering services are typical examples.) In some instances, full-cost-plus schemes have been employed in attempts to motivate and control by transforming expense centers into pseudo-profit centers. Such schemes are exercises in fantasy and mysticism that only generate conflict and confusion. All methods of allocating expenses are arbitrary and only result in the creation of "soft" and "funny money" items in budgets, as well as obscure performance evaluations.

Controllability also presents a few unique problems. Some inputs, such as a supervisor's salary, may be direct with respect to a unit yet would not be controllable at that level. Some functions of output also may not be controllable by a particular unit; selling prices imposed upon some revenue centers by higher headquarters are examples.

All expenses are controllable at some level in an organization over time. Activity reports should identify and relate those inputs and outputs that are traceable to and controllable by the unit or level to which they are addressed. The process is not an easy one. Furthermore, the traceability and controllability of an input often changes as the cost objective (the unit or level) changes or is segmented.

Behavior. Input data (costs and expenses) should also be classified in accordance with their behavior or variability in relation to changes in activity. Three cost-behavior patterns are commonly used: variable (direct input/output relationship); mixed (less than direct changes with activity); and fixed (those that do not tend to change with activity). Usually, the most prevalent costs and expenses fall into the troublesome mixed category, and require separation into their fixed and variable components before they can be projected or assessed.

Determinations of the traceability, controllability, and variability of input-output data are crucial to responsibility accounting. They form the foundations upon which standard cost, flexible budget, and other possible evaluation systems rest.

Standard Costs. Initially, activity reports based upon standard costs were considered to be practicable only for production centers. This selectivity was the natural result of the relative importance of the manufacturing process, and because the input-output relationships lent themselves to engineered determinations. However, since many firms have recognized the value of some of the basic concepts of standard costs, in the management of other responsibility centers, an overview is useful here.

Standard costs refer to the prices and quantities of inputs that *should be* used to produce *a unit* of output. The standard-setting process requires the analysis of historical and projected input costs and their classification according to traceability (direct or indirect with respect to products) and estimated variability, in total, with volume. Standards should be practical (tight, but reasonably attainable) and kept up to date if they are to promote economy and efficiency.

Actual product costs by component (materials, labor, and manufacturing overhead) can then be compared with the established standards, and the differences (variances) reflected in activity reports as exceptions for possible management attention.

Also, the variances for each component can be further analyzed as to source (price and quantity for variable components, budget and volume variances for the fixed components). Given the sources of variances, management is then in position to determine the causes by querying those subordinates in positions of control. The level of sophistication employed in standard cost systems usually depends upon the nature of the product or process and the degree of real competition within the industry.

Many aspects of standard costs can be used by important responsibility centers other than those engaged in the production process. The only real, basic change regards the cost objective. In other words, the classification of costs or expenses (according to traceability and variability) would be based upon the activity engaged in rather than a unit of manufactured product.

Flexible Budgets. Logical extensions of standard-costing concepts are known as flexible budgets. Standard costs focus upon the unit costs of products, whereas flexible budgets reflect the total costs of activities, whether manufacturing or otherwise. Consequently, flexible budgeting procedures can be employed to manage all sorts of important activities, whether operated for profit or not, so long as the information system is geared to trace and accumulate inputs and outputs to the particular responsibility centers.

The term is somewhat of a misnomer today. As its title implies, flexible budgeting was first used to project the results of operations over several levels of activity or volume. However, since an approved budget can reflect only one level of activity, flexible budgeting concepts have proved to be most useful in *ex post facto* adjustments of budgets. Knowledge of the patterns of cost behavior for specific activities permits the inputs originally budgeted for *expected levels* of activity to be adjusted to the amounts reasonably allowable for the *actual levels* of operation. The differences reflected are logical exceptions for management consideration. Also, logic dictates that the cost or expense elements contained in performance reports be separated into categories in accordance with their *controllability* at the authority level to which the report is addressed.

Reporting Criteria. As activity reports gravitate up the management ranks their nature and content change.

Reports addressed to lower authority levels generally focus upon the control of inputs or upon outputs in nonmonetary terms. At middle management levels, both inputs and outputs are reflected, monetary terms predominate, and, if an emphasis exists, output data are generally considered more important. Activity reports addressed to top management tend to be as comprehensive and as concise as possible. Selected, key monetary data may be presented standing alone (such as sales or profits); however, extensive use is made of integrative relationships of inputs and outputs, usually in terms of percentages or other ratios.

In most reporting systems, top-level managers require explanations of certain exceptions in the aggregate data received. Subordinates respond, based upon the findings of their variance analyses and circumstantial factors. Responsive systems and effective subordinates are those that enable unusual variances to be isolated, examined, and acted upon (wherever possible) prior to the receipt of queries from higher authorities. To assist responsiveness, many activity reporting systems contain predetermined criteria for attention and explanation. Common factors are:

- Size—such as more than 10% over or under the allowable amounts in flexible budgets.
- Relative importance to profitability.
- Controllability at the authority level addressed.
- Frequency of occurrence, either actual or potential.

PERFORMANCE MEASURES AND STANDARDS

Methods of performance evaluation were devised for compatability with the roles of responsibility centers and their managers. Attributes of the various measures and standards developed for use with domestic operations will be examined here.

Dualities Involved

Common sense dictated that evaluations should be realistic. Early systems designers believed that, in order to be realistic, performance measures had to be objective—that is, until they learned that many important factors could only be examined subjectively. Today, it is generally recognized that realism is best achieved by a reasonable blend of objectivity and judgment.

Less apparent but more troublesome dualities were encountered in considerations of the elements to be used in measurement, the attributes to be measured, and the spheres of reference.

Two *elements* were required in the evaluation process:

- A measure (or index) of the inputs and outputs, and
- A standard (or benchmark) against which the measure could be evaluated.

For some activities, micro-measures and standards could be determined and applied rather objectively and frequently. For the more complex activities, however, macro-indexes that netted the relationships of many variables were preferred. The macro-benchmarks applied were often mostly judgmental. Due to the inherent complexities and the lag times of information systems, macro-evaluations were performed less frequently.

Two *attributes* had to be measured and evaluated:

- Efficiency—the relationship of inputs and outputs, and
- Effectiveness—the relationship of outputs to company objectives.

Problems concerning the attributes were not that they were so much in conflict, but simply that they were different. Assessments of what was being done called for different approaches than how well the activities were being conducted. The pursuit of fairness also presented the dilemma of differentiating between the results of chance and those of achievement.

The *spheres of reference* presented the most troublesome of all dualities:

- The operating unit or responsibility center, and
- The manager or individual delegated authority over the operation.

Potential conflicts were myriad. Different goals could exist. Different roles, whether real or imagined, were possible. The scopes of operations and effective controls could differ. Also, most information systems suffer from two defects: (1) the lag time between the making of a decision and the reported results, and (2) only the results of alternatives accepted are recorded—no one keeps a record of opportunity costs.

Finally, the components of the dualities cited above interact. Small wonder then, that performance evaluations remain in the realm of art rather than science.

In general, units or activites should be evaluated on the basis of *traceable* inputs and outputs. Managers and subordinates associated with the units should be appraised by relating their *controllable* inputs and outputs.

Flexible Budgets

In the author's opinion, flexible budgets are the most useful and versatile of all the tools available for performance evaluations.

Upon approval, budgets represent both reasonable measures and standards in one. When subsequently adjusted to conform with actual volumes, the variances represent deviations from expected performances. Variance analysis serves as the source of reasoned explanations and the means of improving subsequent projections.

Flexible budgeting methods can be applied to all responsiblity centers in whole or in part. Segmented applications can be tailored to fit and lend themselves well to the consolidation that is necessary as activity reports move up the scalar chain. Redundancies in activity reports can be minimized *iff* the reports are structured into sections identifying traceable and controllable items.

Expense and Service Centers. Input evaluations are usually financial. Activity reports based upon flexible budgeting procedures reflect variances, favorable and unfavorable, in monetary and percentage terms. Where the variances warrant, they can be analyzed into price-efficiency components to assist in isolation of causes. In some cases, time lags may occur between the incurrence of expenses and their benefits. Such factors should be made part of management's variance report.

Measures and standards concerning output evaluations are more difficult and depend upon the nature of the activity.

Outputs of *expense centers* can usually be quantified in nonmonetary terms. Where justified, sophisticated systems examine costs per order, letters typed per hour, credit checks processed per day, and similar measures. Qualitative evaluations of the outputs of expense centers are particularly important, but often only subjective assessments can be made. Where the quality of service outputs is a significant factor, user opinions should be solicited rather than waiting for their complaints.

Outputs of some *service centers* lend themselves to financial measures. Examples are those of power, janitorial, and similar services for which engineered or external standards are available. In other cases, such as plant cafeterias, financial evaluations must necessarily be subjective. Trends in surrogate monetary measures (costs per unit of output) or nonmonetary goals (numbers of output units) are in common use. Qualitative assessments of service-center outputs are necessarily subjective but, unlike those of expense centers, are performed more frequently.

The operations of expense and service centers should be evaluated and *justified* on their own merits, standing alone. Cost-benefit analyses made at the time the centers were established (the expected benefits) should be compared with actual results to determine if the centers should be retained (as is or with modifications) or decentralized, or whether the services should be obtained externally. Granted, judgments concerning convenience of access, turn-around-time, confidentiality, and other subjectivities will be involved, but these benefits will at least have costs against which they can be weighed. Changes in expectations, interdependencies, and other unanticipated events should also be taken into account. Naturally, such evaluations are similar to disinvestment decisions and are not made routinely.

Production Centers. Because of their importance, operations of production centers are often evaluated daily as well as over longer intervals. Activity reports for short periods of time are based upon standard costs, while flexible budgets are normally the basis for monthly evaluations. Both are related. Standards focus upon the *unit costs* of outputs whereas flexible budgets address the *total costs* of inputs and outputs traceable to a given center.

Actual product costs (materials, labor, and manufacturing overhead) are compared with the established standards and variances are isolated for analysis by component (price and quantity for variable components; budget and volume variances for the fixed components). Many systems isolate variances as soon as possible; such as material price variances at the time of purchase, and quantity variances at the time of issue, rather than at completion of production.

Nonfinancial measures, quantitative and qualitative, benefit from the availability of engineered standards.

Revenue Centers. Financial evaluations of revenue centers should also begin with activity reports, in flexible budget format, that relate the revenues actually generated with the expenses allowable for that level of operation. Expense variances are thereby isolated for attention.

Revenue evaluations are usually more significant and complicated. Budgeted and actual revenues can differ because of changes in selling prices and changes in unit volumes. Consequently, the variance between the amounts of revenues budgeted and generated should be broken down into its price and volume components. The price variance is particularly important in those cases where selling prices are administered by higher echelons. Quantity variances are always important measures since sales volumes govern the hearbeat of nearly every operating unit of an enterprise. Multi-product revenue centers require variances to be reported for each product. Generally, activity reports are further segmented by geographic areas, customer groups, and the like.

Since neither the costs (which presumably affect price) nor the qualities of the items sold are controllable, adjustments must be made for changes in these factors not recognized in budget revisions.

Nonmonetary measures may also be used effectively. Backlog orders, units shipped, market shares, and average collection periods are examples that can be compared with standards or trends.

Profit

The most common macro-measure of economic activity is profit. Although most of the attributes of profit as a measure are well-known, its shortcomings are often ignored. Both will be mentioned briefly, together with some incorrect uses of profit as a standard.

Advantages. Profit (revenues minus identifiable expenses) is the *primary* objective of business enterprises since it is essential for survival and growth. Profit is a convenient measure of the relationships of inputs and outputs. Expression can be in nominal (monetary) or relative (percentage) terms. Also, profits are determined routinely by financial accounting systems for internal and external users. Finally, profits are powerful motivators. Although decentralization made profit centers possible, their motivational aspects made them attractive to DuPont, General Motors, and other giant firms that adopted and popularized them.

As an aside, undoubtedly some top executives believed that, since they were evaluated by profitability, why shouldn't their subordinates be?

Shortcomings. Most of the faults that can be ascribed to profit as a measure are situational rather than conceptual. Therein lies the problem.

Profit is a unidimensional measure. Although profit is a primary objective, most enterprises stipulate other goals formally and, if they do indeed exist, they should also be weighted and measured. Profits may be useful, although rather blunt, measures of *activities* that are independent, however, interdependencies that exist negate the profit-center concept and the use of profit as a measure. Few managers, other than top executives, are really responsible for profits. To apply the measure to *individuals* lacking the commensurate authority is a sham.

Technical problems abound. Profits determined according to financial accounting standards are rather arbitrary. Unless profit measures for internal use can be redesigned to conform more closely with economic realities, uneconomic decisions can easily be made. A related deficiency applies to the instability of the monetary unit. A relatively stable dollar is a good common denominator for measuring and comparing inputs and outputs. In times of changing price-levels, profits stated in nominal dollars become suspect.

An Illogical Standard. Perhaps the most inane uses of profit involve attempts to convert the measure into a self-determined standard.

Admittedly, the usefulness of profit, just as any other measure, is enhanced by comparisons. Flexible budgets are examples of such comparisons. However, flexible budgets represent valid benchmarks because they will have been adjusted to reflect changes in the levels of activity originally budgeted. Nonetheless, some executives find it easy to scan a list of profits reported by various activites—ranked in one order or another—and evaluate not only the activites but their managers as well!

A similar, but possibly less critical, blunder results when executives expect the whole to equal the sum of its parts. In short, the company profit should equal the total reported by the various profit centers. Such expectations lead to wholesale allocations of common expenses that negate the very premises upon which responsibility accounting is founded.

Profit is an equitable measure of the financial performances of independent activities. As a measure of the financial responsibility of managers, "profit" must be recalculated to reflect the manager's contribution, which has been aptly defined as "the result of actions for which he is responsible and which he has taken in the best interests of the company."[3]

Return on Investment

Almost all large decentralized domestic enterprises use some version of return on investment as the primary measure of the financial performances of divisions and their managers.

Return on investment (ROI), or rate of return, is a measure that relates profits with the resources employed in their generation. The concept was popularized by the DuPont Company and was called the "DuPont formula" for many years. The basic formula consists of two relationships:

Return on Investment = Margin X Turnover

where

$$\text{Margin (Earnings as Percent of Sales)} = \frac{\text{Net Operating Income}}{\text{Sales}}$$

and

$$\text{Turnover (Times Capital Revolves)} = \frac{\text{Sales}}{\text{Total Investment}}.$$

Alleged Advantages. The widespread reliance upon ROI as a measure and a standard of the financial performance of domestic operations stems from its alleged advantages:

1. It is a comprehensive device that considers all significant elements in a single ratio.
2. Computation is relatively simple and can be made from data in conventional financial reports.
3. Overall efficiency is expressed since net outputs (operating income) are related with inputs (resources employed).
4. As a relative measure, ROI can be used to make comparative evaluations, both internally (among divisions or with plans and prior periods) and externally (with similar ratios of competitors, the industry, and alternative opportunities).
5. It is an effective, logical motivator. Managers are made aware that resources should be used economically. Goal congruence benefits also. Profitability measures, such as ROI, affect the fortunes of companies and chief executives. If subordinate managers know their fortunes also depend upon ROI, they will act to maximize the ROI of their operations and the company.

Caveats. Many of the alleged advantages of ROI should be viewed with caution. Some are conditional, others are flawed.

Although the comprehensiveness of ROI may be a desirable attribute, it can be a fault as well. All macro-measures net and conceal the results (both good and bad) of factors outside the effective control of divisions or their managers.

Searches for simplicity often result in simplex considerations of complex matters—a systematic fault common to model builders. Data in conventional accounting reports can provide macro-measures of efficiency, but they cannot indicate effectiveness. Accomplishment and accounting profit are not synonymous concepts.

At first thought, relating earnings with capital employed is more desirable than looking at earnings alone. However, a multitude of problems concerning the components of revenues, expenses, and resources arise in practical applications.

The interdependencies common to complex enterprises obscure the relationships of revenues and expenses with subunits. Divisions often furnish products or work for other units. The monetary amounts assigned to the goods and services exchanged are known as *transfer prices*. These prices are often in excess of cost and are often dictated by the headquarters. In such cases, it is difficult to identify what and who are being evaluated.

Definition of the investment base is particularly troublesome. The common bases in use and their attributes are shown in Appendix 3A. Although the asset compositions of divisions tend to vary with circumstances, companies usually select a single mold, create artificial conformity, and consider the resulting measures to be comparable. In all fairness, however, almost any investment base selected can bias the measures of attributable assets and profit. Experience indicates that selecting investment bases compatible with the circumstances peculiar to the divisions result in more equitable activity evaluations. Of course, ROI was not developed nor intended to evaluate manager performance and should never be used for that purpose.

The validity of ROI as a comparative measure (or common denominator) of results, whether internal or external, depends upon several factors. Operating circumstances must be similar or appropriate allowances should be made. Not all investments and activities require the same time to generate returns; ROI focuses only upon short-term results. Most divisions operate with a mixture of assets having various risks; yet, the use of ROI as a comparative measure assigns the same average risk to all investments. If ROI is to be used as a benchmark, then someone has to establish what is an acceptable rate (or range) of return.

As a motivator, ROI can easily encourage managers to make short-run decisions contrary to the best long-run interests of the enterprise. Less productive assets can be scrapped prematurely. Expenditures for maintenance, repairs, and equipment overhauls can be deferred. Inventory levels may be manipulated. Even more costly, perhaps, are the results of inactions—the profitable opportunities not undertaken by the most productive divisions. What manager of a division posting a current ROI of 30 percent would undertake an investment with an estimated 22 percent yield? However, if the other divisions are earning returns of only 15 to 18 percent, the company will have lost an attractive opportunity. The above scenario is made possible because ROI looks at profits only as percentages—and percentages can't be deposited in the bank.

Residual Income

Development of the residual income concept is credited to the General Electric Company. Residual income (RI) is a refinement of ROI and makes use of percentages and dollars to evaluate profitability.

The name is derived from the process employed:

$$\text{Divisional Income} \quad - \quad \text{Investment Charge} \quad = \quad \text{Residual Income}$$

The investment charge is a percentage rate (representing imputed interest, cost of capital, or a minimum ROI) applied to the resources employed. Divisional income dollars in excess of the investment charge represent earnings above the threshold rate established.

Residual income methods are favored because they reduce suboptimal decisions and enhance goal congruence. By focusing upon earnings in dollars, managers are encouraged to accept investment opportunities promising rates of return greater than the investment charge.

Residual income also improves upon ROI conceptually. The same scale is used to state earnings and investment. Earnings represent flows. By application of a rate for the investment charge, the static amounts of balance sheet assets are also presented on a flow scale.

A final, important advantage of RI over ROI is its flexibility. ROI applies only one rate to assess earnings on assets. Residual income methods can assign various rates to asset groups based on turnover time, degree of risk, controllability by the manager, and similar criteria.

Although residual income compensates for some of the defects of ROI, in whole or in part, the other caveats cited earlier remain in contention.

Both ROI and residual income methods require the establishment of benchmark rates or standards. If the threshold rates are too low, earnings may tend to depreciate. If the rates are abnormally high (or appear to be so), motivation will tend to suffer, desirable opportunities may be foregone, and the evaluation process will become a mock exercise. If the rates are changed too frequently, the results can also be demoralizing to operating managers.

Not-For-Profit Techniques

Given the ever increasing levels of governmental and other nonprofit expenditures, improvements in efficiency and effectiveness should be everyone's concern. Unfortunately, such is not the case.

Governmental and nonprofit accounting systems are designed to facilitate compliance reporting. The central purpose often is assurance that expenditures (inputs) do not exceed the amounts appropriated or approved. Performance cannot be measured or evaluated since outputs are not specified. Four different systems have been employed in attempts to improve efficiency and effectiveness with varying success. One method still holds promise.

The first attempt was known as the Planning-Programming-Budgeting System (PPBS). The program originated in 1960 and the first concerted application was made by the Department of Defense beginning in 1961. On paper the system looked good. The planning phase identified objectives, the programming segment addressed how the objectives were to be attained, and the budgeting operation determined the related costs. Since the outputs rarely, if ever, could be quantified in monetary terms, PPBS was similar to the budget of a gigantic service center. Unsatisfactory results over a ten-year trial led to virtual abandonment of PPBS in 1971. Several reasons for failure can be conjectured. The mountains of paperwork created was the official reason cited. However, the real problems most likely were: the unwieldy scope, the maze of interdependencies among activites, and the reluctance of civilian and military personnel to subject their performances to more stringent evaluation procedures.

Management by Objectives (MBO) was selected by the federal government to replace PPBS in 1973. MBO was actually PPBS segmented into small components with the end purpose of improving budget allocations. Although MBO concepts underlie the flexible and master budgeting systems of the private sector today, they atrophied due to inattention within the government sector.

Zero-Based Budgeting (ZBB) was popularized by Peter Pyhrr in 1970,[4] subsequently tried by several states, and applied by some federal agencies in 1979. As most individuals correctly surmise, government agencies tend to spend the amounts appropriated whether needed or not—if the monies aren't used this year, next year's budget will most likely be reduced. The basic concept of ZBB is to approach budget submissions of each activity afresh, rather than build upon the inefficiencies of the prior period. In short, the need for and scope of the activity is to be justified first, then the resources needed are to be determined. The major fault of ZBB encountered in the government sector also afflicted early trials in private industry—a ream of justification material was often prepared to accompany a one-page budget request. Industry has learned to limit justifications to one or two pages. The government sector, in the main, has yet to learn this lesson.

The most recent efforts to control the costs of government are collectively known as "Sunset Legislation." The regulations applicable in a handful of states and to some federal agencies effectively write ZBB concepts into law. Basically, activities are examined, usually in staggered fashion each five or six years, and those that cannot be justified are discontinued.

It appears that government and other nonprofit operations can benefit most by adopting those systems and techniques that have proved beneficial in the private sector. MBO systems, together with the addition of selected managerial accounting techniques to supplement governmental methods, hold the greatest promise. New accountings that measure and relate inputs and outputs to activities are sorely needed.

The time and expertise of leaders in the business community and the accounting profession have been instrumental in enabling the federal government to phase in supplemental accrual accounting procedures and publish prototype consolidated statements. Similar cooperative undertakings should filter down to the agency levels and eventually to the activity segments. Politicians, however, are prone to call for efficiency and effectiveness so long as they are to be applied to someone else's bailiwick. Civil Service underlings have no motivation for change. Progress will be tortuously slow.

UNRESOLVED ISSUES

The major dilemmas involving the responsibility accountings and performance evaluations of domestic operations concern interdependencies and attitudes. Problems of interdependencies are technical and are often magnified by transfer prices and other related techniques of cost allocation. Attitudinal problems persist because of human inertia.

Transfer Prices

The objectives of domestic transfer-pricing practices have been: (1) to control operations, (2) to motivate managers, (3) to enhance decision-making, and (4) to evaluate both operations and their managers. Over time, the *pursuit of equity* among interdependent divisions has become the primary goal.

Three types of transfer prices are in common use with domestic operations: cost-based, market-based, and a hybrid form known as "dual pricing." The attributes of each type are summarized in Appendix 3B.

In the past also, problems concerning control were myriad. Admixtures of responsibility centers with varying degrees of independence precluded the selection and dictation of any single type of price or system. Companies that were highly decentralized replaced the objective of control with the goal of *coordination*.

In effect, the quest for coordination combined the second and third objectives cited above. The transfer prices that were preferred were those that would encourage managers to make decisions that were in the best interest of themselves and the company, without unduly constraining managerial autonomy. The decision to establish transfer prices by the mechanism of negotiation rather than dictation preserved autonomy, but all the other circumstantial problems remained. Units often had different marketing positions, strategies, and capabilities to negotiate. Also, congruent decisions generally required a broader data base—cost as well as market prices.

Finally, the end purposes of transfer pricing—performance evaluations—called for valid measures that were equitable and compatible with the various roles of the units and their managers.

Needless to say, dogmatic approaches to domestic transfer prices were impractical. No single transfer price or system was possible. The trade-off selected by most decentralized domestic firms was the preservation of local autonomies as much as possible with the recognition and acceptance of the costs of occasional suboptimal decisions.

Captive domestic units (those that provided goods and services solely to sister units) and other activities with significant interdependencies required different approaches. All too many companies were so captivated by profit centers that cost-plus transfer prices were implemented in order to create "pseudo profit centers." Over the years, reams of articles criticizing such schemes have been published.[5] The gist of these criticisms has, perhaps, been best summarized in the typical, precise British fashion: "Revenue which is not revenue, transfer prices which are not prices, and profit centres which do not earn a profit, are mystical inventions. They are fictions which cannot serve as a basis for action."[6]

Cost Allocations.   All allocations of costs are spin-offs of transfer pricing. Indirect assignments of service-center and other manufacturing overhead costs to production centers are required. All other cost allocations are discretionary.

Unnecessary allocations of costs serve no useful purpose and only further compound the effects of natural interdependencies that exist. The traceability of inputs to units and their controllability by managers are impaired.

Discretionary allocations of cost should be approached with caution. Better yet, they should be avoided altogether.

Human Inertia

Top executives who evaluate others are themselves judged, usually by ROI, earnings per share, price-earnings, and other financial measures of profitability. Consequently, it is quite understandable that they would tend to be reluctant to adopt other measures for evaluations of activities and appraisals of subordinates.

Data in conventional financial reports are comprehensive, routinely available, familiar, and relatively easy to understand. Managerial accounting reports emphasize segments of the enterprise, involve additional expense, deal with less familiar terms (such as contribution and segment margins), and require different standards to be developed and used.

However, most chief executives realize that macro financial measures are often inappropriate yardsticks to apply to the activities of segments. Also, they want managers to receive credit where credit is due. As a consequence, an ever increasing number of firms have recognized that the significant amounts of time and money customarily devoted to budgeting can yield substantial benefits if properly applied —and if given support and emphasis from the top.

Budgets can be tailored to fit the particular roles and circumstances of the units. The results projected can be examined for reasonableness, from both the circumstantial and total enterprise viewpoints. Subsequently, budgets can be adjusted, where necessary, to reflect the inputs allowable at the output level actually achieved. The original and adjusted budgets serve as reasonable standards to evaluate activity performance. These same reports, segmented by controllability at various authority levels, also serve as equitable benchmarks for the appraisal of management contributions. Explanations of the variances reflected provide better understandings of the results or profits produced, particularly when supplemented by relevant nonmonetary data.

Appropriate attention to the efficiency and effectiveness of segments, not only makes a complex enterprise manageable, but contributes a great deal toward assuring its overall profitability.

NOTES

1. Charles T. Horngren, *Introduction to Management Accounting,* 4th ed., (Englewood Cliffs, N.J.: Prentice-Hall, Inc., 1978), p. 251.

2. Frederick Herzberg, "One More Time: How Do You Motivate Employees?", *Harvard Business Review,* January-February 1968, p. 57.

3. Richard F. Vancil, "What Kind of Management Control Do You Need?", *Harvard Business Review,* March-April 1973, p. 86.

4. Peter A. Pyhrr, "Zero-base Budgeting," *Harvard Business Review,* November-December 1970, pp. 111–121.

5. John Dearden, Professor at Harvard Business School, has perennially dissected the problems of profit and ROI concepts. The following articles appeared in the *Harvard Business Review* (starting pages and topics are shown): "Problem in Decentralized Profit Responsibility," May-June 1960, p. 79 (fixed asset base); "Problem in Decentralized Financial Control," May-June 1961, p. 72 (current asset-base); "Limits on Decentralized Profit Responsibility," July-August 1962,

p. 81 (conflicting profit goals); "Mirage of Profit Decentralization," November-December 1962, p. 140 (levels of profit responsibility); "New System for Divisional Control" (with Bruce D. Henderson), September-October 1966, p. 144 (transfer prices); "Appraising Profit Center Managers," May-June 1968, p. 80 (performance evaluations); and "The Case Against ROI Control," May-June 1969, p. 124 (summary of problems).

For a classic article, also see Billy E. Goetz, "Transfer Prices: An Exercise in Relevancy and Goal Congruence," *The Accounting Review*, July 1967, pp. 435–440.

6. M. C. Wells, "Profit Centres, Transfer Prices, and Mysticism," *Abacus*, Vol. 4, No. 2, December 1968, p. 180.

APPENDIX 3A

INVESTMENT BASES AND THEIR ATTRIBUTES

Selection of the asset base to be used in return-on-investment and residual-income calculations poses three questions: which assets, how are they to be measured, and when are they to be measured?

I. WHICH ASSETS?

A. Traceable Assets—all assets directly identifiable with the activity.

- Relatively easy to isolate and identify.
- Includes assets financed externally and noncontrollable by local management.
- Comparability among divisions doubtful.
- Not relevant for manager or activity evaluations.

B. Assets Employed—traceable assets in use.

- Idle assets may indicate inefficient use of resources *if* all are locally controlled.
- Equitable where headquarters requires activities to carry surplus assets.
- Compatible with investment-center concept.

C. Controllable Investment—traceable assets controllable by manager less controllable debt.

- Preferred by advocates of controllability.
- Relevant to appraise managers; unsuitable for activity evaluation.

D. Total Assets—traceable assets plus an allocation of headquarters' (common) assets.

- Preferred by advocates of comparability.
- Activity evaluations distorted by allocations of common assets and inclusion of resources financed externally.

E. Net Investment—total assets less non-interest bearing liabilities.

- Appropriate for macro-evaluations of activities.
- Most comparable with cost-of-capital concepts.
- Most compatible with interests of top executives.

F. Stockholders' Equity—traceable assets financed by equity.

- Not measurable, except arbitrarily, if the capital mix of the headquarters company includes debt.
- Preferred by outside analysts to evaluate *total* company.

G. Parent Equity in Subsidiary—total assets less local debt and equity financing.

- Appropriate for macro evaluations of investments in controlled, but less-than-totally owned, activities.
- Relatable with parent's cost-of-capital.
- Frequently applied to foreign subsidiaries and ventures.

II. HOW TO MEASURE ASSETS?

A. Original, Historical Cost.

- Routinely available from financial accounting records.
- Rough surrogate estimate of replacement cost in times of rising price-levels.
- Not consistent with input/output data in income statements.

B. Net Book Value—original cost less accumulated depreciation.

- Widely used.
- Routine basis of financial accounting reports.
- Satisfactory for routine evaluations of performance.
- Unreliable denominator: changes over time; biased by age-mix of assets and all methods of depreciation (implicit interest depreciation injects the least amount of bias).
- Not consistent with concepts of economic (real) income during periods of price instability.

C. Current Cost—amount required for current replacement of existing assets *in kind*.

- Inputs related to outputs in common dollars.
- Protects financial capital; relates economic sacrifices and incomes.
- Assumes steady-state technologies and competitive environments.
- Subjective; not comparable; difficult to assess.

D. Current Replacement Value—amount required for current replacement with asset of *equivalent productive capacity*.

- Recognizes technological changes as well as competitive and industry peculiarities.
- Protects capital in the form of productive capacity.
- Eliminates past mistakes (outmoded equipment and plant).
- Comparable with economic income concepts.
- Equates company survival with productive capacity.
- Highly subjective; extremely difficult to assess.

III. WHEN TO MEASURE ASSETS?

A. At a Point in Time—at the beginning, end, or other point in the accounting period.

B. Over Time—at amounts representing simple, moving, or weighted averages.

APPENDIX 3B

DOMESTIC TRANSFER PRICES: TYPES AND ATTRIBUTES

Most domestic transfer prices could be classified as cost-based or market-based. Each category contains several variations that were designed for special purposes. A hybrid form (dual pricing, which uses cost bases in combination with others, and is widely used for foreign transfers) is also used occasionally for domestic transactions.

I. COST-BASED METHODS

Captive and other dependent domestic units normally use cost-based prices for horizontal transfers (to similar levels of production and distribution) and vertical transfers (to successive levels). Oligopolists, with little fears of competition, and other firms that favor more centralized controls also tend to favor cost-based transfers. Difficulties are created for those units that produce outputs for both internal consumption and external sale.

As a general rule, cost-based transfer prices are readily understood, accumulated routinely, and are relatively simple and inexpensive to apply. They are generally the most logical means of accounting for internal transfers of outputs from cost centers.

Four common variations of cost-based methods are used domestically, and each has its own peculiarities:

A. Full Cost (Standard or Actual):

- Advantages:
  - They lend themselves to systematic use over time.
  - Fixed cost inclusions conform with normal cost and budget systems, as well as facilitate long-run decisions.
  - They are easy to justify internally and externally (to regulatory agencies).
  - Use of standard costs prevents the passing on of normal variances, while enabling unusual costs (for rush or special orders) to be added.
- Disadvantages:
  - Cost of capital employed by transferor is ignored.
  - Decision making can be impaired unless costs are segmented into variable and fixed components.
  - Profits will accrue only to final transferees.
  - They are not compatible with intermediate operations that are decentralized.
  - Actual costs pass inefficiencies along to transferees.

B. Full-Cost-Plus:

- In some instances, increments are used to cover costs of capital. Generally, the increments represent pseudo-profits for cost centers converted into artificial profit centers. Where market prices do not exist, full-cost-plus prices can satisfy "arm's-length criteria" of the U.S. Internal Revenue Code, Section 482.

- The increments only lessen further the usefulness of full-cost data for decision-making, unless the price components are identified separately.

C. Variable Cost (Standard or Actual):

- Normally, variable costs are separately identified *segments* of transfer prices since their usefulness is limited to control and decision making:
  - Relevant costs that change with activity are isolated for control.
  - Lowest cost input decisions (make or buy) and special, short-term decisions (distress pricing, special orders) are enhanced.
  - They are used by vertically integrated firms to facilitate cost aggregation and as a basis for pricing outputs.
- Deficiencies of variable-cost transfer prices all relate to their incompleteness:
  - Only losses can accrue to transferees.
  - They are furthest removed from market considerations and can invite dumping and other charges of unfair competition.

D. Variable-Cost-Plus:

- Seldom used, and then primarily by companies employing contribution approaches to pricing.
- In common with variable costs, lowest possible (floor) pricing levels are identified.

II. MARKET-BASED METHODS

By definition, market-based transfer prices are as adequate or as deficient as the marketplace with which they relate.

A. General Advantages:

- Compatible with the concepts of autonomous units.
- External market prices enhance profit as a measure of performance.
- Market prices stimulate efficiency (control of inputs) and effectiveness (awareness of consumer needs).
- Opportunity costs (profits forgone on outside sales) are recognized when internal transfers are considered while operating at near-capacity levels.
- Conform with arm's-length and similar fair business guidelines.

B. Common Shortcomings:

- Impractical if intermediate or final markets are ill-defined or nonexistent.
- Uneconomic decisions can result from internal transfer considerations when operating at less than full capacity.
- Market prices must be adjusted downward to reflect savings in distribution and marketing costs.

C. Negotiated Prices:

- Are used to amerliorate shortcomings of market-based prices, including the absence of viable markets.
- Prices are compatible with concepts of autonomy, profitability, and arm's-length criteria.
- The above are contingent upon the preconditions that the negotiators bargain from positions of similar autonomy, strength, and knowledge of market factors.
- Negotiations can be time consuming and prices are not amenable to systemization.

III. DUAL PRICING

Although the variant methods of dual pricing defy description, they are generally adopted in order to reconcile the conflicting objectives of control, decision-making, and performance evaluation.

Dual pricing, as the name implies, records an internal transfer at two prices—usually one is cost-based, the other can be tailored to need. Normally, dual pricing is most useful for transfers from cost centers to other types of responsibility centers. Such transfers might be recorded at cost-out, market-in (to enhance cost control and confidentiality) or, alternatively, market-out (to add synthetic profits to the cost center) and cost-in (to assist decision making by the transferee).

Most drawbacks surround the additional costs of record keeping. Complaints regarding the double-counting of profits are cosmetic since all intercompany profits must be eliminated upon consolidation. Dual-pricing can help in the elimination process if the synthetic profits are recorded as unrealized.

Note: In June 1980, the National Association of Accountants published a study, *Transfer Pricing: Techniques and Uses,* authored by Ralph L. Benke, Jr., and James Don Edwards. The "general rule" recommended for domestic transfer prices was in two parts: standard variable cost plus opportunity cost. The first part assisted control and decision-making. Opportunity cost (excess of market price over standard variable cost) was added for equitable treatment of transfers between profit centers. Naturally, in the absence of a market price or a reasonable substitute, the opportunity cost would be zero.

4
International Phenomena

In the preceding chapter, responsibility accountings and performance evaluations were described in the context of the domestic U.S. environment. Unresolved issues were found to remain, even though domestic units operate within a relatively uniform set of environmental circumstances. Transnational operations are inherently more complex.

Different national environments present significant challenges as well as opportunities—these two elements, in combination, represent the real attraction of international business. In order to cope with diversity, MNEs have developed a variety of organizational structures. Operating units tend to have multiple roles that often seem in apparent conflict. The parent or headquarters functions as the synthesizer, coordinating the efforts of the several parts in the best long-run interests of the whole.

The above phenomena introduce a maze of interacting variables that further compound the problems of evaluating overseas activities and their managers. Reasonable solutions are still being sought.

MULTIPLE ENVIRONMENTS

By definition, multinational enterprises operate in multiple domiciles, each having different national environments—political, sociocultural, legal, and economic. Perhaps the only safe generalization is that the environments are similar yet different. Each acts and interacts, further complicating the coordination of widely dispersed operations. Successful MNEs have prospered because they learned to adapt. The process of adaptation, however, produced mutant forms of activities having various roles and responsibilities.

Political Spheres

Individuals not engaged in international business may not realize that the game involves three players—home and host countries, as well as the MNE. Conflicts of interest occur, both real and imagined, over the control of resources (inputs) and the distribution of wealth (outputs).

Home countries are predominantly developed countries. Initial concerns regard the economic uses of the resources exported: financial, material, human, and technological. Subsequent concerns usually involve domestic capital needs, losses of tax revenues, exportation of jobs, and balances of payments. Often, as evidenced in the United States, concerns eventually gravitate toward other diseconomies: such as the effects upon competition of vertical oligopolies and political payoffs. Finally, many home countries also attract foreign investments and fears of foreign takeovers of domestic industries are generated. In sum, home countries are (or become) host countries as well. All the above lead to a variety of political pressures upon MNEs.

Host-country concerns tend to vary, in number and intensity, with the stages of economic development that exist. Naturally, emerging nations possess the most inherent concerns: national sovereignty; exploitation of resources and capital; stability of foreign-exchange and labor markets; technological dependence; and control of MNE activities involving competition, tax evasion, social responsibility, and political influence.[1] Host governments assess and compare the potentials of the above risks with those of the economic benefits of a proposed foreign investment. Usually, governments are willing to surrender some sovereignty for economic benefit. Should subsequent conditions alter the nature or extent of the risks, political overtures usually address sovereignty, exploitation, independence, and similar emotional forms of nationalism. The typical results are additional layers of restrictions that change the rules of the game.

The MNE is not only an active player in the game, but an arbiter as well—it must continually adjust in order to placate home and host governments. The MNE can adopt, assimilate, and reconcile conflicting political forces because of its size, primarily, and because of the flexibility acquired in its search for comparative advantage on a global basis. In short, the MNE can (and does) manipulate its resources on a worldwide basis, using them wherever the opportunities

Perlmutter recently added his idea of the form the MNE will be forced to adopt in the near future if it wishes to survive and grow.[3] Alternative options would result in divestitures and other contractions of operations. Perlmutter's concept, paraphrased below, calls for:

- A "transnational network," or "TNN," having affiliations with a wide variety of firms, consortia, and operating concessions in all sectors of the globe.

Today's stockholders would become "stakeholders" in the TNN, and would include employees, trade unions, governments, and similar influential interests. Management decisions would become more difficult and tend to be the products of compromise rather than fiat.

The evolution of the TNN appears to be a logical and inevitable compromise. MNEs have received dubious "evaluations" of responsible performance by developing and industrial nations alike. Parent company interests transcend national boundaries and are not controllable by any single government. Operations of local units are subject to the control of host governments, but effective influence is often achieved only as the result of undesirable conflict.

The TNN could evidence the fact that foreign investment is not a zero-sum game. Each participant can realize incremental benefits and harmonize objectives. Reports addressing the total effects upon the local balance-of-payments should be developed and issued regularly. Value-added statements could properly disclose the positive-sum benefits actually produced. The variety of stakeholders would mandate that evaluation bases other than profit be used, and these measures could be tailored to fit the interests represented. National governments would also tend to become more comfortable as they reacquire more effective control over local redistribution of income and wealth.

It has been said that the world affairs of economics are too important to be delegated to politicians. The international cooperation inherent in organizations such as the TNN would enable our future worldspace to be shaped at least as much by concerned stakeholders as by politicians.

are best and the risks least. (In fact, the veritable size and flexibil
of MNEs have motivated the emerging countries to ask the Unit
Nations for programs to improve their negotiating abilities.)

There is little doubt that MNEs are capable of causing all the ho
country disruptions mentioned earlier. There is also little doubt th
some MNEs have been disruptive: the American oil company me
dlings in Mexico in the 1930s; United Fruit Company's exploitatioi
of the "Banana Republics" in the 1950s; the more recent alleged cla
destine affairs of ITT in Chile; and the illegal payments by America
aircraft companies are cases in point. (Even legal political contribu
tions present thorny issues: for instance, British Petroleum was 6!
percent government-owned when it contributed $1.5 million to Italiai
political parties.)

The large majority of MNEs realize that it is in their own best long
run interest to be good citizens in host countries. They also realize
that all governments may become hostile at *some* time, but not all at
the *same* time. Playing according to the rules will serve to minimize
political hostility and punitive legislation, thereby preserving the
free-market environments in which MNEs flourish.

National Orientations. Multinationals have been classified according to
their spheres of reference by Professor Howard Perlmutter[2] as follows:

- Home-country oriented (ethnocentric)—parent company domi-
  nation. Centralized control; "foreign" subsidiaries considered as
  branches of parent. Common treatment of first foreign operation.
- Host-country oriented (polycentric)—foreign operations adapted
  to local conditions and markets. Investments viewed as long-
  term. Common frame of reference today for established MNEs.
- Global oriented (geocentric)—a nearly stateless enterprise. Parent
  company location is circumstantial. World market opportunities
  addressed. More of an ideal concept than a practical possibility

A fourth category seems to be necessary today to accommodate th
joint-venture operation—it could be called *duocentric* for conformity
These organizations, in which ownership and control are divided equa
ly (or nearly so) between two investor firms, are essentially partne
ships. They are particularly appealing to developing countries and a
often the only form of entry possible into controlled economies.

Sociocultural Milieus

Multinational operations are complicated by cultural as well as geographical distances. The social and cultural environments represent a melange of structures, institutions, attitudes, customs, and values that defies description. Industrialized societies often reflect the most similarities, although significant differences are also common—Japan and Sweden, for instance, differ from most other developed countries. Understanding the peoples of the developing nations tends to be most difficult for managers of multinational firms. Yet, if these managers wish to be successful, they must be (or learn to become) students of people.

The social structures of most underdeveloped countries tend to be well-defined and rigid. Typically, two strata exist—the rich and the poor—with a wide gulf in between. Social mobility is usually rare or nonexistent. Abundant labor is often a major local resource and capital-intensive operations of foreign investors can readily appear to be socially irresponsible.

Social institutions of emerging nations also tend to be archaic. Religion affects perceptions of, and the values attached to, what is right and wrong, material gains, self-improvement, and the future itself. Government institutions are often ineffective—independence altered the faces of those in power but not the methods. Educational systems typically focus upon law, medicine, and preservation of the social niceties of the landed gentry. Opportunities for technical and business education are exceptions, if they exist at all.

It is imperative that MNEs recognize two peculiarities of the sociocultural milieu: (1) that ways of thinking change slowly, but (2) that change is inevitable. The first requires that operations recognize and assimilate local conditions. Expectations, reports, and evaluations must reflect the effects of attitudinal differences toward productivity, responsibility, loyalty, budgeting, time, and supervision. The second peculiarity recognizes that, over time, operations in host countries will generate social changes. Higher levels of standards-of-living and future aspirations of sufficient numbers of people exert pressures upon social structures. All sorts of problems can result if these changes are not anticipated and accepted. MNE and host government officials should identify, plan for, and chart the progress of those social goals mutually agreed upon. Although social accounting has received little more than lip-service in the United States, its application is mandatory for local reportings and evaluations of foreign operations.

Legal Systems

The absence of an international law consitutes a mixed blessing for multinational operations. While the MNE cannot be effectively controlled by any single external power, neither is there any power to turn to for the resolution of international conflicts. MNEs must rely upon themselves for survival.

The legal systems of most Western societies and some Asian countries are based on either one or a combination of two frameworks:

- Civil law—derived from Roman Law or the Napoleonic Code, or
- Common law—established by the judicial process over time.

Civil laws are prescriptive—they specify what shall be done. Consequently, civil law frameworks tend to be inflexible, if not rigid. Maintenance of the status quo has the advantage over change, whether or not intended.

Common laws are proscriptive—they stipulate actions that are prohibited. Since the judicial process is continuous, flexibility and response to change can be accommodated readily. New layers of laws and regulations affecting business are generally responses to the unethical conduct or reporting abuses of an ill-advised few, yet all become subject to the additional restrictions and the costs of compliance.

The legal environments of host countries, although differing widely, define the rules of the business game. MNEs must learn and attempt to abide by the rules in the scores of countries in which they operate. Different rules are often applied to foreign and domestic firms, even though comparable treatment may be stipulated.

Regardless of their peculiarities, the regulatory environments provide host governments with control over the game by means of three "aces": the powers to legislate, to tax, and to expropriate. The first two can promote or prohibit foreign investment, as well as adopt all sorts of nuances in between. Playing the last ace brings the game to an end.

Statutory environments affect all aspects of host country operations and determine many. Entry laws determine what sectors will be open to foreign investment, the form and extent of foreign ownership, and, quite often, the locations of plant sites and the infrastructures required. Regulations also can prescribe the levels of: domestic ownership and management, indigenous resources to be employed, foreign-exchange holdings, capital and dividend repatriations, as well as interest rates and other fees to be levied by the parent or affiliated firms.

Tax legislation is particularly vexing. A wide variety of alien types of taxes are encountered, with an even wider variety of rates and taxable bases. Tax administration systems can be classical, split-rate, or imputed. Special tax treaties, tax incentives, and tax holidays serve to simplify as well as further confuse. Needless to say, international tax-planning literally borders upon the impossible.

Last, but not least, companies acts and tax laws affect reporting practices. Diversities in depreciation allowances, inventory valuations, and treatments of investment incentives impact reported incomes. The effects of all such divergences from generally accepted accounting principles in the United States must be removed upon preparation of consolidated statements by the U.S. parent. However, should financial performances of foreign operations be evaluated in the context of host or home country environments; before or after actual or potential tax liabilities?

Mention should at least be made here (and will be expanded upon later) that the MNE holds the fourth "ace" of the game—transfer pricing. MNEs can (and do) use transfer prices selectively to ameliorate (if not circumvent) almost any control imposed by a host government.

Economic Environments

The MNE was the first institution that attempted to marshal and manage economic resources on a worldwide basis. The inherent potential for economic efficiency holds great promise for the peoples of all nations. Some of this promise has been realized.

According to the broadest, on-going study of the effects of MNEs begun by Harvard University in 1965, MNEs have effectively supplied capital needs, reduced oligopoly control, enhanced compeition, and increased consumer choice within industrialized countries.[4]

The jury is still out regarding the net effects upon the economies of developing nations. The ambivalence of many host countries toward the MNE has been captured in traditional British humor:

> It fiddles its accounts. It avoids or evades its taxes. It rigs its intracompany transfer prices. It is run by foreigners, from decision centers thousands of miles away. It imports foreign labor practices. It overpays. It underpays. It competes unfairly with local firms. It is in cahoots with local firms. It exports jobs from rich countries. It is an instrument of rich countries' imperialism. The technologies it brings to the third world are old-fashioned. No, they are too modern. It meddles. It bribes. Nobody can control it. It wrecks balances of payments. It overturns economic policies. It plays off governments against each other to get the biggest investment incentives. Won't it please come and invest? Let it bloody well go home.[5]

All the environmental factors mentioned thus far impact economic affairs in one way or another. Add to that the realization that MNEs operate within a patchwork of national economies of different types, in different stages of development, and with different growth patterns. Local businesses vary in form, ownership, size, and complexity. Competition may come from other MNEs or not exist at all. Here again, perhaps the only generalization possible is that MNEs prefer to work in, and rely upon, economies employing relatively free market mechanisms.

The variables that affect operating decisions of domestic U.S. firms are multiplied and accentuated. Multiple, instead of single, inflation rates must be coped with. The goals of transfer pricing are compounded. Short- and long-term tax strategies must negotiate a labyrinth of systems and rates. Information systems must synthesize a confusion of procedures that attempt to control, coordinate, report, and evaluate a hodgepodge of interrelated activities.

Exchange Rates. International economic dilemmas are dominated by one unique affliction—the absence of a universal currency or common unit of account. While space prohibits a detailed examination,[6] an overview is essential. Foreign-exchange considerations, from both internal and external viewpoints, generate serious impacts upon the conduct and evaluation of transnational operations.

Without a universal currency, international business transactions are confronted by two problems:

- Conversion—the *physical exchange* of one currency for another in settlement of business transactions.
- Translation—the *expression* of financial transactions and statements recorded or denominated in one unit of account into another.

Solutions to both the above problems are approached by the use of devices called "exchange rates"—ratios by which one currency is traded for others. By definition, exchange rates are appropriate mechanisms for physical exchanges (conversions) of different currencies, and for expressions (recordings) of transactions denominated in other than local currencies. Exchange rates were not designed for translating foreign-currency financial statements. However, they are the only convenient means available today.

Money serves two functions: as a medium of exchange, and as a store of value. Exchange rates can possibly perform the first function but not the latter. Value has been described as "the worth of a thing is what it will bring." Locally, the value attached to a given currency is its purchasing power—the goods and services it can command within its national environment. Internationally, the relative values of currencies should reflect their purchasing-power parities. Exchange rates, unfortunately, do not reflect the relative purchasing-powers of currencies.

Monies require some form of common denominator or standard. Over time, various international standards were employed. No standard exists today. Initially, under the *gold-bullion standard,* governments defined and redeemed their currencies in terms of gold (mint parities) that, in turn, established their exchange rates. Subsequently, various pressures upon gold holdings brought about the *gold-exchange standard.* Governments continued to define their currencies with respect to gold (official parities), but only the United States continued to redeem its currency in gold. This latter point effectively created a *gold-dollar standard* that was used by the International Monetary Fund (IMF) from its inception (in 1945) until 1970. At that time, the IMF created special drawing rights (SDRs)—or additional borrowing powers for member countries—to compensate for temporary deficiencies in gold and dollar holdings. The SDRs added a *"paper gold" standard*. In 1973, the international monetary system was effectively dismantled by two events. The United States cancelled the gold convertibility of the dollar, and permitted it to float. And, the Organization of Petroleum Exporting Countries (OPEC) declared economic warfare on the rest of the world by quadrupling the price of crude oil—and monetizing "black gold."

Each of the standards mentioned above served as a common denominator for the international monetary system. Although each had its innate and circumstantial defects, an identifiable basis for exchange rates was established, as well as reasonable parameters or bands, within which the rates moved over time. Today, the floating-rate "system" is actually the *absence* of any system. Outside their national boundaries, currencies have no common denominator. They have been transformed into commodities to be bartered along with all other goods and services in international trade. Money, in the international sense, has become a *circular concept*.

Exchange rate fluctuations in the recent past have been unusually volatile, both in frequency and amplitude. Moreover, there are no reasons to expect a return to reasonable stability in the near future. In the long run, the real value and exchange rate of a currency will continue to be determined, as it has been in the past, within the goods and services markets of the particular country. In the short to medium time-frames, exchange rates will be determined by the whims of the private financial markets. (This condition will persist until the international community tires of financial disorder, brings the OPEC countries in step with the rest of the world, and restores to the IMF the stature, authority, and resources it requires.)

Foreign-Currency Translations. The need for and practice of translating foreign-denominated transactions are as old as international trade itself. Early traders also recognized and accepted the risk that money prices might vary between the time a transaction was made and recorded, and the time it was settled. The differences (conversion gains or losses) represented adjustments to the costs or profits originally anticipated. Contemporary participants also accept the above as peculiarities and risks associated with trade across national boundaries.

Today, foreign-currency *financial statements* are also translated, and for several purposes:

- To prepare consolidated statements,
- For the convenience of users,
- To direct and control foreign operations, and
- To evaluate performances of foreign operations and their managers.

Consolidated financial statements. In the United States, consolidated financial statements are designed to report on and evaluate the economic entity as a whole rather than the separate legal entities. Where U.S. parent firms are concerned, component statements of foreign subsidiaries must first be adjusted (restated) to conform with U.S. accounting principles, then be expressed (translated) into terms of U.S. dollars. Several methods of translating statements have been employed in the United States and elsewhere, namely: (1) current-noncurrent, (2) monetary-nonmonetary, (3) current rate, and (4) temporal methods. The peculiarities of the various methods are not particularly relevant here. Their similarities are. Each method produces a difference whenever an item is translated at a rate other than that existing at the time it was originally recorded. No problems are presented by the differences attached to items sold, consumed, settled, or otherwise disposed of—they are reflected in current income as realized (conversion) gains and losses from closed transactions. Many problems are attached to those differences pertaining to unsettled or open exchanges. These open exchanges can be sorted into two components: those that will be realized in the near future (such as open payables and receivables), and those with indeterminate or doubtful realizations (noncurrent assets, deferrals, equities, and the like). The differences related to translations of open exchanges should be labeled for what they are—unrealized translation differences—reported by component (major currencies and potential realizabilities), and deferred, pending realization or subsequent adjustment as rates change over time.[7]

Financial Accounting Standard No. 8. Prior to January 1, 1976, the effective date of *Statement of Financial Accounting Standards No. 8 (FASB-8),*[8] U.S. parent MNEs applied various methods of translation (about equally divided between current-noncurrent and monetary-nonmonetary). Transaction (conversion) gains and losses were reported in current income, but material translation differences were processed through reserve accounts wherever available. The historical strength of the U.S. dollar enabled many of the older MNEs to build up significant, favorable translation differences. These cushions were used to absorb unfavorable differences as they arose.

FASB-8 required that the cushions be eliminated and that all translation "gains and losses," as well as transaction gains and losses, be reflected in current income. Realized gains and losses were commingled with translation (or paper) differences that might never affect cash flows. In effect, *FASB-8* required U.S.-based MNEs to report their foreign operations as if they had been conducted in the United States, in U.S. dollars, *and* were to be liquidated tomorrow. That display of economic nonsense triggered a rash of other uneconomic actions.

Financial journals were replete with reports of divestments of otherwise profitable foreign ventures by small and mid-size MNEs—economic evaluations became overshadowed by scare evaluations. The plights of other mid-sized MNEs to protect against "paper losses" generated a bonanza in foreign-exchange consulting fees for U.S. banks.[9] The larger MNEs were not motivated to overreact, at least initially. They benefited from ITT's $50 million lesson in 1974 that trying to outguess the vagaries of foreign-exchange markets is a zero-sum game. They also benefited from internal or structural "hedging" —the translation "exposures" of the multiplicity of currencies dealt in tended to be offsetting. Over time, however, the effects of paper gains and losses upon reported earnings per share[10] motivated even the larger companies to incur the significant costs of amelioration. The Monsanto Company established, in May 1970, a multilateral (intracorporate) netting facility in Switzerland (Monsanto Finance) monitored from Brussels (by Monsanto Europe). Intracorporate transactions represented half of all Monsanto's European settlements and, with that volume, annual savings in conversion costs alone were estimated at 1.5% per million dollars. Netting also provided additional intangible benefits related to the control of liquidity and net foreign exchange exposure.

Where intracorporate volumes have permitted, similar savings in conversion costs, and centralized management of exchange exposures, have been realized by the use of a reinvoicing center—a central point through which all transactions of an MNE's worldwide subsidiaries are processed. The center determines the most favorable national currencies in which the transactions are to be denominated, nets offsetting flows, and identifies and manages the remaining exposure. (International Harvester, Gillette, and Eli Lilly are examples of MNEs that have initiated centralized exchange-management systems such as those mentioned. Since start-up costs and break-even volumes are substantial, many large U.S. banks now conduct feasibility studies for interested firms.)

The results of major studies of the economic effects of *FASB-8* merely confirmed what was surmised. An FASB-sponsored study published in 1979[11] found that: (1) some firms had increased the hurdle rates for overseas investments; (2) others had refrained from foreign ventures that were otherwise desirable; and (3) that concerns of exchange risk had diverted the attentions of most managements from profitability to cash-flow evaluations. The latter finding led to the belief that managements tended to "overemphasize" the effects of *FASB-8* "gains and losses" upon reported earnings, while shrouding evaluations of future local earnings and similar important factors. (That emphasis should not have been surprising since *FASB-8* required the nebulous exchange "gains and losses" to be disclosed prominently, whereas the attendant costs of exchange management were buried, and the costs of opportunities foregone were never recorded.)

A research study of the impact of *FASB-8* sponsored by the Financial Executives Institute[12] found that: most respondents (52%) had revised their foreign capital-mix and many (32%) reported resultant increases in money costs; a significant number of firms (68%) decided to incur the real economic costs of hedging in order to minimize paper losses; and the large majority (80%) of executives decried the management time diverted from the real problems and opportunities of foreign operations.

The foregoing narrative should illustrate that *FASB-8* multiplied the fictions inherent in consolidated financial statements. The greatest disservice, however, was the diversion of emphasis from the real economic performances of entities and their segments by sanctifying myopic evaluations in U.S. dollars. In effect, financial evaluations suffered from regression to a home-country orientation and its attendant fallacies. (Although reluctantly, the FASB issued a proposed amendment to *FASB-8* in late August 1980 that will return to square one—transaction gains and losses will be reflected in current income; translation differences will be deferred in the equity section.)

The lesson should be clear. Exchange rates and translated financial statements introduce economic illusions that can impair macro- and micro-evaluations of entities. Their use as tools to evaluate past performances or future economic decisions can only be attempted at great risk.

Convenience translations.   Financial reports are often expressed in terms of currencies other than the reporting currency for the convenience of certain users.

An increasing number of MNEs are adopting the practice of furnishing reports in several national languages and currencies to promote better understandings by local stakeholders. Usually, the exchange rate existing at the date of the report is applied to all the amounts, thereby preserving the relationships among the data.

Internally, convenience translations may be of value to managers who have not become accustomed to thinking in more than one currency. However, the essence of the statements (data relationships) must be preserved.

Direction and control.   Other than for convenience, translated statements are of little value to local managers.

Regardless of the roles assigned to the various subsidiaries, their operations will be subject to host-country rules and environments. Accounting and reporting requirements of the host country must be satisfied. In some instances, statutory recordkeepings may be archaic —designed to make work rather than decisions. In other cases, accounts will be required to conform with local tax regulations, and be of little value to management. In most cases, the parent firm will also levy accounting and reporting requirements either in local or parent-country currencies. In all cases, local operating decisions must be made in light of local conditions. Consequently, most sub-sidiaries keep multiple sets of records. One will be used by local managers to direct and control operations, and it should be in terms of the local currency.

Performance evaluations. Foreign-currency financial statements lose much of their relevance outside the context of their particular domiciles.

For activity evaluations, foreign statements could simply be expressed in another currency (convenience translations), or they could be restated to conform with the accounting principles of the parent as well. Convenience translations are valid measures of financial performance *iff* the foreign activities are independent profit centers *and* if the profits generated are to be repatriated to the parent as they are earned. The operating characteristics peculiar to each domicile would be retained in the income statements, and the one-way flows of profits would be expressed in the parent's currency. (Of course, the usual cautions would apply to balance sheet items since the amounts, before or after translation, would rarely represent economic values.) *Restated* translations are invalid measures of activity performance. To reconstruct the results of foreign operations as if they had been conducted in the parent country and in the parent's currency is an exercise in fantasy. Evaluations based upon such fantasies are myths. Nonetheless, since U.S. accounting and reporting standards require such aberrations to be conjured routinely, some executives are prone to use them to assess foreign activities, as well as to compare them with their domestic counterparts.

There are no valid reasons for translating foreign operating statements in order to evaluate the performances of local managers. Foreign operations are conducted within given domiciles and in terms of local currencies. Whether or not financial performances are primary measures of foreign operations, local managers tend to have imperfect to no effective control over exchange exposures or fluctuations in exchange rates. To presume controls where none exist is to perform illusory evaluations.

STRATEGIC ROLES

Worldwide pursuit of comparative advantage has led to the evolution of MNE organizations structured from global perspectives. National frameworks have been transcended and their concepts are no longer appropriate. A variety of organizational forms exists, with no apparent consensus. Structures that have evolved were influenced by many factors: attitudes of chief executives, perceived objectives, natures of products, sizes and complexities of the parent firms.

Initially, foreign operations were primarily branch operations, controlled much as if they were in Chicago or San Francisco. The first foreign subsidiaries were treated as step-children; concerns over the safety of investments overshadowed those of profitability. Eventually, foreign investments were undertaken for their potential earnings in local currencies in accordance with local conditions. Today, multinationals are cosmopolitan—networks of operations generate and reinvest earnings in multiple locations and currencies; nationalities are no longer primary considerations. Operating units perform a variety of interdependent and strategic roles. The synergistic effects negate customary approaches of independent and relative evaluations of the subsidiaries.

Financing

The large majority of MNEs exercise centralized control of financial activities, either from the parent or regional headquarters. Some MNEs (such as Exxon) regularly deal in over a hundred currencies. The most desirable trade-offs and exposures require the expertise and market information available only at a centralized facility.

Financial activities represent the most sophisticated and adaptable of all the functional areas. Commercial and merchant banks have cooperated with MNEs to thwart the policies of countries and national banks, providing financial resources where needed, and creating new resources if necessary—such as Eurocurrencies.

Financings of local units vary. Different inflation rates and exchange controls create variances in credit policies, inventory levels, financial structures, and their related costs. The leads and lags applied to intracompany loans and other payments affect the money costs and cash flows of subsidiaries and parents alike. Some units function as funnels to channel earnings to parents; others serve as low-tax reservoirs for resources to be redeployed wherever needed.

Manufacturing

As on-site manufacturing replaced the earlier emphasis on international trade by MNEs, networks of interdependent affiliates were formed.

Today, sales by MNEs are estimated at $700 billion, or roughly one-fifth of the gross world product. The growth rate of MNEs worldwide averaged nearly twice that of the world economy, until the OPEC debacle contorted international statistics. According to the U.S. Department of Commerce, foreign operations represent one-third of the total volumes of over 200 U.S. corporations. Also, the Commerce Department estimated that, for the period 1966 to 1971, one-fourth of total U.S. exports represented transfers from U.S. parents to their overseas subsidiaries.

As early as the end of 1977, foreign operations of at least 10 U.S. non-oil MNEs accounted for more than one-third of their consolidated sales and/or profits (Table 4-1). Had intracompany transactions not been eliminated the foreign shares would undoubtedly have been even greater.

Table 4-1. Magnitudes of Foreign Operations Reported by Selected U.S. Multinationals for 1977.

| | FOREIGN PERCENTAGES OF 1977 TOTAL | | |
COMPANY	SALES	OPERATING PROFITS	ASSETS
Coca Cola	44%	58%	45%
Colgate-Palmolive	56	63	54
Dow Chemical	45	35	48
Ford Motor	35	44*	47
IBM	50	45*	48
ITT	51	52	45
Johnson & Johnson	41	50	44
Pfizer	53	64	56
Standard Brands	34	35	42
Xerox	44	35*	47

Note: * denotes operating incomes (after allocations of common corporate expenses); operating profits would be greater than percentages shown.

Manufacturing subsidiaries have a variety of roles. They seek out favorable cost environments. They follow competition as well as initiate it. They protect technologies and patents, and begin new life cycles in new environments for products that have matured at home. They represent solutions to host-country pressures for increases in local investment and value-added increments to products.

Intermediate components and finished products—including imports to the parent domicile—are manufactured, assembled, stored, and transferred from country to country. Differences in costs, economies of scale, modes of manufacturing, and host-country environments all influence the roles, contributions, and profitabilities of the subsidiaries. Few will be comparable.

Sourcing

The primary roles of some foreign subsidiaries do not involve local generations of profit. Common examples are those units established to assure access to and dependable supplies of raw materials. The extractive and agricultural industries are cases in point.

Other units are organized to ameliorate the effects of tariffs, quotas, exchange and price controls, and similar trade barriers. Still other subsidiaries are expected to function as profitable waste baskets— they are sent fully depreciated, dilapidated equipment and obsolete goods, charged at new prices, and expected to generate the same ROIs as their more competitive sister units.

Marketing

There is little question that the present phase of the MNE evolution concerns the pursuit of markets, a diverse and difficult field of endeavor.

The "marketing concept" stipulates that products should be attuned to customers' needs. Some marketers like to believe they create needs or, at least, they tend to equate the absence of an item with an unfilled need. Regardless, the cultural differences cited earlier present a wealth of opportunities for different products and operations. In some cases, the perishable nature of the product itself will influence how operations will be conducted. In still others, the reduction of distribution costs will be the primary functions of local or regional subsidiaries.

Since the marketing function determines the pulse rate of most enterprises, even relatively small increases in market shares by each unit in a global network add up to significant increases in aggregate demand, economies of scale, and overall profitability.

Synergistic results. Each unit contributes to its own profitability and enhances that of its affiliate and parent units as well. Such contributions are difficult to evaluate.

Transfer Pricing

In the preceding chapter, the pursuit of equity was cited as the objective of domestic transfer prices. Outside the United States, equitable treatment of subunits is, at best, an afterthought, if it is considered at all.

MNEs must, and do, consider equitable divisions of profits with host governments. Transfer prices may represent amounts assigned to flows of goods and services among subunits of an *economic* entity. However, host governments consider these transfers as revenue-producing transactions between and among separate *legal entities*— and host countries expect a reasonable share of the profits generated. What is considered to be "reasonable" will depend upon circumstantial factors, but most host countries will not complain so long as the MNE does not appear to be too greedy.

International transfer prices are managed. They are devised to serve a multitude of purposes, the end results of which are to maximize benefits to the MNE as a whole. As a general rule, transfer pricing schemes are used to reduce or circumvent the effects of regulatory constraints, to enhance profitability, to control the locales in which profits accrue, to minimize total tax liabilities, and to control intracompany cash transfers. No single system can accommodate all circumstances.

Naturally, transfer prices designed to achieve the above objectives cannot serve to guide the decisions made by local managers. Moreover, they impact significantly the accounting data normally used to evaluate local activities and their managers. Dual transfer prices as well as parallel transfer pricing systems have been employed with mixed success. In most cases the decision bases of local managers have been improved. However, little success has been evidenced in removing the biases in data used for evaluation purposes.

COORDINATIVE MANAGEMENT

In the domestic milieu, the increasing size and complexity of corporate firms required that control give way to decentralization early on. In the international realm, multinational operations mandate that much of the autonomy associated with decentralization must yield to co-ordination, if the best interest of the total entity are to be pursued.

Coordination strikes a reasonable balance between autonomy and control. Those functions considered to be vital to the entity as a whole are selected, integrated, and managed from a central or regional headquarters. The remaining activities are decentralized. Only a central unit has access to internal and external information in the depth and scope necessary to assess certain problems, the interdependencies that exist, and the implications of decisions. The exercise of coordination also circumscribes those activities that will be controllable by local managers.

Naturally, the process of coordination will vary between and among companies at a point in time, as well as within a given MNE over time. All firms will not consider the same functions to be critical. Also, the relative importance of functional areas or specific activities will change with time and circumstance.

As is typical of most dilemmas, problem recognition and understanding are most important. Today's multinational enterprise is not a decentralized company. A different perspective is required.

From the viewpoint of conventional methods, coordinative management is an alien approach. It is essentially a process whereby the several operating units of the worldwide network are forced to cooperate, rather than go about their separate pursuits. To use accounting jargon, the parts must articulate. Usually, managers will be required to meet more frequently to discuss existing, emerging, and anticipated problems. The strategic roles of some units will need to be revised more often to accommodate change. Policies guiding local decisions will tend to become more variable as the relative importances of their focal points rise and fall in ascendancy. Management information systems must become more flexible and responsive to the changing demands of managers at all levels.

Coordinative management is much more dynamic than conventional systems. Perhaps the analogy that depicts coordinative management best would be the modern art form called the "mobile," in which a variety of abstract forms are loosely assembled in various ways, balanced, suspended in midair, and set into motion by kinetic energy. Subordinate forms are located at many levels, with various horizontal and vertical connections all emanating from a central form at the top. Each form contains a center of gravity or focal point (the operating unit) surrounded and affected by its local environments. Given a static total environment, the mobile is still. As air currents move around the whole figure or its separate parts, some forms are set in motion, often with different speeds and directions. The parts set in motion will affect certain other parts directly, and will influence the stability of all other parts indirectly as vibrations are transmitted over the network of connecting linkages to the central form. The position of the central form may also be forced to change. By repositioning, however, the central form maintains the overall balance, adjusts its own center of gravity as well as that of each of the subordinate parts, and acts to restore equilibrium.

Executives of MNEs are not naive. The realize that they manage differently today. Whether or not they choose to attach one name tag or another to the process is irrelevant. What is important, and tends to go unrecognized, is the effect of coordinative management upon the roles of subunits and their managers. New evaluation methods must be developed.

Activities are called upon to play a variety of strategic roles dependent upon organizational structures and environmental considerations. Strategic roles and short-run profit motives are not compatible. Primary reliance upon profit-based measures has become obsolete— and could easily mislead. Reporting alternatives other than single-purpose consolidated statements should be examined. General-purpose financial statements also will have limited usefulness. Subsidiary statements in local currencies (or translated for convenience) may be appropriate starting points for activity evaluations. Augmentations will be found necessary since different reports will be required to address various objectives and the interests of an assortment of stake-holders.

Managerial evaluations will prove to be the most difficult. As with activities, evaluations should be in accordance with the management-by-objectives (MBO) concepts that parallel coordinative management. The interdependencies that exist will dictate that managers should be evaluated by their *total* contributions—those accruing to their own units, other affiliates, and the parent. The identification, measurement, and assessment of these contributions will call for multiple performance criteria that are controllable. No single measure or specific set of measures or techniques has yet been found to be appropriate. Measures will have to be tailored to fit the particular circumstances, and approved and revised as circumstances change.

The above issues are not amenable to simplex approaches or solutions. Activity evaluations, however, tend to be less troublesome since inputs and outputs are more readily traceable. Managerial contributions, on the other hand, are plagued not only by problems of traceability, but the more perplexing issues of controllability as well. Consequently, evaluations of overseas managers tend to be mere reflections of the financial evaluations of their activities—if they are performed at all.

Whether or not admitted, executives of domestic firms have not been entirely satisfied with performance evaluations of U.S. operations and managers. If the problems regarding performance evaluations within a homogeneous environment cannot be resolved, then there is little hope for satisfactory resolutions of the more complex issues surrounding international and multinational operations.

Performance evaluations are managerial problems primarily, and accounting problems secondarily. Management must identify the objectives of activities and the contributions expected from, and controllable by, their managers. Accountants must then address methods of measuring, charting, and reporting results as they are achieved.

Costs are involved. But benefits also accrue, not the least of which is the enhancement of management effectiveness (and profit) that comes from simply a better understanding of the intricacies of one's own enterprise.

NOTES

1. These concerns are examined at length in Elwood L. Miller, *Accounting Problems of Multinational Enterprises* (Lexington, Mass.: Lexington Books/ D. C. Heath & Co., 1979), Chapter 2.

2. Howard V. Perlmutter, "The Tortuous Evolution of the Multinational Corporation," *Columbia Journal of World Business,* January-February 1969, pp. 9–18.

3. Howard V. Perlmutter, "Alternative Futures for the Multinational," in: "Proceedings, Second Annual International Business Conference," Saint Louis University, December 16, 1976, p. 23. © Saint Louis University School of Business and Administration.

4. An address by Frederick T. Knickerbocker, in: "Proceedings, First Annual International Business Conference," Saint Louis University, December 1, 1975. Unpublished, Saint Louis University School of Business and Administration.

5. *The Economist,* London, January 24, 1976, p. 68.

6. For a detailed examination, see: Miller (note 1), Chapters 7 and 8.

7. John K. Shank and Gary S. Shamis, "Reporting Foreign Currency Adjustments: A Disclosure Perspective," *The Journal of Accountancy,* April 1979, pp. 59–65.

8. Financial Accounting Standards Board, *Statement of Financial Accounting Standards No. 8,* "Accounting for the Translation of Foreign Currency Transactions and Foreign Currency Financial Statements," (Stamford, Conn.: FASB, October 1975).

9. "Banks Cash in on FASB-8," *Business Week,* December 6, 1976, p. 104.

10. James J. Kerley, Executive Vice-President, Finance, Monsanto Co., address to the Conference Board, February 14, 1979. Adapted in: "Statements in Quotes," *The Journal of Accountancy,* July 1979, pp. 79–81.

11. Thomas G. Evans, William R. Folks, Jr., and Michael Jilling, *The Impact of Statement of Financial Accounting Standards No. 8 on the Foreign Exchange Risk Management Practices of American Multinationals: An Economic Impact Study* (Stamford, Conn.: FASB, 1979).

12. John K. Shank, Jesse F. Dillard, and Richard J. Murdock, *Assessing the Economic Impact of FASB No. 8* (New York: Financial Executives Research Foundation, 1979).

5
The Nature of Measurement

An aura of mysticism seems to surround the process of measurement. Identifying and assigning numerical values to things has long been considered an honorific activity. Some of the mystique has been contributed by the objects being measured, such as, the distance to the sun, or the structure of an atom. Much of the aura, however, can be attributed to the use of mathematics, a language almost everyone learns to various extents, only to have it atrohpy from nonuse.

Little aura attaches itself to more mundane measurements made by businessmen and accountants—although the latter group does benefit from the tendency of the uninitiated to consider them mathematicians rather than arithmeticians.

Nonetheless, so long as those associated with business hold it out to be an activity that generates postive-sum benefits, they had better be prepared to identify and measure those benefits. Accounting, as the language of business, attempts to maintain charts of the various activities and express the benefits produced, as well as their attendant costs, usually in monetary terms.

Financial accounting has addressed total entities, primarily. Managerial accounting has focused upon operating segments and their managers. Both processes involve measurement. Problems often arise when macro-measures are applied to micro-units, or when the natures of the measurements themselves are not understood.

MEASUREMENT SYSTEMS

Almost every business and accounting journal will contain one or more articles belaboring problems of measurement. Some will address the difficulties inherent in the subject under consideration, such as, changing price-levels. All too many will reflect the frustrations caused by attempting to do what cannot be done—transform fields of endeavors that are social into natural sciences.

To the extent that journeys into the abstract are made in the pursuit of knowledge, perhaps the only resulting detriment is that portion of the journals rendered unintelligible. On the other hand, the resources used in searches for ideal systems waiting to be discovered are diverted from the efforts needed to make practical systems more meaningful and useful.

Ideal Systems

Most often, ideal measurement systems are defined as integrated, coherent wholes. The use of standardized principles, terms, units, and methods enable measurements taken at micro-levels to be summarized and employed at successive- and macro-levels as well.

The objectives focus upon cause-effect, input-output relationships. Measurements should be quantifiable, both from the standpoint of precision and of their capability for mathematical manipulation and analysis. Expression in terms of a common denominator, such as dollars, enhances comparability. Direct, as opposed to surrogate, measures are preferable, and all should be neutral or without bias. The measures should also be consistent, cost-effective, and clear. The last attribute simply means that the information produced should reflect what it purports to measure, appear to be reasonable to the user, and not tend to be misleading.

Practical Systems

For the so-called social "sciences," ideal systems are little more than illusions.

Searches for integrated, coherent structures are futile. An excellent example is the present scurrying about by the FASB in search of a conceptual framework for accounting.[1] (Although never actually admitted, the FASB is seeking to discover a model founded upon immutable truths with which it can defend its pronouncements, thereby shielding itself from business pressure and further "politicization."[2])

Practical subsystems are achievable. Complex systems can be understood and examined by addressing their component parts that are manageable. The nature of the operations of each segment can be taken directly into account. Objectives may involve the acquisition of benefits from external sources (such as sales), the provision of goods or services internally, or some combination of both. The objectives identified will also identify the system of measurement that will be most meaningful and useful. The units of measurement will tend to vary with, and be determined by, the nature of the activities to be measured. Eclectic approaches will, in many instances, preclude expressions of the measures selected in terms of a common denominator. However, that is not all bad since the unrealistic assumptions and structural defects associated with most common denominators will have been avoided.

Surrogate measures will often be found most useful. Many service centers, for instance, engage in a variety of unstandardized activities involving managed costs. Although costs usually represent valid measures of inputs rather than outputs, it may be that operating within the constraints of budgeted costs will be the only practicable financial measures of the performances of some centers. Of course, many forms of nonfinancial output measures can (and should) be developed *and* related to the financial costs.

Practical approaches provide practical solutions. Not scientific, perhaps, but not misleading either.

OBJECTIVES TO BE MEASURED

The important items and operating aspects controllable by each responsibility center should be identified. Naturally, these items will vary in number and in kind.

Wherever possible, the objectives should be quantified to assist measurement and evaluation. Attempts to construct graphic portrayals of activities have proved to also be tests of their measurability. Not all things can be quantified and explained meaningfully in the language of numbers. However, virtually everything can be expressed and explained in the language of words. Each language has its particular values and purposes.

Starting with definitions of the objectives related to particular activities conforms with the management process itself. Chief executives establish strategic (long-range) plans dealing with effective allocations of resources given the existing and expected environmental constraints. Lower management echelons translate the strategic goals into tactical (mid-term) plans—the process of management-by-objectives. At the operating levels, near-term plans (usually covering one year) are developed in the form of budgets that express the objectives in financial terms. The more effective budgets also include relevant nonmonetary data, as well as the assumptions upon which the budgets were constructed. The budgets are then reviewed for conformity with overall company objectives and approved, as submitted, or following adjustments agreed upon. Thereafter, the management information system is tasked with charting and reporting progress toward the approved goals, whether financial or nonfinancial.

From that perspective, it should be evident that there is no realistic way to assess overall conditions in one measure. The objectives must be subdivided into practical components that, upon evaluation, will be indicative of their contributions toward the welfare of the whole.

The various operating segments and their particular objectives will determine the nature and frequency of the measurement process, as well as identify the most appropriate units of measure. Managements should select the best measuring tools available.

UNITS OF MEASUREMENT

An appropriate unit of measurement exists, or can be devised, for every objective, activity, or thing. Some are more direct, significant, and readily identifiable than others. Some are familiar and comfortable. Others are not familiar, and therefore suspect.

Quantitative measures of things that can be counted are desirable since they can be expressed in various systems or scales:

- Ratio scales—systems having natural zero-points with which observations or performances can be compared. Common examples are: return on investment, and percentages of net income, contribution margin, and plant capacity used.
- Interval scales—systems with no zero point; equal differences between items (intervals) indicate equal differences in values. Numbers of units sold or returned, and numbers of shares traded are examples.

- Ordinal scales—items are ranked by numbers in order of significance. Higher numbers can signify better performance (ranked by sales) or inefficiency (ranked by costs per order).
- Nominal scales—items are merely classified by type and quantity. Determining overseas sales outlets that carry inventories and those that do not, and showing the number in each category is an example.

Fortunately, most items to be measured within the operating parameters of an enterprise can be quantified, either directly (in terms of units of input or output) or relatively (in terms of financial units of money). Other objectives, such as some product characteristics, can only be measured in qualitative terms.

Unfortunately, measurement in a single unit is not always practicable. For instance, a firm usually wishes to maximize the outputs of acceptable products or services within reasonable constraints on input costs. Monetary, nonfinancial, and qualitative units must be used, singly and in combination. Standards or benchmarks (topics of the next section) must also be constructed—someone must determine what is acceptable and reasonable. Consequently, an honest (yet unacceptable) answer to the question "how are we doing?" may well be "it all depends!".

Monetary and qualitative measures pose the most problems. Costs are accounting measures of inputs; revenues are accounting measures of outputs. Both are monetary measures. Their validity depends upon the stability of money as a common denominator. The amounts in money terms are the products of unit prices (P) times unit quantities (Q). Whenever P is unstable, accomplishment or growth in *real* terms requires that emphasis be placed upon Q. (This rather simple change in emphasis seems to be much more desirable than proposals to replace historical costs by any of the other bases suggested: current or replacement costs; or the value bases—present, economic, opportunity, and exit values.) Changes in real terms (quantities produced or sold) could be compared readily with changes in nominal terms (production costs or sales revenues in dollars). Similar techniques could be applied to nearly every important item in financial statements. The ability to cope with the real impacts of changing price-levels upon a firm or segment, acting within its particular environment, would be determined. Disclosures would be simple and understandable.

(This disclosure method, championed by the author, is called "inflation explanation."[3] Since the FASB "decided not to decide" in its *Statement No. 33*,[4] the SEC has required that the effects of inflation upon reporting companies will be *explained,* effective with fiscal years ending after December 15, 1980.[5] It will be interesting to see how companies and accountants—as well as the SEC—will respond. Many companies do not seem to be fully aware of the SEC requirements as yet.)

Qualitative measures also present dilemmas, as those involved with "social accounting" (measurement and evaluation of the social performance of large companies) will attest.[6] Sometimes things that cannot be counted directly can be expressed on a *pseudo-numerical scale.* Items can be assessed (as unacceptable, poor, fair, good, and excellent), assigned values from zero to four, and treated much the same as quantifiable items. In other cases, surrogate measures are possible, such as the use of "shadow prices," but, quite often, narrative descriptions will be the best measuring tools available. The latter should be recognized as no more subjective than the future values or probabilities interjected by some accountants and operations researchers. Narrative descriptions, supported by available data, continue to be the most representative and useful assessments of local environments by foreign subsidiaries.

Performance evaluations should address the effectiveness and efficiency of activities and their managers. These objectives point toward different units of measure.

Effectiveness means doing the right something, which may refer to inputs (such as sales orders) or outputs (products or services). Physical measures in units are often the most direct and useful initial measures of performance. Attention should also be given to qualitative measures, such as: the sales-mix of orders, product qualities, timeliness of deliveries, and the like. Such measures are alien to financial information systems and, unfortunately, to all too many management information systems.

Efficiency, or doing something right, tends to emphasize dollar measures. Properly designed systems of standard costs and flexible budgets can routinely examine both quantity and price variances of inputs and outputs. Most important factors will be given attention so long as the "netting" aspects of variances are recognized, and the qualitative impacts of quests for efficiency are not overlooked.

The greatest benefit that accrues from considerations of the topics mentioned thus far is the realization that enterprises and their segments pursue multiple objectives. Profitability is certainly an important one, but it is only one dimesion of short- and long-run plans.

STANDARDS

Measurements become much more useful when they can be measured themselves by comparison with some benchmark. These bases of comparison are known as standards.

Standards may be classified into two general types:

- Normative, or absolute, and
- Nonnormative, or relative.

Normative standards indicate what should be or take place by means of predetermined norms or benchmarks. Norms can be established in a variety of ways: by reference to past performances; by estimates of what is reasonably attainable, given the circumstances; based upon state-of-the-art or engineered estimates; and, of course, simply by fiat.

Normative standards benefit from two advantages, one of which is moot. Normative standards are relatively easy to apply in practice. They are also favored for their objectivity, but that attribute depends upon how the norms were established. Someone must determine what "should be." Subjectivity necessarily exists, but in design rather than application. Subjectivity—or, judgment is a better term—is not *malum per se*. Business and accounting, as arts, are steeped in the exercise of judgment. But that judgment must be regarded as sound, or at least not in conflict with common sense. Reason dictates that, as conditions change, standards must also be updated.

Where performance evaluations are concerned, recognition of the multidimensional aspects is critical. Each activity may suggest the need for multiple measures. For instance, a marketing center may call for assessments of: sales mix; contributions by product and sales representative; numbers of customers called upon, added, or lost; sales returns; customer complaints; and the like. Also, the interests or objectives of activities often require resolution; for example, marketing prefers generous inventories to minimize back orders during the selling season, whereas, manufacturing wants to level production runs, lowering costs of making products but increasing costs of financing inventories—and adding a bit more gray to the controller's hair. Trade-offs must be agreed upon and reflected in existing standards.

Recognition of the multiple dimensions to be considered will go far toward preventing management myopia—the belief that a single measure or standard can evaluate multiple and conflicting goals.

Budgets, tailored to fit the circumstances, and adjusted to conform with actual levels of activity, will be found to be the best *primary* standards of performance. *Secondary* standards should be used as supplements to assess important factors not addressed routinely within the budgets (market shares, new products developed, numbers of customers, orders processed, backlogs, and similar items).

Relative standards do not require norms to be established. Instead, current results or values are compared with those of prior periods, other subsidiaries, competitor firms, or the particular industries.

In practice, relative standards are often used because they are convenient. Objectivity can further be enhanced wherever comparisons can be made with external values.

The major requirement of relative standards is, of course, that the activities or results must be *comparable*. If not, the effects of situational or structural differences are commingled with those of performance. Recognition of this defect is relevant whenever overseas activities are compared with each other or with their domestic counterparts.

REPORTING ASPECTS

It was stipulated earlier that a management accounting system should provide the right information, to the right people, at the right time. A good system will do the above at the lowest possible cost.

What information is right will depend in large measure upon the people concerned, as well as the other way around.

The levels to which measurement reports are to be addressed will indicate the objectives involved, as well as the most appropriate measurement systems and standards to be employed:

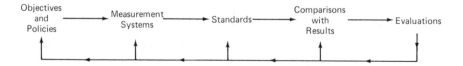

Operating levels will also affect the nature of the measurements reported. In general, the lower the echelon, the greater the detail. Consequently, the data should enable integration as it flows upward. At all levels, the information should be as clear-cut, easy to understand, and concise as possible. (This author has particular aversions to inch-thick computer printouts, encoded gobbledygook, and similar products of papermills that are held out as information systems. If information cannot be communicated intelligibly it ceases to be information.) The measures should be relevant to (or controllable by) the level for which the data have been prepared. The usefulness of quantifiable measures can be enhanced by comparative displays, such as trends over time.

Environments and situations will also affect what data are right. As money becomes a defective common denominator, dollar amounts lose much of their relevance. Units sold become more useful indicators of activity than dollar sales. Similarly, dollars of receivables and inventories become less meaningful than the numbers of day's sales outstanding or covered by inventories. Caution should be exercised, however, where composite measurements are involved or attempted, because of problems of mixes and weights. Internal composites (sales mixes) usually call for segmented measurements and evaluations. Also, applications of external composites (various price indices) do not really express measurements in common or constant dollars, but rather in common or constant bundles of goods and services. Care must be used to assure that the right bundles are selected.

Experience indicates that the problems associated with keeping measurements in step with changing circumstances are often exacerbated by computer technicians. Such situations are paradoxical since, if computer programs and systems could remain static, there would be little continued need for the services of EDP technicians. Regardless, more and more companies, frustrated by the resources wasted on false starts and ineffective EDP systems, have enlightened their computer technicians that systems are to serve the needs of management rather than the whims of systems designers.[7]

The natures of the people or managers concerned will also affect the natures of the measurements and the manners in which they are reported. Some executives are comfortable with and prefer graphical presentations supported by concise written explanations.[8] They find them easy to understand and remember. These reporting and evaluation methods will be examined later. Suffice it to say here that computer-generated graphics is a field that is expanding rapidly and may hold great promise.[9] However, the old warning that "figures don't lie, but liars figure" should be heeded since graphic measurements can produce misleading inferences if they are constructed improperly.[10]

Concise written narratives are not easy either. In the author's opinion, the young person entering business today with the knack for assimilating masses of detail and summarizing them in a one-page report has his or her future assured.

The last (but certainly not least) criterion of reported measurements is timeliness. The best designed measures and reports are of little value if they are not made available when decisions are to be made or corrective actions can be taken. In practice, unexpected changes in environments, operations, or needs for information are accommodated by means of special or "flash reports." However, should one-time or as-necessary flash reports become routine aspects of information systems, then that symptom would indicate that the systems are no longer responsive and should be examined.

SUMMARY

Evaluations of complex enterprises and interdependent activities require a variety of measures. Macro-measures are suitable for application to the enterprise as a whole. Micro-measures are necessary to identify and assess the contributions of the component parts to the whole. Both approaches contain something of value. Either-or attitudes do not.

NOTES

1. *FASB Discussion Memorandum: Conceptual Framework for Financial Accounting and Reporting* (Stamford, Conn.: Financial Accounting Standards Board, December 2, 1976).

2. For example, see Marshall S. Armstrong, "The Politics of Establishing Accounting Standards," *Journal of Accountancy,* February 1977, pp. 76–79; and David Solomons, "The Politicization of Accounting," *Journal of Accountancy,* November 1978, pp. 65–72.

3. Elwood L. Miller, *Inflation Accounting* (New York: Van Nostrand Reinhold Company, 1980); also, "What's Wrong with Price-Level Accounting," *Harvard Business Review,* November-December 1978, pp. 111–118.

4. Financial Accounting Standards Board, *Statement of Financial Accounting Standards No. 33,* "Financial Reporting and Changing Prices" (Stamford, Conn.: September 1979). Large firms were required to disclose, as supplementary information: selected data in common or constant dollars, as well as current costs, together with *explanations* and *discussions* of the data. Additional information was encouraged to be disclosed to assist user understanding.

The AICPA lost face by stipulating that the data and explanations be *unaudited.*

All but a handful of reporting firms presented the data required, stated that the information was not indicative of the effects of inflation upon their companies, but remained silent concerning the actual effects.

5. The SEC was understandably irked by the shortcomings of *FASB-33,* the renegings of professional responsibilities by the AICPA, and the absolute refusals by reporting firms to explain the effects of inflation (note 4, above).

Consequently, on September 2, 1980, the SEC issued four *Accounting Series Releases* (ASRs 278–281), totalling 354 pages, that integrate annual reports with the SEC's Form 10-K. One purpose stipulated by the SEC was the reduction of redundancies and costs of reporting. However, firms were also required to expand management discussions of operations to include the effects of inflation.

Also important is the fact that the four *ASRs* require generally accepted accounting principles to comply with SEC rules—an authority the SEC always possessed but exercised only when the private sector seemed unresponsive to user needs.

Although annual reports may become more informative and useful, the author, as a member of the accounting profession, would much rather have seen his profession be a leader of change rather than a follower.

6. Committee on Social Measurement, American Institute of Certified Public Accountants, *The Measurement of Corporate Social Performance* (New York: AICPA, 1977).

7. "A Corporate Viewpoint," an interview with Walter Wriston, Chairman of Citicorp, by Randolph L. Denosowicz, in: *The Columbia Journal of World Business,* Fall 1977, pp. 125–128.

8. George B. Blake, "Graphic Shorthand as an Aid to Managers," *Harvard Business Review,* March-April 1978, pp. 6–8, 12; see also, Gregory M. Leivian,

"How to Communicate Financial Data More Effectively," *Management Accounting,* July 1980, pp. 31–34.

9. "The Spurt in Computer Graphics," *Business Week,* June 16, 1980, pp. 104, 106.

10. Johnny R. Johnson, Robert R. Rice, and Roger A. Roemmich, "Pictures that Lie: the Abuse of Graphs in Annual Reports," *Management Accounting,* October 1980, pp. 50–56.

6
Studies and Opinions

Performance evaluation has been a continuing topic of interest over the last 25 years or more. During that period, more than a score of studies have been conducted. Several are under way at this time. The more relevant aspects and findings of eleven studies will be examined here.

Since all works are constructed (to various extents) upon those of others, previous studies seemed to represent appropriate places to begin. The problems encountered were rather frustrating at first. However, after sufficient sifting and winnowing, the sense of a trend or change (perhaps metamorphosis is a better term) over time evolved.

After nearly two decades of practice and experience, most observers would expect to find general improvement, not only in purposes, but methods as well. Whether or not refinements have occurred seems to be moot, and opinions will tend to vary with perspectives and points of view. Suffice it to say here that changes have taken place—and are continuing to evolve. What is presented here represents a still picture of a moving scene. Unfortunately, changes in contemporary practices seem to represent responses to external stimuli more than changes in the ways of thinking internally.

The problems encountered in examining the studies are mentioned here as caveats to all that follows. The foremost problem, of course, was the lack of comparability. Few studies could be considered as replicable—then or now. This fault is typical of studies of things social and is not peculiar to research in business, in general, or performance evaluation, in particular. Sizes of the populations studied were quite different, ranging from slightly more than two dozen or so to nearly two thousand firms. Differences in the composition of the firms studied were also prevalent in such areas as the sizes of the firms, the industries in which they were engaged, and the various emphases they placed upon international operations. Different time periods also were reflected; however, this difference was desirable.

Moreover, no matter how objectively a study (or this book, for that matter) is begun, all reporters of ideas are forced to interject colorings of their own opinions. Multiple or vague responses to some key questions often require subjective interpretations by those who study the behavior of others. Responses by firms to questionnaires and responses obtained in subsequent personal interviews with executives of those same firms often differed. Did the individual replying to the questionnaire respond as he or she believed things were done, or as he or she wished them to appear? Where multiple criteria were said to exist, some executives disavowed any purposive rank ordering, yet one would seem to be necessary.

As a consequence, it is not at all uncommon to see something in a different light each time a study is read again.

EVALUATIONS IN THE SIXTIES

As developed in chapter 3, the twin concepts of decentralization and profit responsibility came under close scrutiny in the United States in 1960. Challenges of accepted practices of performance evaluations emanated primarily from the academic sector and continue today.

The initial and majority of the challenges posed in the sixties focused upon the unsound reliance upon profit and ROI as measurements of the performances of *domestic* activities and managers. Foreign operations did not come under intensive scrutiny until the dawn of the seventies.

The issue deserving emphasis here is if, in fact, the *manner* in which popular evaluation measures were being applied to domestic activities was defective, how valid were these same measures when applied to foreign operations conducted within dissimilar environments?

For the sake of continuity, the studies in this chapter will be presented in chronological order and, where appropriate, in the following format: description of the study, major findings, and the comments and opinions of this author.

Mauriel and Anthony (1966)

In early 1966, Mauriel and Anthony published the results of a study conducted of the evaluation methods used by large U.S. firms.[1] No attempt was made to isolate and differentiate domestic and foreign operations.

Description of the Study. Two sequential surveys were conducted for two purposes: (1) to identify the extent of reliance upon the responsibility concept of the *investment center;* and (2) to determine how the *profit* and *investment* components were defined and measured.

In the first segment of the study, 3525 large U.S. companies (sales of $20 million or more) were polled. Slightly less than one-half (47%) were manufacturing firms; the remaining 53% were engaged in agriculture, transportation, and service industries. Responses were received from 75% (2658) of the companies polled and, of these, 1603 (or 60%) indicated that they had two or more investment centers.

The second phase queried 1378 of the 1603 firms regarding how they evaluated their investment centers—the remainder were eliminated for various reasons. Some 981 firms responded. Of these, 130 indicated that they misinterpreted the original questionnaire. Consequently, the responses from 851 companies (68% of the 1248 considered eligible) served as the basis for the second phase and purpose of the study.

Major Findings. One important finding cited was the "rapid growth" in the use of the investment-center concept to evaluate operations. One-half[2] of the original 2658 companies had two or more investment centers and employed return-on-investment (ROI) or residual-income (RI) measures, alone or in combination, to evaluate activity performance. Also, of the 851 companies that applied investment-center measures routinely, more than half initiated the practices after 1955, and more than one-third after 1960.

What disturbed Mauriel and Anthony most was the finding that the depreciation methods used for external financial reporting by 97% of the firms were also used to compute the profits of investment centers. They were concerned, and rightly so, that operations were being "misevaluated"—measures designed to serve external purposes were being used to assess internal performances.

Comments and Opinions. The study indicated clearly that investment centers had replaced profit centers in popularity. Also, as might have been expected, the movement from profit to investment centers increased with the size of the firms. Similarly, nearly one-fourth of the smallest firms (sales of $20 to $35 millions) had not yet adopted profit-center concepts.

Clearly, ROI was the predominant measure used. Although 7% of the firms professed to use RI only, and another 23% reported using some combination of RI and ROI, the researchers believed that the numbers actually using RI were overstated since only 11% responded to specific RI queries, such as rates employed. Somewhat disturbing was the finding that only slightly more than half (51.4%) of the firms using ROI established different target rates for investment centers operating under different circumstances.

In sum, by the end of 1965, ROI had become the predominant measure of activity performance by large, U.S. companies. Unfortunately, almost all (97%) of the firms may well have constructed the measures incorrectly, and nearly half applied the same standard (target rate) to activities they may or may not have operated under like circumstances.

Little indication of logical progress was evident. Moreover, the study did not attempt to identify the methods used to evaluate the performances of managers, nor of overseas activities.

The Zenoff Discussions (1967)

In mid-1967, David Zenoff reported the results of his discussions with the financial executives of thirty prominent U.S.-based multinational enterprises.[3] The foreign operations of these firms represented one-sixth of the total overseas volumes of all U.S.-based MNEs. Zenoff's primary purpose was aimed at developing a feeling of the "attitudes" of the executives toward their foreign subsidiaries.

In Zenoff's opinion, overseas operations were considered as profitable "stepchildren" by their American parents. This characterization was applicable to firms having a long, successful history in international business as well as the relative neophytes.

The report dealt with discussions concerning three topics primarily: flows of funds to the parent, tax planning, and capital budgeting.

Various approaches to "slicing the foreign earnings pie" were noted. One group of firms followed the practice of first ascertaining the total amount of funds needed by the parent, then determining the sources (from what subsidiaries) and the forms that minimized overall taxes (dividends, fees, royalties, etc.). A second skittish group of parents used what is now called the "cash cows"[4] approach—subsidiaries were told to borrow to the hilt locally and repatriate all their eanings each year. The third group (which was termed "permissive") adopted the long-term attitude—the foreign operations were considered to be bona fide businesses and were expected to be operated as such, i.e., by reinvesting earnings, improving viability, and paying dividends when financial positions and conditions warranted.

Tax planning was found to be elementary "juggling," if exercised at all, although some parents were awakening to its necessity. Most firms, however, sought to avoid "penalty" taxes—host-country levies for paying too much or too few dividends.

Zenoff was also concerned over the capital-budgeting "methods" encountered. Frequently, no quantitative evaluations were made. In other cases, returns on investments were computed in the foreign currencies, rather than in U.S. dollars either before or after U.S. taxes. Finally, little evidence was found of the "worldwide-pool-of-funds" concept in which overseas and domestic investment proposals competed on some sort of comparative basis.

Comments and Opinions. Much of what follows benefits generously from hindsight. Nonetheless, some of Zenoff's opinions were paradoxical, even considering the state-of-the-art of international business in 1967.

Certainly, many foreign operations of that period suffered from "stepchild" status. Those parents believed that sooner or later competition would dry up their cash cows, so the milking process had to be performed efficiently. However, the other so-called "permissive" companies had already developed the long-term international outlook coveted highly today.

The virtual inattention to tax planning was probably the result of the milking process—little forward thinking need be employed if parents embraced policies calling for repatriations of foreign incomes in full as earned. Juggling, perhaps, but not planning was required.

The absence of a worldwide-pool-of-resources concept should not have been at all surprising then—or now. The principle of a worldwide tax domain exercised by the United States created two pools of resources, one domestic and one foreign. It is, and has been, generally advantageous from an after-tax viewpoint to fund foreign and domestic expansions from their own particular resource pools. Also, evaluations of foreign operations, before and after the fact, seem to be appropriate *only* in terms of foreign currencies and foreign environments. To do otherwise would reflect the short-run viewpoint of a one-way flow of funds, at best, or, since most investments are medium- to long-term in nature, reflect an attitude of parochialism.

The frequent absence of quantitative assessments of foreign investment opportunities perplexed Zenoff then—and might even today, since that absence persists. As mentioned earlier in reference to the measurement process, the manipulation of numbers is possessed of a certain amount of mysticism, even though the numbers may represent sheer "guesstimates" of the results of events some years hence, founded upon particular assumptions.

(Persons with quantitative orientations abhor the prevalent contemporary practice of employing the simple payback method in evaluating investment opportunitites, when sophisticated, discounted-cash-flow methods seem so much more rational.)

Approaches to capital-investment decisions, then and now, are often colored by the circumstances. Some companies may be faced with a wealth of opportunities competing for limited funds. For other firms (and possibly a majority), the real problem lies in identifying opportunities that might be available. For still other companies, there is little real choice if a competitor establishes himself in a desirable overseas market area. Finally, the favorable environments and incentives peculiar to some overseas areas, such as Ireland, call for strategic planning, rather than quantitative considerations.

There is little question, however, that Zenoff's discussions established the fact that many U.S. multinationals, circa 1967, were more concerned over the safety of their overseas investments, and one-way flows of funds, than they were over long-term profitability, much less its measurement.

The Mauriel Survey (1969)

In May 1969, John Mauriel published the results of a series of interviews (begun in 1966) with the executives of 15 multinational "giants" (sales over $5 billions).[5]

Description of the Survey. The objectives of the interviews were to determine the differences, if any, between domestic and foreign systems of control and performance evaluation.

Major Findings. Mauriel found that the multinational veterans he surveyed had outgrown their initial strategic concerns over the establishment of foreign operations. Overseas subsidiaries were in place, long-term commitments had been made, and the companies turned their attention to problems of control and performance evaluation. Similarities and differences between domestic and foreign approaches were found.

Similarities. Standard domestic budgeting and financial control systems were emphasized. Small teams of traveling advisors from the headquarters also provided some assistance as required.

Profit and investment centers were in common use. Applications of ROI were relatively recent but growing in popularity (12 of the 15 firms were calculating ROI and/or RI regularly). Those same companies, however, did *not* use ROI or RI as the *primary* evaluation measure. In many cases, profit as a percentage of sales was considered to be more important, particularly for those activities that were not well established as yet. Other firms, such as the 3-M Company, realized that ROI or RI represented an important, yet single, ingredient of the overall evaluation process.

The majority of the firms were "actively involved" in their overseas operations—the "stepchild" caricature was noticeably absent. (A few parents, however, continued to evidence a home-country attitude by stipulating that *they* managed their foreign operations.)

In most of the firms Mauriel studied, the overseas subsidiaries were organized as segments of an "autonomous international division." That division was responsible for shepherding foreign operations and generating the profits and/or rates of return budgeted.

Differences. As might be expected, many of the differences were environmental, yet some were conceptual and serious.

Environmental differences were induced by foreign currencies, the lack of managerial accounting expertise on the part of indigenous personnel, and the infrequent opportunities for two-way informal communication. Also, the dearth of external data available in many locations not only made budget preparations more difficult, but often precluded the use of external benchmarks with which to evaluate performances.

The conceptual differences discovered were most relevant. In the process of translating foreign-currency statements, most companies incorrectly equated changes in exchange rates with the effects of changes in local prices. Also, only rough estimates, if any, were made of the effects on overseas operating performances of the "big decisions" reserved for and made by the headquarters. (Some companies reportedly made "intuitive allowances" from the standards applied to domestic operations.) Naturally, all the above conceptual differences impacted foreign operating results and their evaluations, and the effects could have been favorable as well as unfavorable.

Comments and Opinions. Several noticeable changes in management attitudes and approaches were evidenced.

First, overseas operations were considered to have come of age. However, that observation may have been produced by the fact that Mauriel studied only the very large, veteran MNE firms.

Second, multiple criteria were being used to evaluate the performances of both domestic and foreign activities. Here again, the size and maturity of the companies studied may have accounted for the absence of tunnel vision or management myopia.

Third, overseas managers were being afforded opportunities to participate in the establishment of their operating budgets. What was not clear was whether the participative approach was the result of the initiative of the international division or the parent headquarters. Regardless, it represented welcome relief from the former parochial attitudes.

Fourth, but not least, was the presence of international divisions within organizational structures. Managements of international divisions evidenced the requisite interest, appreciation, and expertise necessary to coordinate operations in dissimilar environments.

(Although the passage of time usually engenders progress, things international are often exceptions. The trend over the last decade or so away from international divisions to global product divisions seems to be a giant step backward. Few product managers have the requisite interest in, or the desire to learn about, the peculiarities of international operations. Rather than a movement toward globalism, such reorganizations may actually represent regressions toward parochial, home-country attitudes.[6])

International managers must be students of people as well as products. Witness the humorous, yet costly, blunders that have been publicized, e.g., attempts to market an automobile in South America where "Nova" means "No go," or uses of slogans that, in translation, mean "Corpse by Fisher" or "Emerge from the grave with Pepsi!". (Then again, perhaps the examples of international boo-boos cited shouldn't be all that surprising since American auto manufacturers have yet to recognize the type of product the majority of their domestic market really prefers.)

CHANGES DURING THE SEVENTIES

The 1970s ushered in the era of the multinationals. As the operations of MNEs increased in importance geometrically, so did the level of interest in those operations by concerned stakeholders.

The subject of performance evaluations attracted particular interest for several reasons. Academics and some segments of the business community were interested in the validity and equity of the methods used. These same groups were joined by other stakeholders (including governments and international organizations) who realized that defective performance evaluations might easily disrupt the flows of capital and other critical international resources. Finally, the nature of MNE operations had changed considerably. Free-standing subsidiaries became interdependent units without clear-cut demarcations. One U.S.-based manufacturer of agricultural machinery combines an engine (made by its U.K. subsidiary) with a transmission (produced in its French plant) and an axle (from its Mexican subsidiary) and sells the tractor (assembled in its U.S. plant) in all its world markets. Naturally, just how the transfer prices attached to these intracompany flows of goods and services were handled in performance evaluations created considerable interest.

Financial Executives Research Foundation Study (1971)

In 1971, Edward Bursk and three colleagues reported the findings of a study sponsored by the Financial Executives Research Foundation.[7]

Nature of the Study. The study was designed to examine and codify the financial control systems of multinational companies. The procedures and the financial reports of 34 multinational enterprises were examined. Each of the MNEs had executives who were members of the Financial Executives Institute.

Major Findings. Ancillary to the central purposes of the study, yet relevant here, was the fact that 32 of the 34 companies (94%) placed primary emphasis upon the profit performances of their foreign subsidiaries. Actual profits compared with budgeted profits was the principal measure of performance evaluation. ROI was considered second in importance for a variety of reasons, followed by comparisons of actual and budgeted sales.

The study also concluded that more attention needed to be given to the development of methods to separate evaluations of the performances of managers from those of their activities.

Comments and Opinions. This FERF study concurred with many of the findings by Mauriel mentioned previously.

Perhaps the most important aspect of this study was its recognition of the *dual nature* of performance evaluations. The effects of changes in exchange rates, and other variables not normally controllable by foreign managers, called for somewhat different evaluation procedures than those being applied to activities.

The McInnes Survey (1971)

Also in 1971, J. M. McInnes reported the result of his survey of the financial reporting and evaluation systems used by thirty U.S.-based, medium-sized MNEs (with annual sales of $100 to $300 millions).[8]

Major Findings. Only minor differences were found between the financial reporting systems prescribed for use by domestic and foreign units. The major difference, of course, related to foreign-currency information. Financial data in U.S. dollars and in foreign currencies were being reported: 50% of the firms asked for data in both dollars and local currencies; 30% wanted U.S. dollar information only; 17% required data in local currencies only; and 3% stated that the situation determined the reporting currency.

Basically the same techniques were used to evaluate domestic and foreign operations. The measures used, in their rank order of importance were: ROI, budget comparisons, and historical comparisons.

Comments and Opinions. Two aspects of the McInnes survey should be noted. First, an increasing awareness of the need for both U.S. dollar and local-currency information is relevant. Also, this survey was the first to report the primacy of ROI as a measure of the performance of foreign activities.

Report of the AAA Committee on International Accounting (1973)

The 1971-72 Committee on International Accounting of the American Accounting Association (largely an organization of accounting educators) was charged with investigating and identifying the accounting problems produced by multinational enterprises.

The committee's report, issued in 1973, was the most thorough, yet concise, examination of the accounting problems of MNEs issued to that time.[9] (In fact, many collegiate-level courses were built around the report since appropriate texts were not available then.)

Nature of the Investigation. The committee examined the nature of the MNE, the diverse environments in which it operates, its strategies, and the accounting problems unique to (or exacerbated by) international operations.

Major Findings. Seven "major problem areas" were identified and addressed:

1. External Reporting
2. Taxation
3. Financial Planning
4. Transfer Pricing
5. Currency Translation
6. Performance Evaluation
7. Information Systems

Neither profit nor ROI were considered to be valid measures for use in performance evaluations. Several reasons were cited. The interdependencies that existed in foreign operations prevented any "clear cut cleavage" between related units. In addition, parent headquarters made many of the important decisions that affected the profitabilities of the units. Also, the prevalence of managed transfer prices shifted local incomes among subsidiaries to produce the best advantage for the MNE as a whole.

Other barriers to performance evaluations noted were: the necessity to rely on raw data, since on-site visits were infrequent; and the lack of comparability of the data obtained from foreign subsidiaries.

Performance evaluations by MNEs at that time were considered to be "limited." Most often, foreign subsidiaries were evaluated quantitatively—by traditional financial statements "mentally adjusted for extenuating circumstances." Appraisals of local managers, where made at all, were often subjective—"based on personal impressions." (The committee added, however, that subjective evaluations of managers were lesser evils than quantitative attempts that would necessarily be grossly invalid.)

The committee stressed that MNEs recognize the need for two evaluations: (1) how the *entity* used its resources, and (2) the ability of the *local manager*.

In the committee's opinion, MNEs indicated a willingness to place greater emphasis upon budget variances in making evaluations. The committee cautioned that budget variances in activity reports be segregated into items controllable and noncontrollable by local management. Such distinctions would be necessary if valid dual evaluations were to be made using a single report.

Other measures suggested as supplements were: nonmonetary quantitative factors, internal audits, and "point systems" for weighting achievements of various objectives other than profitability.

Comments and Opinions. The AAA committee contributed a fund of knowledge regarding the uninvestigated areas of that time. Perhaps the most valuable contribution was the recognition that performance evaluations did not represent a separate, self-contained problem area. Instead, it was an amalgam of the residues of assorted transfer pricing, currency translation, and responsibility accounting practices.

Given the diversity of causes and effects, the committee suggested (but did not seem to give its whole-hearted support to) the use of flexible budgets, segmented into controllable and noncontrollable items.

Apparently, knowledgeable accountants (and managers) of that time were still seeking out *normative* approaches that would be valid when applied to diverse situations. The Holy Grail was still being pursued, although the cortege may have become smaller.

Vancil's Contribution (1973)

Operations of all forms of complex organizations, not only multinationals, received intensive scrutiny during the early 1970s.

The most valuable contributions of many who shared their thoughts with others during that period were often in areas other than originally intended. An article by Richard F. Vancil was one example.[10]

The basic thrust of the article focused upon the matrix form of organization which, in Vancil's opinion, held great promise. In short, the matrix organization might well achieve the efficiency of functional forms as well as the effectiveness of product structures. (See the section on hybrid forms in chapter 3.)

Vancil's real contributions were in two other areas. First, the basic frameworks of responsibility accounting were presented. Most chief executives circa 1973 had probably never been introduced to those concepts formally—or had simply forgotten them.

Second, Vancil exposed rather skillfully the abject reliance upon profit as a panacea measure by most executives. Pseudo-profit centers were being erected at will, even though few managers were "responsible for profits in any meaningful sense of that term."

Vancil's closing statement regarding profit (borrowed in part in chapter 3) is furnished in full, below, since it is a gem:

> Profit should be used as a measure of financial responsibility only when it is possible to calculate it in such a way that a manager's "profit" increases as the result of actions for which he is responsible and which he has taken in the best interest of the company.[11]

The Robbins and Stobaugh Classic (1973)

Without a doubt, the classic of all articles examining the performance evaluations of foreign operations and their managers was that authored by Robbins and Stobaugh in the fall of 1973.[12]

Nature of the Study. Some 39 U.S.-based MNEs were visited, their executives interviewed, and their records examined. Also, the annual reports of an additional 150 MNEs were studied. A gamut of size existed. For the smallest, one-fifth of its $100 millions in sales was generated overseas; the sales of the largest was in the billions.

Major Findings. Most companies had established their foreign operations as "strategic systems." The profits expected from any particular unit were given only crude consideration, if at all. These factors were forgotten, however, during subsequent evaluations. Consequently, performance evaluation was described as "one of the most misunderstood and confused tasks" of that time.

Almost all (95%) of the firms evaluated their foreign units in exactly the same way as domestic units—by ROI in one form or another. That measure was found to be applied even to captive units for which the transfer prices (and profits) were determined by the parent. Small wonder, then, that ROI was called the "bent measuring stick."

(Many of the MNEs reported the use of budgets but only as *supplementary* evaluation devices.)

Insofar as currencies were concerned, managements were about evenly divided—44% used local currencies, 44% U.S. dollars, and 12% used both forms. As might be expected, the firms using local currencies reflected somewhat more realistic attitudes toward the intricacies of foreign operating results. The other half, however, retained their parochial attitudes rather stubbornly.

Realistic budgets, tailored to fit the particular circumstances of each unit, were recommended as replacements for ROI and/or all other inflexible, insensitive evaluation approaches. The effects of headquarter's fiddlings with transfer prices and other arbitrary allocations would also be ameliorated.

The usual problems that might be encountered in budgetary systems were recognized but were considered to be amenable to control. Regardless, tailored budgets (even if their inherent faults persisted) were considered to be better measuring sticks than ROI.

Common sense dictated that, if foreign subsidiaries functioned as strategic segments of MNEs, it was foolish to evaluate them as if they were independent entities.

Comments and Opinions. Robbins and Stobaugh (to borrow from the vernacular) put it all together. They looked at what was being done at the time, found that performance evaluations of overseas activities violated common sense (as well as reality), and stated that tailored budgets were the best measuring sticks. Little more can be said.

The Reece and Cool Study (1978)

In mid-1978, Reece and Cool shared the results of their study of financial performance evaluations.[13] The scope of the study was generally comparable to that of Mauriel and Anthony some twelve years prior.

Description of the Study. The Fortune "1000" firms were queried and 620 responded. Information was sought concerning: the use of profit and investment centers, how investment centers were evaluated, definitions of profits and assets, and how the performances of investment centers were compared.

Major Findings. The observations and conclusions made by Reece and Cool are presented in the order of their four purposes and, where appropriate, are compared with the findings of Mauriel and Anthony.

Use of centers. Almost all of the 620 respondents (96%) used either profit centers (22%) or investment centers (74%). Use of such centers increased with size; 80% of the firms using neither center reported sales under $500 million. Size was also a factor in the length of time that centers were used. Recent adopters (within 5 yrs) were primarily small firms.

Longevity comparisons made with the Mauriel and Anthony study were debatable. Reece and Cool reported that nearly all (94%) of their study group used such *centers* more than 5 years (and some 38% more than 25 years), whereas only two-thirds of the Mauriel and Anthony group reported more than 5-years' use. However, it should be noted that the Reece and Cool responses applied to both *profit and investment* centers, whereas Mauriel and Anthony studied the use of *investment* centers only.

One valid conclusion that could be made, however, was that more firms were using some form of profitability center and, although the use of profit centers declined somewhat (5%), investment centers had increased significantly (21%). (See Table 6-1.)

Evaluations of investment centers. What changes are observed in the methods of evaluating investment centers during the 1966-1978 period depends, in large measure, upon how the results in the Mauriel and Anthony and Reece and Cool studies are perceived. (See Table 6-2.)

If the Reece and Cool results are compared with those of Phase I of Mauriel and Anthony, the use of ROI increased significantly (by 13%), with offsetting decreases in dual measures (both ROI and RI) and in RI standing alone.

Somewhat different conclusions might be reached if the Reece and Cool findings were compared with those of the more refined, Phase II of the Mauriel and Anthony study. In this case, slight declines would be reflected in the use of both ROI and RI *standing alone,* with offsetting increases reported in the use of dual and "other" measures. (The "other" measures were not specified by Reece and Cool.)

Definitions of profit and investment. Reece and Cool found that only 40% of the firms continued to use the same methods of determining profit for evaluations and financial reportings. The majority (60%) made adjustments to exclude allocations of taxes and common corporate expenses, such as administrative and interest charges. (The Mauriel and Anthony study did not address the determination of profit directly.)

Any positive effects that might be attached to the above findings were more than offset by the manner in which companies calculated depreciation expense—which impacts computed profits. Little change had occurred in 12 years: the same depreciation methods were used for evaluation and external reporting purposes by 97% of the Mauriel and Anthony and 92% of the Reece and Cool respondents.

Calculations of investment bases had changed. Use of net book values increased from 73% (Mauriel and Anthony) to 85% (Reece and Cool).

Comparative evaluations. Both studies gathered information regarding how target ROI rates and/or RI charges were established. The relevant data have been assembled in Table 6-3.

Table 6-1.   Reported Uses of Profit and Investment Centers, 1966 and 1978.

| | STUDIES AND DATES | | | |
| COMPANIES HAVING: | MAURIEL AND ANTHONY* 1966 | | REECE AND COOL 1978 | |
	NUMBER	%	NUMBER	%
Neither profit nor investment centers	497	20%	26	4%
Profit centers	688	27%	135	22%
Investment centers	1326	53%	459	74%
Totals	2511	100%	620	100%

Sources: Mauriel and Anthony study[1], Exhibits IA, C, and IIA; Reece and Cool study[13], Exhibit I.

Note: The Mauriel and Anthony data from Phase 1 of their study have been adjusted to reflect errors in initial responses they discovered in Phase II as follows: 147 subsidiaries were reported twice as investment centers; 130 other firms reported using investment centers, whereas profit centers were correct. Therefore, profit centers were increased from 558 to 688; investment centers reduced from 1603 to 1326; and the total respondents reduced from 2658 to 2511.

Table 6-2.   Reported Evaluation Methods of Investment Centers, 1966 and 1978.

| | MAURIEL AND ANTHONY 1966 | | | | REECE AND COOL 1978 | |
| | PHASE I | | PHASE II | | | |
COMPANIES USING:	NUMBER	%	NUMBER	%	NUMBER	%
ROI only	838	52%	593	70%	299	65%
Both ROI & RI	665	42%	193	23%	128	28%
RI only	100	6%	65	7%	9	2%
Other					17	4%
No response					6*	1%
Totals	1603	100%	851	100%	459	100%

Excluded from *Phase II because*:

Reported twice	(148)	*"No responses" were not re-
Invalid response	(130)	moved since effects were con-
Financial inst.	(77)	sidered to be minor.
No response	(397)	
	851	

Sources: Mauriel & Anthony study[1], Exhibits IA and IIA; Reece & Cool study[13], Exhibit V.

Table 6-3. Reported Uses of Target ROI Rates and/or RI Charges, 1966 and 1978.

COMPANIES REPORTING:	MAURIEL AND ANTHONY 1966	REECE AND COOL 1978
Target ROI rates:		
Depend on circumstances	51%	64%
Same rate, all centers	38%	7%
None assigned	—*	23%
Residual Income charges:		
Same rate, all assets	76%	81%
Rates vary with assets	6%	19%
Same rate, similar assets in		
all centers—yes	70%	58%
—no	7%	38%

Sources: Mauriel & Anthony study[1], Exhibits II I, J, K; Reece & Cool study[13], Exhibits XI, XII.

Note:* Mauriel & Anthony asked if different rates were assigned to different centers. It was not possible to identify from the 11% "not applicable" and "no response" the number of firms not assigning target ROI rates at all.

The little more than a decade of lapsed time between the studies enabled many companies to realize that assigning the same ROI rate to all centers, regardless of the differences in their circumstances, was sheer nonsense. It was unfortunate, however, that it was not possible from the Mauriel and Anthony responses to determine what percentage of the companies did not assign target ROI rates in 1966. On the other hand, it was encouraging to note from the Reece and Cool data that nearly one-fourth (23%) of the firms polled did not assign ROI target rates in 1978. (It would indeed have warmed the heart, had these companies adopted the use of flexible budgets instead.)

Where RI was used, both studies indicate that managements had not learned how to use their tools any better in twelve years. The number of firms applying the same RI charge to all assets actually increased. Note also, however, that the firms using different rates for different types of assets also increased. (This was possible, of course, since the number of firms reporting the use of RI increased.) The question then might well be, have the experienced executives become wiser, while the more recent adopters of RI have their lessons yet to learn?

The answer to the above question may also appear in Table 6-3. Note that the percentage of firms assigning the same ROI rate to similar assets in all centers declined and, also, that those using different rates increased even more. It would appear that experience has engendered wisdom, but it is also clearly apparent that there is much more learning to be done.

Only the Reece and Cool study solicited information regarding how investment centers were ranked (apparently for evaluation) where ROI and RI criteria were used.

Of the total group of firms having investment centers (459 companies), 69% ranked the centers using one or both criteria (some firms reported using ROI and RI). Another 29% stated that no such rankings were made—that response seems more than a little unusual. One reason might be that the target rates were used to motivate rather than evaluate.

Where residual incomes were ranked (by 137 firms), various schemes were employed. The largest segment (46%) used the absolute amounts of RI dollars; the next largest (44%) related the RI dollar amounts to those of the investments, thereby converting profitability back into the ratio that RI was supposed to improve upon. Other popular devices were comparisons of actual and budgeted RI amounts (38%), and RI related to sales (34%).

A much larger group (427 firms) used ROI as a ranking device, and also employed various schemes. The majority of the firms (55%) used the ROI percentage standing alone. The next largest (41%) related actual and budgeted ROI ratios, while nearly the same number (37%) used an amorphous variant (if it could be considered to be ROI at all) whereby profits were related to sales. (This latter scheme would more appropriately represent an alternative to, rather than the use of, ROI.)

Comments and Opinions. Neither of the studies dealt with the effects of foreign-currency translations. It was not a topic of interest when the Mauriel and Anthony study was made, and the Reece and Cool effort simply excluded the matter.

Adoptions of the investment-center concept increased significantly. The use of ROI as a measure also increased, although the exact extent was not determinable since many firms used both RI and ROI. Moreover, nearly all the firms in both studies (97% and 92%, respectively) used the same depreciation methods for purposes of external reporting and internal evaluations.

Differences in the attitudes of the authors of the two studies were almost as apparent as were those of the executives studied.

Mauriel and Anthony made it clear that, in their opinions, both practices lead to "misevaluations." Reece and Cool were not as committal—or were, perhaps, more objective. They expressed their opinions that comparisons of actual and budgeted performances represented the *"most equitable"* method of *ranking* activity contributions[14] and, by implication, the most desirable method of *determining* those contributions as well. However, in their attempts to rationalize why methods that were flawed conceptually were on the rise in many areas, they became more speculative. In their closing remarks, Reece and Cool expressed their belief that financial managers were "aware" of the potential "pitfalls" associated with the uses of ROI, and applications of external reporting approaches to internal evaluations. They assumed that those same managers considered the pitfalls to be more "hypothetical" than real, and closed with a "note of caution" in that regard.[15]

It may well be that financial executives have assured themselves that the systems they use are rational and equitable. On the other hand, it also may be that executives have simply attached greater value to convenience, to compatibility (at least from their vantage point) of internal and external measures, and—last but not least—to their time. (It certainly takes less time to peruse a list of activities ranked by ROIs than it does to assess the real contributions of interdependent activities and their managers.)

This author is convinced that all too many executives have chosen to make convenient evaluations rather than realistic evaluations because they are simply "too busy." Whether those executives are unaware of the weaknesses in their approaches or simply choose to ignore them seems rather irrelevant—both are forms of myopia, with the difference only in degree.

Financial Executives Research Foundation Study (1979)

The classic contemporary study was conducted by Persen and Lessig (of the Business International Corporation) for the Financial Executives Research Foundation and published in 1979.[16]

Nature of the Study. Given the magnitude of foreign operations, and the variety of problems related to their management and evaluation, the study sought to gather insights into how financial performances were being evaluated, as well as how the methods may have changed over time. Particular attention was given to efforts directed toward neutralizing the distortions created by the diverse environments in which foreign operations were conducted.

Of the 400 U.S.-based manufacturing firms polled, 125 responded to the questionnaire. To gain further insights, the chief financial officers of 20 of the participating MNEs were interviewed. The study focused upon evaluations of the financial performances of those overseas activities charged with profit responsibility. In addition, only wholly-owned subsidiaries with ongoing operations (as opposed to newly established) were examined.

The companies studied conducted operations in Europe, primarily, and were rather evenly distributed among three ranges of *foreign sales:* small (less than $100 million), medium ($100 to $500 million), and large (in excess of $500 million).

Major Findings. Perhaps the major, although not necessarily surprising, observation concerned the apparent lack of uniformity found to exist. No single method or system of evaluation was used. In the search for *realistic* approaches, most evaluators found it necessary to make allowances for environmental differences, as well as unexpected changes in the environments, in order to assess how well activities responded to and managed change. As might be expected, objectivity was forced to yield to judgment, in most instances, in order to achieve the realism desired. (That finding alone is gratifying.)

Primary evaluation approaches. Multiple evaluation techniques were common. The number of measures actually employed tended to vary among companies. Also, the particular measures changed in relative importance within a particular company as times and conditions changed. Usually, two or three measures were emphasized; rarely were more than half a dozen emphasized at any one time.

Several other general conclusions were cited. More commonalities of evaluations were evidenced by the larger, veteran MNEs than the smaller neophytes in foreign operations. Methods of evaluating domestic units were *not* simply applied to foreign subsidiaries by the majority of firms. Instead, techniques of assessing profitability were not only revised, but expanded as well by 56% of the companies (some 40% still used the same bases, however).

Another indication of enlightenment was the finding that the large majority (74%) evaluated managerial performance differently than that of the subsidiary. Typically, other criteria were used in addition to profit generations.

Various schemes were reported for making comparative rankings of the financial performances of subsidiaries. The methods are shown below in order of their popularity in use:

- By subsidiary—most popular because it was the simplest to use.
- By product line—second most common overall, and the preferred method used by diversified firms, or those structured along product lines.
- By region—third in popularity, and typical of firms with extensive foreign operations.
- By country—only used by those firms in which countries were synonymous with market areas.
- Other methods were also applied, generally in combination with one or more of the above, for the examination of manufacturing units, sales, and profitability segmented in various other forms.

Measurements used. Persen and Lessig expressed their opinions that measurements of performance tended to evolve with the firm itself. Initially, increases in sales are monitored, followed by relating profits to sales and assets and, eventually, to return on investment. Perhaps that is why the researchers seemed to *condition* their finding concernging the measurement used most widely.

In several places within the study (and emphasized in some), Persen and Lessig stipulated that comparison of actual and budgeted operating results *appeared to be* the predominant measure in use at the time. ROI was ranked third, but a "solidly growing emphasis" was also reported. (Rankings of the top-ten measurements—past, present, and future—are shown in Table 6-4.)

Comparisons of operating budgets were favored by the larger firms, and by about one-half of the smaller companies. The measure ranked

Table 6-4. Performance Measures, Ranked In Order of Perceived Importance In
1979, 1974, and 1984.

FOCUS	CURRENT (1979)	PAST (1974)	FUTURE (1984)
Operating budget comparisons	62%	50%	59%
Contribution to earnings per share	44%	45%	42%
Return on investment	40%	32%	54%
Contribution to corporate cash flow	35%	14%	55%
Return on sales	34%	32%	34%
Return on assets	34%	21%	41%
Asset/liability management	30%	9%	50%
Non-accounting data	16%	13%	22%
Long-term plan comparisons	12%	6%	23%
Return on investment (inflation adjusted)	8%	3%	31%

Source: William Persen and Van Lessig, *Evaluating the Financial Performance of Overseas Operations* (New York: Financial Executives Research Foundation, 1979), p. 68. Reproduced by permission.

second—contribution to EPS—was considered to be more commonly applied to domestic units, since application to foreign subsidiaries was difficult, at best, if really possible at all.

ROI was listed third but an increasing emphasis was discerned. (This observation and the nebulous nature of the EPS item, above, probably account for the reservations of Persen and Lessig. Moreover, impressions they gained in personal interviews often cast doubt upon, if not contradicted, responses obtained in questionnaires.)

Contribution to corporate cash flow, ranked fourth and growing, is a difficult and nebulous measure. Since archaic, one-way flow-of-funds concepts are requisite, this measure would seem to be desirable primarily to the smaller, less-experienced firms. Broader concepts of pools-of-funds employed by the larger, veteran MNEs—particularly in aspects of overall tax planning—would seem to negate the usefulness of cash-flow measures since they would tend to be more circumstantial than anything else.

Most of the other measures seemed to be ancillary or temporal in nature. Return on sales and assets reflected opposite trends, evidently the result of the evolutionary change in emphasis by smaller firms from the former to the latter. The management of balance sheet items, while ancillary, was attracting more attention due to the volatility of foreign currencies and interest rates.

Unfortunately, recognition of the real value of nonaccounting data in times of changing price-levels was not all that apparent. Only slight increases in interest had occurred and were projected.

Comparisons with long-term plans represented a natural fallout from use of the leading measurement. The increase in importance projected should tend to offset some of the over-emphasis that can be attached to short-term results by the use of measures such as ROI.

The lack of current applications of inflation-adjusted measures is understandable, particularly where overseas operations are concerned. The upsurge in projected importance is also reasonable, but probably impracticable. (Perhaps trial-and-error may eventually result in greater appreciation and use of nonaccounting data, in general, and nonmonetary data, in particular.)

Other reported findings indicated that profitability *after taxes* was preferred, whether the returns were related to investments, assets, or sales.

Also relevant was the finding that the apparent leading measurement—operating budget comparisons—was applied monthly by 87% of the companies. Permissible ranges of variances were usually established with explanations required of excesses.

The budget process. Persen and Lessig gleaned the impression that, upon approval, the budget was almost considered to be "a contract" stipulating given amounts of profit and investment. The typical time-frame called for September submissions, followed by reviews, and final approvals in December for calendar-year firms.

The prevailing attitude toward subsequent budget revision was mixed. Almost equal numbers left the budgets intact as revised them. Naturally, those firms that did not revise approved budgets (and treated them as contracts) expected the explanations of variances to include the effects of unanticipated changes in circumstances. Regardless of the approach used, the assumptions upon which the budgets were constructed were as important as the budgets themselves.

Foreign-currency treatments. The "vast majority" of the companies were found to evaluate foreign operations in terms of U.S. dollars. This conclusion was reached despite the fact that 4% used local currencies only and 38% used dollars only. The remaining 58%

stated that *both* currencies were employed; however, the researchers considered that to be impractical, and that one or the other had to prevail.

A minority of firms (13%) used the actual rate (at the time of budget preparation) for purposes of developing the budget and for translating actual results. A slightly larger number (19%) used a projected rate for both purposes. In both the above cases, use of the same rate for budget preparation and subsequent evaluation would produce no translation differences. Such evaluations could be considered as made in foreign currencies.

The large majority (68%) used different rates for both purposes. This approach was equivalent to evaluation in U.S. dollars, and translation differences caused by changes in exchange rates were probable. Most of this group (63%) did not hold subsidiary management responsible for the differences produced—yet, 37% of the firms chose to do so.

When asked to comment on the effects of *FASB-8* upon the evaluation process, 65% reported little impact. The 36% that acknowledged some impact were undoubtedly those companies holding subsidiary managements responsible for the translation differences reportable in income.

Comments and Opinions. Since the opinions of this author were sprinkled liberally throughout the above findings, few are necessary here.

As mentioned early on, it was gratifying to learn that *realistic* evaluations were the objectives of this study group of firms. This fact alone would tend toward diversities in methods and measurements. Rather disconcerting, however, was the finding that 40% of the firms used the same measures and techniques for assessing the performances of foreign and domestic subsidiaries alike.

Some comfort was furnished by the impression of Persen and Lessig that operating budget comparisons "appeared" to represent the leading measurement in use. On the other hand, the third-ranked ROI was reported as having a "solidly growing emphasis"—although the projected rankings of important measurements continued to place ROI second to budget comparisons. It appears that the additional efforts necessary to obtain realistic evaluations may lead some executives to succomb to the convenience of ROI. On the other hand, it may also be that the problems posed by fluctuating exchange rates will produce some benefits—such as impressing upon evaluators the peculiarities of foreign operations and the fallacies attached to computations of ROI in U.S. dollars, almost as if the operations were conducted domestically.

A final comment is necessary regarding the minority of firms that hold subsidiary management responsible for exchange rate variances. It will be presumed that the appropriate authority (the selection of the projected rate to be used for budget preparation, as well as the ability to determine and manage the ongoing exchange exposures) also vests in subsidiary management. Even so, the net total variance produced upon the translations of actual operating results will be composed of two elements—that might not move in the same direction—reflecting two different changes: (1) in local prices, and (2) in exchange rates. (See Figure 6-1.)

If subsidiary managements are given the requisite authorities, and are to be held accountable for exchange-rate differences, then it would follow that someone should also differentiate the effects of management's inability to gauge changes in local-market prices from

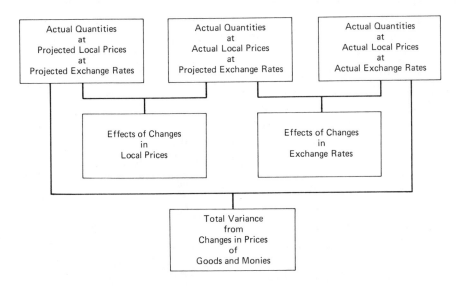

Figure 6-1. Elements of Exchange Rate Variances in Operating Results.

those of attempting to "guesstimate" future exchange rates. Normal-ly, local managers will be more familiar with, and be able to exert more control over, local market prices for their products. Conse-quently, differences caused by changes in local market projections should be given the most emphasis.

MANAGEMENT MYOPIA

The preceding overview of evaluation methods of the sixties and seventies indicates that changes in thinking have evolved, albeit slow-ly and painfully.

Many of the changes noted paralleled the evolution of concerns over the foreign investments themselves. Initially, the primary con-cern was the safety of the investment. Subsequently, interest was shifted to profits, and finally to returns on the investments. There is also some evidence to support the notion that veteran MNEs, at least, have reached, if not crossed, the final threshold toward realistic evaluations. (See Table 6-5.)

There is also little doubt that all too many executives continue to suffer from management myopia. The symptoms are many. Perhaps the most prevalent is the continued fascination over ROI—and in U.S. dollars, at that. Executives afflicted tend to say that they recognize the defects peculiar to ROI, yet argue that it is the best tool available, or that ROI is the only measure understood in the boardroom. The first argument denotes lack of real interest (or laziness), the second dodges the issue—boards evaluate the decisions of chief executive officers, not subsidiary managers.

A second pervasive symptom is represented by an infatuation with measures in U.S. dollars. Regressions to short-run thinking and home-country attitudes are certainly indicated. What may also be present, although not as apparent, is an attitude of complacency—and this could prove to be a pernicious symptom.

Professor Raymond Vernon was intrigued recently over the appar-ent decline in the abilities of American MNEs to compete successful-ly at home as well as abroad. He studied the problem and urged American businessmen to realize that the "cash cows of yesteryear" are no more.[17] No longer can American MNEs be complacent because

Table 6-5.   Rankings of Performance Measures Reported, 1966 to 1979, and Projected to 1984.

PERFORMANCE MEASURES	MAURIEL AND ANTHONY 1966	MAURIEL 1969	FIN'L. EXEC. RESEARCH FOUNDATION 1971	MCINNES 1971	ROBBINS AND STOBAUGH 1973	REECE AND COOL 1978	FIN'L. EXECS. RESEARCH FOUNDATION ACTUAL 1979	PROJ. 1984
Sales Budgets			3					
Profit (ROS)		1	1				5	7
Operating Budgets				2	2		1	1
ROI	1	2	2	1	1	1	3	3
ROI & RI	2					2		
RI	3	2				4		
Historical Comparisons		3		3				
Contrib. to EPS							2	5
Contrib. to Corp. Cash Flows							4	2
ROA							5	6
Asset/Liab. Mgmt.							6	4
Other (Not Specified)						3		

Sources: Constructed from the findings reported in the studies examined in this chapter, together with part of Table 6-4.

Caveats: The measures reported were not entirely comparable in some studies and somewhat vague in others. The forced rankings shown reflect the interpretations of the author in some cases.

of their relative advantages in capital resources, technologies, and niches established in world markets. Real competition now exists from foreign-based MNEs.

Vernon attributed most of the contemporary setbacks of American MNEs to their "parochial" attitudes toward overseas investments. In his opinion, parochialism was the natural result of "one-way" approaches to foreign operations. Vernon cited the preponderance of one-way communication networks. Information flowed two ways, to be sure, but only one-way communication resulted—we talked, they listened. A prime example of the inability of U.S. parents to listen to and learn from their foreign subsidiaries was the U.S. auto industry, according to Vernon. Some overseas subsidiaries of each of the "big three" U.S. auto firms were credited with "mastering" the construction of small cars, whereas their parent firms had yet to accept the signs of the times, much less benefit from the technologies learned.

Two probable causes of the one-way attitudes were offered by Vernon. First, American MNEs evolved with little real technological competition. Products and ideas were originated in the parent headquarters, not in the field. Also, with little real competition (in products or prices), little need existed for more than cursory evaluations of overseas performances. Second, Vernon decried the "premature obliteration of international divisions" for the worldwide product reorganizations so popular in the recent past. In short, domestic product managers were simply ill-suited to recognize and appreciate the diversities of overseas markets. As Vernon put it, they remained as "American as the Dallas Cowboys and apple pie" in outlook and perception.[18]

Vernon urged American MNEs to recognize that foreign competition has arrived in all markets, domestic as well as foreign. There are fewer places to "hide." He stated that the successful competitor will be the one offering the best price, quality, and service.

Vernon's observations seemed to be appropriate for inclusion here for several reasons. His concept of one-way thinking is manifest in those executives who continue to embrace one-way flows-of-funds attitudes. Of most importance is his warning that competition has made the cash cow virtually extinct. If efficiency and effectiveness are to be the real determinants of success in competitive, worldwide markets, then myopic approaches to performance evaluations will have to yield to methods that are realistic. Last, but not least, by taking the time to look at foreign operations realistically, American executives may just find that some of their overseas managers have developed ingenious methods that are transferable to domestic operations.

NOTES

1. John J. Mauriel and Robert N. Anthony, "Misevaluation of Investment Center Performance," *Harvard Business Review,* March-April 1966, pp. 98–105.

2. In phase one, 1603 of 2658 firms (60%) reported use of investment centers. In the second phase, 130 said they had misinterpreted the original questionnaire

and 148 others said they did not have two or more centers, leaving 1325 of 2658, or 50%.

3. David Zenoff, "Profitable, Fast Growing, but Still the Stepchild," *Columbia Journal of World Business,* July-August 1967, pp. 51–56.

4. Raymond Vernon, "Gone Are the Cash Cows of Yesteryear," *Harvard Business Review,* November-December 1980, pp. 150–155.

5. John J. Mauriel, "Evaluation and Control of Overseas Operations," *Management Accounting,* May 1969, pp. 35–39, 52.

6. Vernon (note 4), pp. 153–154.

7. Edward C. Bursk, John Dearden, David F. Hawkins, and Victor M. Longstreet, *Financial Control of Multinational Operations* (New York: Financial Executives Research Foundation, 1971).

8. J. M. McInnes, "Financial Control Systems for Multinational Operations: An Empirical Investigation," *Journal of International Business Studies,* Fall 1971, pp. 11–28.

9. American Accounting Association, Committee on International Accounting, "Report of the Committee on International Accounting," *The Accounting Review, Supplement to Vol. 1973,* pp. 120–167.

10. Richard F. Vancil, "What Kind of Management Control Do You Need?", *Harvard Business Review,* March-April 1973, pp. 75–86.

11. Ibid., p. 86.

12. Sidney M. Robbins and Robert B. Stobaugh, "The Bent Measuring Stick for Foreign Subsidiaries," *Harvard Business Review,* September-October 1973, pp. 80–88.

13. James S. Reece and William R. Cool, "Measuring Investment Center Performance," *Harvard Business Review,* May-June 1978, pp. 28–30, 34, 36, passim.

14. Ibid., p. 46.

15. Ibid., p. 176.

16. William Persen and Van Lessig, *Evaluating the Financial Performance of Overseas Operations* (New York: Financial Executives Research Foundation, 1979).

17. Vernon (note 4).

18. Ibid., p. 154.

7
Innovative Approaches

New ways of doing things are not restricted to the larger companies, yet those introduced by the giants of industry often receive the greatest publicity. Also, since large companies tend to have widespread and varied operations, they would also tend to have more difficulties with performance evaluations, both in number and complexity. Those same firms also have the support staffs and skills necessary to examine problems and develop reasonable solutions.

Many "new" ideas are really not new. They may have been introduced decades ago, yet were not widely adopted for a variety of reasons. In some infrequent cases, innovations employed and proven by a given company were considered too radical for adoption either by competitors in the industry or other firms in the same national environment. In most cases, however, new ideas had to await the coming of technologies that would make them practicable for use by the "average" company.

EARLY INNOVATORS

Three examples of changes in thinking and approach have been selected for mention here. Although others abound, space limited the choices to: one which is unique, as well as alien, to American philosophies; and two early examples of refinements introduced by American companies.

N. V. Philips Gloeilampenfabrieken

Of all the large international industrial enterprises, the Philips Company can be considered innovative in many respects.

Headquartered in Eindhoven, Netherlands, the Philips Company has perennially vied with Standard Oil of Indiana for the 16th and 17th rankings among the largest industrial companies in the world. As a Dutch holding company organized in 1920, Philips N.V. holds more than 95% of the outstanding shares of a network of Philips Industries operating in nearly all the countries of the free world. Although widespread, the company employs a high degree of integration. Operating, management, and accounting practices specified by the parent are followed by all subsidiaries regardless of location.

Among the many unique aspects of Philips' operations, three are relevant here: their accounting system, emphasis upon standard costs, and concept of profits.

The accounting system of Philips N.V., like that of about one-third of the other large Dutch companies, is based upon the current-replacement-value theories suggested by a Dutch professor, Theodore Limperg, in the 1920s. While CRVA theories are outside the scope of this book, suffice it to say here that the primary purpose is to assure protection of the productive capacity of the firm.[1] In other words, assets consumed, sold, and on hand are valued at their costs of current replacement considering technological progress. (CRVA differs from current cost accounting in that the latter stresses replacement *in kind,* ignoring the effects of technology.) Philips modifies traditional CRVA theory somewhat (for managerial use and convenience) since backlog depreciation of fixed assets is ignored. Because of its size and dispersion, the firm is continually constructing and replacing standardized facilities worldwide. Consequently, annual replacement costs approximate yearly depreciation amounts.

Philips employs "accounting for management" in that the company believes that accounting should serve the needs of management decision-making and evaluation. That does not mean that external reporting is relegated to lesser importance. On the contrary, Philips argues that good management accounting is simply good accounting and sees no logical reason to deviate. In countries where CRVA is not permitted in external reports (such as the United States), estimates are used to adjust reported earnings and asset values to the historical cost basis and furnished in supplementary form. (See Figure 7-1.) This practice has been accepted by the SEC.[2]

The modified version of CRVA used represents a highly sophisticated *managerial accounting system,* supported by elaborate standard cost methods based upon internally calculated indexes.[3] Standard

In the United States of America net profit attributable to ordinary shares is customarily determined by reducing net profit by profit-sharing with Supervisory Board. Management and Officers, and with employee pursuant to the Articles of Association on the subject of Profit Appropriation.

Moreover the accounting principles applied by N.V. Philips' Gloeilampenfabrieken in calculating profit differ in some respects from principles customarily followed in the United States.

An attempt is made below to estimate what adjustment to net profit would be required if those accounting principles customarily followed in the United States were applied that differ substantialy from those of N.V. Philips' Gloeilampenfabrieken, viz.:

- Depreciation on property, plant and equipment based on the cost of the assets concerned.
- Cost of sales determined by applying the first-in, first-out method, except to a minor extent, as in the Combined Statements, the last-in, first-out method.
- A write-off period of five years for the amounts paid for the acquisition of participations in so far as the total of such payments in any year exceeds the total net tangible asset value acquired.

The tax effect of the foregoing principles have been taken into account.

The adjustment is as follows:	in millions of guilders	in millions of U.S. $*
Net profit 1976, shown in the Combined Statement of Results	562.5	229.6
Deduct: Profit-sharing with Supervisory Boad, Management and Officers, and employees	-46.0	-18.8
Increase of net profit when applying the aforementioned accounting principles customarily followed in the U.S.	286.6	117.0
Adjusted net profit	803.1	327.8
(including result relating to operations to be discontinued and a provision for estimated losses on disposal aggregating f 40 m)		
Number of ordinary shares of f 10 of N.V. Philips' Gloeilampenfabrieken outstanding at 31 December 1976	170,455,617	

Per ordinary share of f 10 of N.V. Philips' Gloeilampenfabrieken:

Adjusted net profit	f4.71	$1.92
Adjusted net profit, excluding a loss of f 40 m for operations to be discontinued	f4.95	$2.02
Dividend	f1.60	$0.65

Assuming conversion of all outstanding convertible debentures, the adjusted net profit per ordinary share would be f 4.40 ($1.80).

If the method of historical cost had been applied in the past it is estimated that the item Revaluation Surplus as shown in the Combined Statement of Financial Position as at 31 December 1976, would have appeared as follows:

	in millions of guilders	in millions of U.S. $*
Addition to retained profit	1,809.6	738.6
Deduction from property, plant and equipment, stocks, and provision for deferred taxation (net)	1,179.6	481.5
	2.989.2	1,220.1

*converted at the rate of f 2.45 per U.S. $

Figure 7-1. Information for American Shareholders in N.V. Philips' 1976 Annual Report.

costs are estimated each January 1st based upon the replacement costs of fixed assets and inventories. Estimating departments plot trends of specific price levels, calculate index numbers, and apply the index numbers to homogeneous asset groups. Thereafter, index numbers and replacement values are recalculated as often as is necessary, but not less frequently than each January 1st. These index-adjusted standard prices are used to value all inventories (materials, component parts, work in progress, finished goods), cost of goods sold, and fixed assets. Increases and decreases in values are reflected in equity (revaluation surplus) accounts. As a result, two different price variances are recorded: the holding gain, mentioned above, and the "real" price variance (the actual price versus the index-adjusted standard).

Each subsidiary maintains its own accounting department and prepares its own index numbers and financial statements. Budgetary controls, based upon indexed standard prices, enable the company to distinguish real and holding gains, thereby isolating the results of management performance.

Philips' common sense approaches to responsibility accounting also differ from the methods chosen by most American firms. Profits are generated only when a sales transaction with outsiders takes place. All manufacturing activities are *cost centers*. All internal transfers are made at indexed standard prices plus a fixed charge (historically 10%) to cover costs of financing the assets employed. Only marketing activities are treated as *profit centers.*

The concept of profit adopted, together with the maintenance of clear demarcations between the roles of units, simplifies performance evaluations at all levels. Increases in equity are segregated into those of accomplishment (real profits from sales transactions) and those of circumstance (amounts due to changes in specific price levels). Effective employment of capital simply becomes the arithmetic relationship of profits and assets employed, both based upon current value concepts. Of course, cost center evaluations primarily address variances from standards since the investment charge applied to transfers recovers the costs of capital employed.

Other common sense refinements are used to keep prices, profits, and performance evaluations "clean." All foreign currency translations are made using current rates (the temporal method of *FASB-8* would also permit use of current rates where current prices—as in the

Philips' case—are employed). All differences, however, are first applied to revaluation surplus accounts and only the residuals, if any, are reflected in current income. Moreover, Philips' size and immersion into indexation enable its subsidiaries to calculate current "purchasing power rates" that compare the relative buying powers of the Dutch florin (guilder) and local currencies.

One final common sense policy deserves mention. Philips does not permit tax considerations to violate sound business and accounting practices. In most countries, including the Netherlands, CRVA is not acceptable for tax purposes. Consequently, the conservative earnings reported using CRVA, compared with taxation based upon historical costs, usually produce much higher effective rates of income taxation than those reported by competitors. Also, most other important earnings ratios used by analysts and investors place Philips at a disadvantage.

Nonetheless, the Philips Company is convinced that the disadvantages mentioned, as well as the significant costs involved with operating its management accounting systems, are far outweighed by the benefits afforded management decisions and performance evaluations.

As is common to almost all systems, there are some theoretical flaws inherent in Philips' concepts, but they are not relevant here. It is also recognized that Philips' methods were virtually mandated by the hyperinflationary conditions in Europe during the 1920s. Moreover, the innovative approaches were: (1) made possible by the business practices accepted in the Netherlands, and (2) made practicable by Philips' veritable size. However, such factors are neither necessary nor sufficient conditions. They only serve to germinate and enhance the growth of ideas. The ideas themselves—the strivings for realistic approaches—these are the seeds of innovations.

General Electric Company

During its extensive reorganization in 1954, the General Electric Company pioneered at least three concepts: management by objectives, residual income, and the establishment of multiple, measurable goals.

Like many other large organizations in the 1950s, General Electric became unwieldy given its highly centralized, functional organization structure. In order to decentralize, the company stipulated that "objective goals and objective measurements of progress toward these goals" were necessary. Objective measurements were considered to be essential, not only to guide day-to-day managerial decisions, but also to enable managers to "focus attention on the relevant, the trends, and on the future." In short, the company was convinced that the success of its program to decentralize (into some 120 integrated, yet autonomous subdivisions) was dependent upon the development and use of objective goals and evaluations, instead of the more subjective appraisals common to that time.[4]

Eight objectives or "key result areas" were identified as the basis for measuring organizational performance.[5] In each area, the company proposed to construct indexes to evaluate individual divisions objectively and to perform meaningful comparisons between and among the divisions. The key areas identified were:

• *Profitability.* The company was concerned that concentration upon profits as percentages (ROI), rather than in terms of dollars, would induce managers of the more profitable divisions to reject undertakings that would be desirable for the company as a whole. Consequently, the concept of *residual income* was devised by which a charge for the cost of capital was to be deducted from reported profits in dollars.

• *Market Position.* This area attempted to address the effectiveness of the products as well as the efficiency of marketing them. Market shares were considered to be indexes of consumer acceptance that could assess whether the right products were being provided at the right prices. Also, market research devices were planned to determine what sorts of unfilled customer needs existed.

• *Productivity.* A variety of quantitative, input-output relationships were to be employed to evaluate the productivity of labor, management, and capital. These measurements were also to be compared with comparable indexes of competitor firms and industries. Multiple measures were chosen in recognition of the trade-offs often possible between the employments of human, material, and capital resources.

• *Product Leadership.* This area attempted to assess a division's ability to innovate and lead the field in creating and marketing new products. Although various cost measures were to be applied to newly introduced products, market tests of the success of those products remained rather subjective.

• *Personnel Development.* An assortment of measures were to be used to determine: if qualified people were prepared to fill positions where needed (i.e., promotions from within); if personnel inventories were adequate to serve projected needs; and if development programs were made available, utilized, and effective.

• *Employee Attitudes.* Considered a key reflection of management effectiveness, several indirect measures were to be applied, such as rates of: turnover, absenteeism, injuries, employee suggestions, and the like.

• *Public Responsibility.* The abilities of the divisions to function as good citizens within their respective communities were to be evaluated by feedbacks from employees, suppliers, customers, and community organizations. Quantitative measures reflecting levels of employment, wages, local purchases, and similar value-added contributions were preferred.

• *Balance of Short- and Long-term Goals.* Although the seven preceding objectives alone go far toward preventing sole emphasis upon the short term, long-range plans were required to be submitted and reviewed regularly.

Hindsight indicates that General Electric was not able to construct all the objective measurements planned. Neither was the decentralization program successful, at least in its original form. Several reasons can be conjectured.

Since this was the company's first move toward decentralization, perhaps G.E. was overly ambitious. Integrated units do not function very well without some centralized coordination.

Too much dependence may have been placed upon objective measures and standards. Setting goals and devising means for charting progress toward them cannot assure that they will be achieved.

Finally, other than the ordering in which they were presented, there were no weights specifically assigned the eight objectives. Testimonies of company managers during subsequent hearings regarding price-fixing charges in the industry indicated that, from the managers' points of view, the firm emphasized profit generations to the exclusion of all else. If that impression did prevail, the company's actions established the ranking of objectives more clearly than any statements of policy.

Regardless, General Electric's initial move toward decentralization provided new ideas and tools that have proved to be useful when employed properly.

The 3M Company

In an appendix to his 1969 study of the evaluations of foreign operations, John Mauriel[6] described the process developed by the 3M Company. He was impressed by the "comprehensive top management procedures" employed.[7] In fact, the process, excerpted below, would even be considered comprehensive and innovative today.

In 1969, the 3M Company had over thirty overseas subsidiaries in three regions: Europe, Latin America, and the Far East. Each region had a controller who reported to the controller of the international division.

The formal reporting system encompassed the usual monthly, quarterly, and annual reports. Unusual aspects involved: sales budgets in units as well as monetary terms, and total profit budgets segmented by product line. Frequent informal visits by functional staff members also provided assistance and valuable two-way communication.

The annual on-site reviews represented the "capstones" of the evaluation process. A review team was assigned to each area and conducted a "full-dress" evaluation of each subsidiary. Each team was composed of board members and personnel from the international division, usually in equal proportions.

Prior to each annual review, the international or area controller paid an advance visit to each subsidiary, giving whatever assistance was necessary. Also prior to the actual review, team members were furnished briefing (data) books by both the international division and, upon arrival, by the local manager. The briefing books were required to contain the normal financial reports and projections, augmented by any special information considered relevant.

The actual review was of three parts. Local management made slide presentations of the usual financial results and forecasts, turnover reports, and segmented analyses of sales and operations. The second phase consisted of discussions by local management of the progress and/or status of some 18 specified items: 5 in marketing, 8 in manufacturing, 2 regarding the competitive environment, plus trends of financial ratios, forecasts of cash flows, and dividend prospects. The final segment of the review consisted of a general discussion and interchange of information between local management and team members. Not only did the discussions serve as vehicles to exchange useful information, but they also enabled the team officials to make further assessments of the capabilities of local managements.

The review processes of the 3M Company afforded many benefits to parent and subsidiary executives. The related costs were also significant. The parent officials apparently considered that the benefits exceeded the costs and time involved—at least for the thirty or so overseas units concerned.

Most likely, similar evaluations would not be practicable given more extensive overseas operations. However, with minor revisions (such as alternating annual reviews between on-site and parent locations, and adjusting the compositions of the traveling review teams), the same realistic evaluations could be afforded a larger number of locations—and the valuable, two-way educational benefits could be retained as well.

CONTEMPORARY APPROACHES

Over the past decade, many innovations have been made or suggested. Initiatives for change were generated internally and externally. Some of the changes were partial and addressed particular concerns of particular companies. Others represented complete changes in thinking.

Most of the brief examples that follow represent improvements, which will be defined as changes in attitudes and methods that encourage more realistic performance evaluations.

Honeywell, Inc.

Like the majority of U.S.-based multinationals, Honeywell operates with some 100 foreign and dozens of domestic divisions.[8] All are regarded as profit centers. Intracompany transfers amount to hundreds of millions of dollars annually. Honeywell's primary concern has been the design of transfer prices to achieve and maintain equity among its profit centers.

All internal transfers are recorded in dollars regardless of the locations involved. Prior to the debacles produced by floating exchange rates, transfer prices in U.S. dollars were established prior to the start of each year based upon projected exchange rates, costs, and volumes. Once approved, these transfer prices were frozen. Current exchange rates were used to translate subsequent internal reports, but the differences between planned and current rates were not significant as a rule.

Floating rates motivated Honeywell to change its procedures in order to retain: (1) realistic performance measurements, (2) internal accountings in current U.S. dollar equivalents, and (3) practicable procedures.

Honeywell's solution was "dollar indexing." All of the original system was kept unchanged. However, as an actual exchange rate deviated from the planned rate for any foreign location, a new transfer price in U.S. dollars was calculated and applied:[9]

$$\text{New transfer price} = \text{Old transfer price} \times \left(\frac{\text{Current exchange rate}}{\text{Planned exchange rate}} \right)$$

Since virtually all transfers were from manufacturing to marketing affiliates, any increases or decreases in planned costs could be considered for reflection in selling prices. In effect, the above adaptation enabled the company to: (1) eliminate the distortions of floating rates upon the performance evaluations of producing locations, and (2) reflect transfers at current economic costs to selling units, thereby enabling more realistic marketing decisions to be made.

Of course, the relatively minor change in procedure was effective primarily because a reasonable, cooperative system of performance evaluation was already in use. Top management reviewed, approved, and treated as contracts the budget submissions of profit centers. Planned transfer prices and exchange rates were also reviewed and approved. (The transfer prices approved for use by manufacturing units provided for recovery of costs plus a "profit" acceptable to the headquarters and made known to the selling units.) Last, but not least, the headquarters translated all foreign-currency operating statements at current rates, thereby preserving their essence.

Carrier International Corp.

An entirely different attitude and approach was adopted by the Carrier International Corporation.

In the opinion of one top executive,[10] performance evaluations should: (1) be meaningful, (2) be based upon "objective standards consistently applied," (3) use the same standards to evaluate the contributions of subsidiaries and their top managers, and (4) be rational and equitable.

Official operating results in U.S. dollars and in accordance with *FASB-8* were selected as the basis for all major evaluations. Three alternative bases were considered but rejected. Local currency results were considered appropriate for assessing performances of middle managers only. Similarly, translated results using budgeted exchange rates were considered deficient for a number of reasons, but primarily because of potential deviations from official *FASB-8* earnings. A third basis—the official *FASB-8* results with translation "gains and losses backed out"—was dismissed as "irrational." Thus, only the official *FASB-8* earnings were accepted as relevant, since they conformed with the information presumed to be used by the financial community to evaluate the corporation as a whole.

Subsidiary management was held accountable for *transaction* gains and losses, and "shared" responsibility for *translation* "gains and losses" with the international division management. The sharing arrangement normally consisted of recommendations by local managers of possible actions to protect translation and economic exposures, with the ultimate decisions being made by the international division.

At evaluation (and bonus) time, the international manager compared *bonuses* based upon *FASB-8* results and earnings obtained by using the budgeted exchange rates. If he considered the difference "material," he would also consider an adjustment. If, in his opinion, the currency movement would be reversed in the near term, he might adjust the bonus nearer to the amount based upon the budgeted rates. However, if the rate change was considered to be permanent, the smaller bonus would be selected, although the full amount of the reduction might be spread over the next two or three years. Either way, if the judgments of the international manager were correct, the adjusted earnings (upon which evaluations and bonuses were based) would closely conform with official earnings over relatively short time spans.

The method admittedly did not eliminate all subjectivity, but it reportedly avoided "the dangers and pitfalls usually associated with fully judgmental and open-ended approaches which can easily degenerate into popularity contests."[11]

Analog Devices

As a growing company in a growth industry (electronics), Analog's management was particularly concerned about mediating conflict between short- and long-term growth. Moreover, the decentralized company (2000 employees, $130 million sales in 1980) recognized that its executive compensation system had to reinforce both corporate and divisional objectives.[12]

The balanced plan that emerged was two-dimensional—based upon sales growth and return on assets—with both measures "pegged" to industry performance.

Since the firm normally experienced a three-year lag time, on the average, between investment in a project and reasonable return, sales growth was to be measured as a moving average over a three-year (12-quarter) time frame.

Within the electronics industry, a lag time (three months) was also common between recognition of and response to changes in order volumes. Consequently, profitability (return on assets) was to be averaged over a period of three quarters. Return on assets was selected since it conformed most closely with controllability by divisional management. The measure of return selected was profits before taxes and nonoperating expenses. Assets were chosen as a base since divisions had no control over financings or capital structures.

Standards for each of the two measures were based upon (and would follow) the average performances of 15 similar firms that were leaders in the industry.

Quarterly evaluations and payouts were selected for compatibility with external reportings and employee aspirations.

A bonus matrix was constructed annually (at budget time) reflecting the results of various trade-offs between goals established for growths in sales and ROA. The following formula was devised to calculate the bonus factor (K):[13]

$$K = \left(\frac{\text{ROA } \% + \text{bias} + .4 \text{ sales growth } \%}{33}\right)^{4.5}$$

(The bias element, above, was introduced to allow for the depressing effects upon ROA of unusual, strategic investments planned at the beginning of the year. Once determined, the element was held constant during the year.)

The evaluation system contained many desirable features. It was two-dimensional and flexible. It recognized ongoing trade-offs between short- and long-term goals (for 1979, a 2% increase in ROA was equivalent to a 5% rate of sales growth). It also recognized the inherent differences possible among divisions—some would be "cash cows" and others innovators—and both contributions were necessary. Furthermore, since the best laid plans often required adjustment, the bias factor recognized the impacts of strategic corporate plans before the fact (and presumably afterward for any significant midstream changes as well).

Also, the measures chosen were realistic in that they were controllable by division management. Finally, pegging standards to industry leaders prevented the company from falling behind the field while encouraging it to move ahead.

The measures, standards, and applications fit that particular company and industry. Naturally, different firms and environments would require different variables and methods tailored to the circumstances.

Mechanical Improvements

Changes in attitudes and approaches are quite often dependent upon practical means of implementation. Two such means are presented below. Each has promise, given further refinements to make them more equitable and realistic.

Distributable Funds. A performance measurement called "distributable funds" has been suggested to help companies and subsidiaries cope with changing prices.

Basically, funds considered to be distributable are those earnings remaining after the "business capacity" financed by equity has been protected. This approach recognizes the normal increased costs of replacing inventories and productive assets, as well as the increments in working capital prompted by inflation. (See Figure 7-2.)

The concept has the inherent flexibility needed to make it adaptable to a variety of circumstances. It can be applied to foreign subsidiaries in local currencies as well as to consolidated results. Specific or general price indexes, or combinations of both, can be employed dependent upon the assets concerned and the replacement plans of the entities.

Realism is enhanced since impacts upon future levels of working capital are also considered, as well as "gearing"—the perceived ability of the entity to finance by debt some portion of the additional resources required.

On the other hand, the beneficial aspects of inflation are ignored, particularly the ability of the unit or company to recoup some or all

	CURRENT PERIOD	PRIOR PERIOD
Net earnings after taxes, per income statement		
less:		
Funds required for increased costs of: Inventories Productive assets Working capital	Note: Amounts can be in local or parent currencies, as applicable.	
plus:		
Funds obtainable from external debt Distributable funds	———	———
less:		
Dividends	———	———
Resources available for growth	———	———

Source: Adapted from Alfred Rappaport, "Effects of Changing Prices on Management Decision Making and Performance Evaluation," in: Paul A. Griffin (ed.), *Proceedings: Financial Reporting and Changing Prices* (Stamford, Conn.: FASB, 1979), p. 41.

Figure 7-2. Comparative Statement of Distributable Funds.

of the increased costs by means of future increases in selling prices. Also, some mechanical problems would be encountered. Applications to foreign subsidiaries in local currencies (perhaps the most useful of all) would present problems in subsequent translations for consolidated use in the parent currency. Some double-counting would be involved to the extent that relative rates of inflation are reflected in the exchange rates used.

Of course, while the proposal *may* represent an appropriate performance measure of an autonomous activity, the equity of its application to a subsidiary manager would be extremely doubtful and would depend upon a host of considerations.

Ideal Return on Assets. An unidentified pharmaceutical company developed what it termed a "minimum ideal return on assets employed"[15] (MIROAE).

Several aspects of MIROAE and its application are unique. Initially, MIROAE considers the incremental cash flows, ignored by customary inflation-adjusted, return-on-equity alternatives, as requisite for growth. Even more important, a minimum ideal rate is computed at the beginning of the year for *each* subsidiary. As a result, rates of local inflation and taxes are considered, as well as policies regarding growth targets, debt-equity ratios, and earnings repatriations. The MIROAE computed is used as a standard with which the actual performance of each unit is subsequently compared. The following steps in computing the MIROAE are numbered to key with those shown in Figure 7-3:

- Step 1. The minimum return on equity is computed taking into account the desired rate of real growth, adjusted for projected inflation and dividends to be repatriated (in the example, a dividend of 33 1/3% is reflected).

  Also, the return needed to support the after-tax cost of borrowed capital is computed. (No costs are assigned interest-free liabilities.)
- Step 2. The rates computed above are applied to the corresponding components of the unit's financial structure. The portion of assets financed by non-interest liabilities is determined by the actual history of the unit, adjusted for any changes planned.

Step 1.   Required return on

a) *equity*

Real growth requirement	6%
Projected inflation rate	7%
Adjusted growth requirement $(1.06 \times 7) + 6 =$	13.42%
Repatriation policy: Dividend $\frac{1}{3}$ of profits 66.7% reinvested: $13.42 \div 66.7\% =$	20.12%

b) *borrowed capital*

Projected local interest rate	8%
Tax on profit before tax	45%
After-tax interest rate	4.4%

c) *Noninterest liabilities*	0

Step 2.   Required return on assets employed

Balance sheet item	% of total assets	req. return on assets
Noninterest liabilities	10 ($\times 0 =$)	0%
Debt	22.5($\times 4.4 =$)	.99%
Equity ratio $\frac{1}{3}$	67.5($\times 20.12 =$)	13.58%
		14.57%

Step 3.   ROAE after tax $14.57 \div (100 - 45)$ $\qquad = \qquad$ 26.49%

Step 4.   ROAE after tax including overhead allocation $(13.20 + 26.49)$ $\qquad = \qquad$ 39.69%

Step 5.   Corrected ROAE minimum $(39.69 \div 1.1)$ $\qquad = \qquad$ 35.9%

Source: William Persen and Van Lessig, *Evaluating the Financial Performance of Overseas Operations* (New York: Financial Executives Research Foundation, 1979), pp. 141-142. Reprinted with permission.

Figure 7-3. Computation of Minimum Ideal Return on Assets Employed.

The debt-equity ratio (in this case 1:3) is the norm established by company policy and need not agree with the actual ratio of the unit.

- Steps 3 and 4. The rate obtained above is adjusted to allow for local taxes and allocations of corporate overhead, respectively, and in turn. (In the example, corporate overhead represented an after-tax burden of 13.20%.)
- Step 5 corrects the projected MIROAE (computed as above on data at the beginning of the year) for compatibility with the actual return (computed on averages for the year).

As with most measures and standards, the MIROAE concept holds problems as well as promises.

Where foreign *subsidiaries* are involved, the computations should be made in terms of local currencies. Little net realism would be gained by attempts to recognize the peculiarities of foreign environments in terms of the parent currency.

Also, realistic evaluations of local *managers* should be begun with rates *before* corporate overhead allocations, then further adjusted for the effects of any other factors not locally controllable. One such factor deserving attention involves the estimated rate of local inflation. Although the rate is held constant in the computations of projected and actual rates of return, the effects of any difference between estimated and actual inflation rates would be reflected in actual operating profits. Any allowances to be made should be based upon the local manager's authority to react to unforeseen economic events.

In addition to the benefits cited earlier, comparability among units is enhanced by holding a constant debt-equity ratio for all units. This is made possible since depreciation (however recorded locally) is added back before actual rates of return are calculated for the subsidiaries at the end of the period.

Japanese Multinationals

General insights regarding the approaches of two Japanese-owned MNEs are presented here as a refreshing study in contrasts.

It should not be considered at all unusual that Japanese-based MNEs have come of age. As the second largest industrial nation in the world, Japan served as headquarters for 750 MNEs (out of 1700 listed companies) at the end of 1978. Together these companies operated some 5,800 overseas affiliates with a net direct investment in excess of $22 billion.[16] Moreover, six Japanese-based MNEs were among the 50 largest industrial companies in the world at the close of 1978, and four of the six advanced in the rankings since 1974. (See Table 7-1.)

Mitsui & Co., Ltd. One of Japan's largest general-trading companies, Mitsui controls 128 foreign affiliates. Operations are controlled through an Overseas Planning Division in the headquarters and by general managers in three regions: America, Europe, and Oceania. Local currency accounting data are sent directly to the headquarters each month by each affiliate, as well as through the regional manager (for the addition of his comments prior to submission to the headquarters).

Because of the diversity of its operations and modes of doing business (and as much due to the Japanese penchant for understatement), Mitsui alleges that it "has not yet succeeded in developing an effective control system over subsidiaries based abroad." Common measures tracked routinely are growths in net sales and profits, each in local currencies. However, top management readily admits that "figures are not always decisive" where evaluations are concerned. Heavy emphasis continues to be placed upon "continuous personal contacts and observations."[17]

Table 7-1.   Japanese MNEs Included in the Fifty Largest Industrial Companies in the World, 1974–1978.   (Sales are in $ Billions.)

	1978		1977		1976		1975		1974	
	Sales	Rank	Sales	Rank	Sales	Rank	Sales	Rank	Sales	Rank
Toyota Motor	$12.7	20	$9.6	28	$7.6	35	$7.1	34	$5.9	38
Matsushita Elec. (Panasonic)	10.0	34	6.8	48						
Nissan Motor	9.7	35	7.6	44	6.5	44	5.4	47		
Nippon Steel	9.5	36	8.9	32	8.0	31	8.7	19	8.8	20
Mitsubishi Ind.	9.2	39	8.0	42	6.1	49	5.6	44	5.7	41
Hitachi	9.1	41	8.2	39	6.6	42	5.9	42	6.2	37

Source: Prepared from data on the "Fifty Largest Industrial Companies in the World" in various issues of *Fortune* magazine.

Sony Corporation. This world-famous firm operates 20 subsidiaries in 13 countries. Overseas units forward standardized financial reports in local currencies to the headquarters each month.

Performance evaluations are made monthly and annually by the "Top Management Conference" at headquarters. Net sales, operating profits, and net earnings are among the measures examined. All evaluations are made in terms of local currencies. Exchange differences, produced upon subsequent consolidation, are not considered at all in assessing subsidiary operations.

As a general rule, top management takes no action so long as the trends of the measures cited are favorable. Where declining trends become apparent, subsidiary managers are "given the opportunity to discuss problems to be solved"[18] during special meetings held at least semiannually.

Comments and Opinions. Many Japanese managements will stipulate that their "overseas"—rather than "foreign"—subsidiaries have not yet been regarded as autonomous profit or investment centers. They indeed may never be. Independence of a corporate family unit seems as alien to their thinking as the word "foreign" is to their vocabulary.

It is widely known that the Japanese are an austere, homogeneous, cooperative, and adaptive people. The fealty of the samurai warrior to his lord has its counterpart in the loyalty of the industrial worker or manager to his company. These characteristics, aided by American seed capital and technology, enabled the Japanese to transform a pile of rubble into the second largest industrial nation in the world.

In this author's opinion, Japanese firms benefit at the outset, whether at home or abroad, from manager and employee traits that American firms attempt to create (if not control) by various motivation and reward systems. Moreover, the traditional lifetime employment practices have encouraged Japanese workers to speak up to improve methods and working conditions. All too many workers in other societies seem prone to grumble or quit.

Traditional Japanese value systems and practices tend to made controls based upon figures seem rather ineffective, if not alien.

That is not to say that Japanese firms have no inept workers or ineffective managers. Upon identification, such persons are generally assigned tasks for which they are better suited—and in which they can cause little disruption or disharmony. Face, as well as fortune, is saved. In many respects, it could be said that the "Peter Principle"[19] was a Japanese innovation.

As is the nature of things, the Japanese culture will change as international relationships introduce more heterogeneity. In the process, it would be desirable if, as the Japanese learn from others, we can also learn to benefit from them.

GRAPHIC COMMUNICATIONS

Many executives will agree that the invention of graphs is second, perhaps, only to the wheel.

One of the first widely publicized uses of graphic presentations by chief executives was reported by the vice-president of finance of one of Mexico's ten largest companies.[20] Prior to resorting to graphs, the executive waded through some 150 pages of data each month in order

---

General Data (Actual/Budgeted, where applicable):

- Sales—in dollars
  - —in units
- Pretax earnings
- Contributions:
  - —by division
  - —by product line
  - —by territory
- Variable income to sales
- Return—on assets
  - —on equity

- Turnovers
- Days—of receivables
  - —of inventories
  - —of payables
- Working capital
- Cash flow
- Capital budget
- Market shares
- Stock prices
- Earnings per share

Productivity and Cost Control:

- Sales—per employee
  - —per payroll dollar
- Overhead to sales
- Standard Variances

- Numbers of employees
- Maintenance and Repair
- Unit costs—production
  - —distribution

Responsibility Center Items:

- Key areas measurable and mutually agreed upon
- Segmented data should coincide with items selected for total company to facilitate comparison and consolidation.

Figure 7-4. Examples of Performance Data and Other Subjects Useful to Graph.

to monitor the progress of his company and its 25 or more responsibility centers. That pile of paper was winnowed down to just one page, with 20 graphs on each side. One side contained charts on the company's performance; the other tracked the important aspects of the national economy. Similar sets of charts depicting relevant performance data were also prepared for the divisions and major responsibility centers—*at the requests of the managers!*

Although data to be graphed will vary among companies and units, examples of useful subjects are shown in Figure 7-4.

Charts and graphs have long been popular vehicles for presenting information in annual reports. The same attributes that make graphic representations desirable in external reporting make them valuable for internal use as well:

- Complicated data and trends can be presented in a form that is easy to understand and remember. Graphics speak a "universal visual language." Perception and retention is increased, particularly given limited amounts of analysis time.
- Important relationships and trends can be highlighted more effectively than by using an array of numbers.
- Appropriate topics can also be readily identified for graphic presentations in annual reports.
- Used in related groups, graphics can present concise, effective, and efficient overviews of a company and its segments.
- The flexibility of selection and design permit key areas peculiar to individual companies to be selected and monitored. Management by exception is facilitated since potential problem areas may be identified readily.
- Graphics can be updated easily and promptly. Information is available earlier and in convenient form.
- If the same series of charts are distributed to all top managers, they can serve as the basis for scheduled as well as impromptu discussions. At budget time, the charts for the current period often serve as useful points of departure.
- Graphic monitoring systems have also proven to be successful early-warning devices for production and other middle-managers. Programs such as "key indicator management," based upon reasonably attainable standards, facilitate control of operations —and identify charts to be used in presentations "upstairs."[21]

- Perhaps one of the less appreciated attributes of graphic communications is attitudinal. As monetary measures lose much of their usefulness during times of price turbulence, managements may become willing to examine charts expressed in terms of units, if only as supplements to monetary data.

Graphic approaches are not panaceas by any means. Some managers feel uncomfortable with charts. Others are hesitant to rely upon them other than as starting points for question or discussion. For those persons, the traditional numerical reports can continue to serve as complements, rather than supplements.

Implementations of graphic means of communication are simple and relatively inexpensive, even when computer-assisted. Moreover, the subjects selected for charting can be assembled in a gradual, piecemeal fashion. Care should be exercised, however, to assure that the charts are constructed properly and are not misleading.[22] (Selected examples of useful graphs have been furnished in Figures 7-5 through 7-8.)

In summary, graphic presentations can reduce "information indigestion," improve management effectiveness, and conserve the most valuable management resource of all—time.

SERVICE SECTOR INNOVATIONS

As mentioned in preceding chapters, innovative approaches to measurement and evaluation techniques within service industries have appeared in phenomenal numbers in recent years.

Both profit and nonprofit service organizations have recently discovered (or rediscovered) responsibility and cost accounting systems. Many service industries in the private sector, whether providing tangible services (restaurants and retailers) or intangibles (insurance companies, banks, airlines) have recognized that their survival today may well depend on reliable cost information. Public sector industries, notably hospitals, realized belatedly that the alternative to cost containment and control was government regulation. These were powerful motivators.

There is little doubt that public accounting firms have been most instrumental in providing the systems and advisory services necessary. Many firms in the service sector have not had the expertise nor the

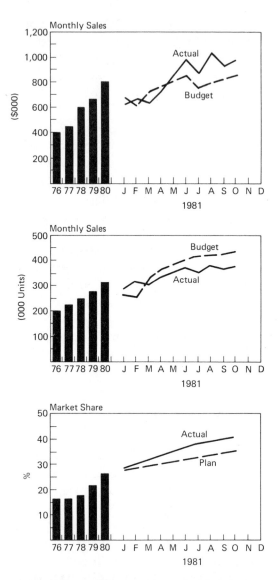

Notes: Items may be segmented by division, product line, or region, as appropriate.
Some charts for overseas operations may be plotted in local currencies as well as dollars.
In some industries, timely comparisons with competitors or industry averages are practical.

Figure 7-5. Examples of Sales Graphics.

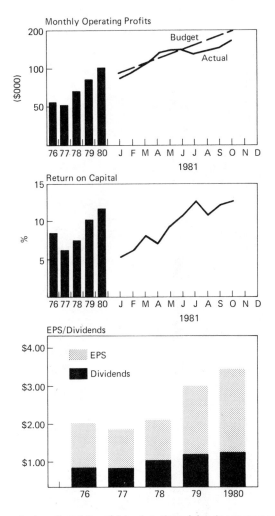

Note: Some companies have found it useful to plot selected data in constant as well as nominal dollars.

For example, the rate of earnings (for the company and for shareholders) can be compared with the rates of change in specific or general prices.

Figure 7-6. Profitability and Earnings Graphs.

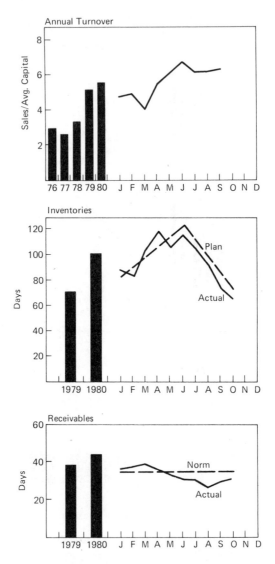

Note: Other items might include:

- Productivity (in various terms).
- Overhead related to sales/costs
- Payrolls related to sales

Figure 7-7. Selected Turnover Charts.

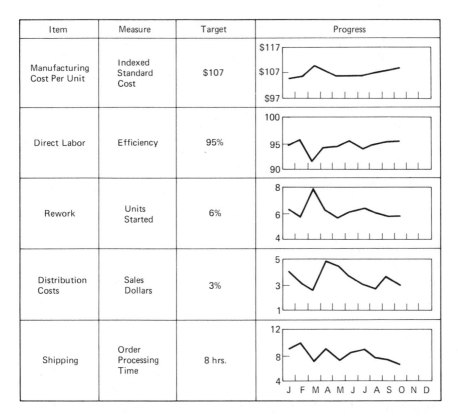

Item	Measure	Target	Progress
Manufacturing Cost Per Unit	Indexed Standard Cost	$107	
Direct Labor	Efficiency	95%	
Rework	Units Started	6%	
Distribution Costs	Sales Dollars	3%	
Shipping	Order Processing Time	8 hrs.	

Source: Adaptations prepared from the more than forty key operating indicators in Robert L. Janson, "Graphic Indicators of Operations," *Harvard Business Review,* November-December 1980, pp. 164–170.

Figure 7-8. Examples of Operating Indicators.

time to commit to the design and installation of responsibility accounting systems. In fact, most of the medium to larger size accounting firms have assembled specialized sections to assist clients in service industries, such as hospitals and insurance.

Planning, management by objectives, key item reports, performance standards, contribution margin reporting, segment analysis, and budgeting have become the new jargon of the service industries. Nearly every issue of the house organs of the "Big 8" accounting firms will feature at least one article describing successful applications of responsibility accounting within the service sector.

The pride of accomplishment evident in most of the cases is justified and well earned. Hospitals, for example, lend themselves to measures of efficiency and effectiveness even less readily than do multinational enterprises, although the same complexities of organization and conflicting goals exist in both. Moreover, hospital administration presents two distinct dimensions: one highly professional, the other nonprofessional. In addition, hospitals have historically relied upon qualitative assessments of performance and, even then, most of those evaluations rarely permeated below departmental levels. Finally, voluntary trustees represent top management and, usually, lack the time and expertise necessary to administer performance surveillance. Given these handicaps, it is particularly gratifying to learn that practicable performance measures and standards have been devised and implemented for all hospital activities save those performed by the medical doctors.[23] (The latter area could have been covered as well, had the medical practitioners been willing to develop the standards of performance necessary.)

NOTES

1. For a detailed examination, see Elwood L. Miller, *Inflation Accounting* (New York: Van Nostrand Reinhold Company, 1980), chapter 6.

2. R.C. Spinosa Cattela, "An Introduction into Current Cost Accounting and its Application Within Philips," *Notable Contributions to the Periodical International Accounting Literature—1975-78* (Sarasota, Florida: American Accounting Association, 1979), p. 110.

3. Ibid. See also, A. Goudeket, "How Inflation is Being Recognized in Financial Statements in the Netherlands," *Journal of Accountancy*, October 1952, pp. 448-452; and "An Application of Replacement Value Theory," *Journal of Accountancy*, July 1960, pp. 37-47.

A more detailed exposition was published as "Philips NV," 1968, Case No. 9108003, by the Intercollegiate Case Clearing House, Boston.

4. *Professional Management in General Electric*, Book III (New York: General Electric Company, 1954), p. 113.

5. *Planning, Managing, and Measuring the Business* (New York: Controllership Foundation, 1955). Part 5 was furnished by R.W. Lewis of G.E.

6. John J. Mauriel, "Evaluation and Control of Overseas Operations," *Management Accounting*, May 1969, pp. 38-39, 52.

7. Ibid., p. 52.

8. Duane Malmstrom, "Accommodating Exchange Rate Fluctuations in Inter-company Pricing and Invoicing," *Management Accounting*, September 1977, pp. 24–28.

9. Ibid., p. 26.

10. Gerard J. Dietemann, "Evaluating Multinational Performance under FAS No. 8," *Management Accounting*, May 1980, pp. 49–55.

11. Ibid., p. 55.

12. Ray Stata and Modesto A. Maidique, "Bonus System for Balanced Strategy," *Harvard Business Review*, November-December 1980, pp. 156–163.

13. Ibid., note to exhibit, p. 159.

14. Alfred Rappaport, "Effects of Changing Prices on Management Decision Making and Performance Evaluation," in: Paul A. Griffin (ed.), *Proceedings: Financial Reporting and Changing Prices* (Stamford, Conn.: FASB, 1979), pp. 37–44.

15. William Persen and Van Lessig, *Evaluating the Financial Performance of Overseas Operations* (New York: Financial Executives Research Foundation, 1979), Appendix, pp. 139–142. This section is adopted from the material in the appendix cited.

16. Yukio Fujita, "Internal Performance Evaluation in Japanese Multinational Companies," *Collected Papers*, American Accounting Association's Annual Meeting, Honolulu, Hawaii, (August 21–25, 1979), pp. 41–44.

Also see: Peter F. Drucker, "Behind Japan's Success," *Harvard Business Review*, January-February 1981, pp. 83–90.

17. Fujita (note 16), p. 44.

18. Ibid., p. 43.

19. L.J. Peter and R. Hall, *The Peter Principle* (New York: Bantam Books, Inc., 1969).

20. George B. Blake, "Graphic Shorthand as an Aid to Managers," *Harvard Business Review*, March-April 1978, pp. 6–8, 12.

Also see: Gregory M. Leivian, "How to Communicate Financial Data More Effectively," *Management Accounting*, July 1980, pp. 31–34.

21. Robert L. Janson, "Graphic Indicators of Operations," *Harvard Business Review*, November-December 1980, pp. 164–170.

22. Johnny R. Johnson, Robert R. Rice, and Roger A. Roemmich, "Pictures that Lie: the Abuse of Graphs in Annual Reports," *Management Accounting*, October 1980, pp. 50–56.

23. Charles M. Ewell, Jr., "Measuring Managerial Effectiveness in the Hospital: It Can be Done," *Arthur Young Journal*, Summer-Autumn 1978, pp. 24–32.

8
Revaluation

At this point it may prove to be useful to construct a brief synopsis of the problems, partial solutions, and unresolved issues delineated in the preceding chapters.

As has been developed, performance evaluations involve a variety of related issues. Some semblance of structure may serve as a point of departure for the suggestions and speculations in the final chapters.

RELEVANT CONSIDERATIONS

Most companies are unique in one respect or another. They may operate within a number of dissimilar environments, evidence various stages of multinational development, and occupy different niches in domestic and international marketplaces.

The perspectives and perceptions of company executives also differ concerning strategies, values, roles of people, and the future.

Consequently, all companies will not face the same problems or promises. The perceived needs for improvements in performance evaluations will vary both in number and importance. Not all the considerations that follow will be relevant in all cases.

The ordering followed is not hierarchical necessarily. It is somewhat functional or procedural in that answers to considerations in one area will help solve (or eliminate) issues in subsequent areas. Some very fine lines separate the classes of considerations presented. Some items might have been placed in another category with little difficulty.

Attitudinal Issues

In the final analysis, performance evaluations represent people judging people. Attitudes are particularly relevant.

Much like beauty, realism and fairness are subjective appraisals. They are also circumstantial and variable. Although perfection may not be attainable, most methods of performance evaluation can be improved insofar as both attributes are concerned.

Perhaps only curiosity need be aroused at first. How good are we? Critical looks may indicate areas that might be improved. What changes should be made? However, only realization that improvements will produce real benefits will determine what changes *will* be made.

For convenience, the most important attitudinal issues have been depicted in Figure 8-1. (Occasional perusuals of this and subsequent related figures might also encourage and assist ongoing revaluations of ways of thinking.)

Coordinative, symbiotic approaches to management may suggest collaborative evaluations. The maze of objectives and variability of effective controls may lead to considerations of multiple measures— as well as generate concerns over the information indigestion that might result.

Perspectives of foreign operations should be examined. How overseas activities are perceived will affect how they should be assessed.

Recognition of dualities will help determine the numbers and natures of the evaluations desired. The relative validities of profits and budgets as measures of accomplishment should be assessed initially and subsequently as circumstances warrant.

Last, but not least, executives must consider their own positions. The costs and risks of change should be compared with the corporate benefits that may accrue from more realistic assessments of productive activities and people.

Conceptual Concerns

Much like selections from columnar menus in Chinese restaurants, the preceding attitudinal factors will help address many of the conceptual concerns summarized in Figure 8-2.

The fundamental concern, perhaps, involves acceptance of the potential trade-offs between and among objectivity, subjectivity, convenience, and realism.

Interdependencies and decisions orchestrated by the headquarters will also present dilemmas. Solutions to some problems may call for

1. Should realism be the primary objective?
   (a) If an ideal system is impossible, can the existing system be made more realistic?
      • Should the best information available be selected as a reasonable compromise?
      • Should multiple objectives and trade-offs be recognized?
      • Need the effects of interdependencies be isolated?
   (b) Is performance evaluation a collaborative enterprise?
      • Would participation in goal-setting by local managers enhance realism, understanding, acceptance, and goal congruence?
   (c) Is controllability a precept of realism?
      • Need authority and accountability be related to controllability and contribution?
      • Are the results of contribution and circumstance separable?
   (d) Are unidimensional approaches to multidimensional situations realistic?
      • Would acceptance of multiple measures lead to analysis paralysis?
      • Is deviation from customary financial reporting concepts necessary? Is it wise?

2. What perspective is appropriate?
   (a) Are different evaluations necessary for domestic and foreign operations?
      • Do environmental variables and strategic objectives make foreign operations unique?
      • Would recognition of uniqueness obviate comparability?
      • Can resources be allocated rationally without comparability?
   (b) Should a home- or host-country attitude prevail?
      • Which operating results are real—those in foreign currencies or translated dollars?
      • Is there any valid, overriding reason to translate foreign-currency operating results for internal, management purposes?
      • Can the interests of foreign and parent-company stakeholders be harmonized?
   (c) Should the short- or long-term outlook govern foreign operations?
      • Is the focus to be on one-way flows of funds from cash cows, or overseas expansion, or both?
      • Would more emphasis upon the medium- to long-term outlook enhance competitive postures abroad and at home?
      • Should the time spans of evaluations conform with those of objectives and strategies?

3. Should dualities be important considerations?
   (a) Is there any real difference between efficiency and effectiveness?
   (b) Are different evaluations of activities and their managers needed?

4. Should profitability remain supreme?
   (a) Are all managers responsible for profits?
   (b) Is the "bottom line" equivalent to accomplishment and contribution?
   (c) Can comprehensive measures conceal as much as they reveal?
   (d) Should the effects of corporate orchestrations be recognized? If so, how?

5. Are budgets, tailored to fit the circumstances, appropriate tools to plan, coordinate, and evaluate activities?
   (a) Would similar devices be useful to assist local managers to operate and control, as well as serve to evaluate their contributions?
   (b) Since the subsequent evaluations would only be as valid as the budgets they were based upon, can optimism/pessimism in budgets be minimized?
   (c) Are budgets worth their time and costs?
      • Would ex post facto evaluations alone be more realistic, since actual responses to known conditions can be assessed?
      • Should budgets be relegated to proforma roadmaps?

6. Is the risk that changes in ways of thinking may be misunderstood internally and externally affordable?
   (a) Would the efforts to communicate and educate be worth their costs?

Figure 8-1. Attitudinal Issues.

1. Is objectivity synonymous with realism?
   (a) Are there too many factors in the evaluation process that can only be judged on a subjective basis?
   (b) Are normative methods realistic in all situations?

2. What are the roles of units and managers?
   (a) Where the roles of each are multiple, should rankings or weightings be considered?
   (b) Are there effective or potential conflicts among strategic and multiple roles?
      • Where conflicts are possible, who should determine the trade-offs desired?

3. Have interdependencies obscured the clean demarcations between units?
   (a) Is a decentralized structure compatible with the best interests of the corporate family?
   (b) Are units really autonomous?
      • Should they be?
   (c) Are interdependencies relatively unimportant?
      • Should they be ignored or assumed away?
   (d) Should responsibility centers be redefined or reassembled into different groupings?
      • Would a worldwide product line organization ameliorate the distortions of most interdependencies?
      • Would the rapport of the international division with local markets be sacrificed?
   (e) Can transfer prices accomplish strategic goals without violating independence, congruent decisions, and equitable evaluations?

4. Do comprehensive measures (such as ROI and RI) assess the performances of activities, local managers, original investment decisions, or some combination of all the above colored by changing times and circumstances?
   (a) Is it desirable to disaggregate such measures by component and contribution?
   (b) How should profits and investments be defined?
   (c) Can control and use of assets really be shared?

5. If budgets are to be used as part of the evaluation process, should they be considered as contracts or estimates?

6. Are financial and managerial accounting concepts compatible?
   (a) Have the concepts been violated by confusion?
   (b) If consolidated statements depict a mythical entity, can the restated and translated components be considered real?
   (c) Financial accounting *presumes* that all accounts will be converted into dollars, whereas only dividends and international settlements will be converted by going concerns.
      • Will residual assets be used locally and affected more by changes in local purchasing power than by exchange rates?

Figure 8-2. Conceptual Concerns.

some revisions in present organizational structures. Perhaps the natures of some subsidiaries will have changed significantly from the time they were last examined. Responsibility accounting may have become a misnomer. Maybe activity accountings (for units) and authority accountings (for managers) are more appropriate labels today.

It may also follow that the old reliable macro-measures of financial accounting now produce misleading results when applied to micro-units. More reliance may need to be placed upon managerial accounting tools that can be related with activities and their segments.

Conceptual approaches toward consolidated statements, foreign currency differences, and budgetary tools may also call for critical examination.

Situational Aspects

Fair warning must be given that the situational aspects in Figure 8-3 may prove to be the most disconcerting of all. However, the attitudinal and conceptual frameworks developed will provide valuable assistance.

The realism traditionally accorded normative methods of evaluation may be found to be undeserved, or, at best, suspect.

Moreover, translated foreign-currency results may be construed as economic illusions. Searches for reality may lead to further considerations of current practices of foreign exchange management. Customary hedging may be found to be a zero-sum game in which costs and economic losses are identical over time. Real conversion gains and losses—actual and potential—may have to be segregated from translation differences for proper management considerations. The translation differences themselves may be cast in a different light, as well as responsibilities for the differences.

Shared authorities may denote shared responsibilities and evaluations. The synergism afforded by coordinative management may be expected to create some uncomfortable moments.

Eventually, some of the tax-planning staff may complain that the information they are supplied with is inadequate. Separate financial reports, official copies of properly certified local tax returns, certified original receipts for local taxes paid, and amounts of dividend repatriations for each year, for each foreign subsidiary, may be required.

1. Does realism depend upon the particular situations of companies and their component parts?
   (a) Should different environmental conditions elicit different expectations?
      • Should situational approaches be substituted for normative methods?
   (b) Can foreign statements be evaluated realistically outside the contexts of their national environments and currencies?
   (c) Are local- or parent-country accounting rules to predominate in assessing operating results?

2. Is comparability of complex enterprises possible, other than in the broadest macro-terms?
   (a) Are foreign and domestic subsidiaries comparable?
   (b) Can foreign operations be considered comparable?

3. Does coordination affect controllability?
   (a) Should the impact of headquarters' manipulations on operating results be identified?
      • Do *managed* transfer prices in use overseas also "manage" to violate the controllability of local managers?
      • Can responsibility for complex aspects, such as exchange differences, be shared?
   (b) How are factors outside the control of the corporation and its managers to be recognized?
      • Should responses to the unforeseen be evaluated by reactions as well as results?

4. Are cash flows to the parent more situational than anything else?
   (a) If sources and amounts of cash flows are based upon tax and other regulatory considerations, are they meaningful evaluation criteria?
   (b) Can flows other than actual repatriations and other receipts be assessed realistically?
      • Would they be meaningful?

5. What tax effects should be considered: local, parent, both, or neither?
      • Will the choice depend on the perspective and on the authority level to be evaluated?

6. Is local management participation in foreign currency decisions a function of the relative size of the subsidiary more than of management capability?

7. Should the volume and depth of internal data be a function of the relative size, importance, and risk of overseas units?

8. How can the lack of regular, informal communication with overseas managements be offset?
      • Should evaluation mechanisms also serve as early-warning devices?

Figure 8-3. Situational Aspects.

Often, consolidated information will not do, and a form of LIFO layer-cake must be constructed for each foreign subsidiary.

Further conversations indicate that there are all sorts of differences between U.S. and foreign tax rates, bases, and incentives—not to mention the timing differences. Former concepts of foreign earnings— before or after taxes—take on different meanings. Current practices of comparing foreign earnings, or of relating specific earnings with specific investments may seem less realistic and comfortable.

Measurement Questions

The stout heart needed to resolve the three preceding series of issues faces two more. The issues become somewhat less difficult, but also less interesting.

Measurement questions, in particular, may often be important yet, just as often, tend to be mundane. This, however, is the milieu of accountants (and other number-movers) who can help with (as well as confuse) the measurement questions in Figure 8-4.

The multiplicity of measures that seem to be needed may confound evaluators as well as those to be evaluated. But, no single measure yet devised, accounting or otherwise, can be expected to accomplish the many purposes intended. Caution is needed to assure that correct responses will be triggered on the part of the managers, and other concerned stakeholders as well.

Circumstances will likely convert two questions into real dilemmas —the relevance of monetary data, and the traceability of inputs and outputs.

Lacking a common denominator, money in the international sense may be found to have become a circular concept. Currencies may be recognized as commodities much like the goods and services for which they may be exchanged. As commodities, the "values" of currencies can fluctuate in response to *their* respective supplies and demands— and the whims of international bankers—rather than what they can purchase in their respective national economies. Some alternatives for money measures may need to be designed for internal use—and they can serve as important escape valves. However, since money measures will continue to be required for certain internal and external purposes, ingenious methods will need to be devised to prevent such measures from misleading managements and other users.

1. Do multiple objectives call for multiple measurements and standards?
   (a) If several measures are adopted, will they trigger correct responses from managers?

2. How can inputs, outputs, and objectives be related?
   (a) Can reasonable measurements and standards be devised and changed as necessary?
      • How are the contributions of interdependent units and their managers to be identified, isolated, and measured?
      • How is synergism (the contributions of an activity to others and the headquarters) to be reflected?
   (b) Should all criteria be quantifiable?
      • Are qualitative aspects equally important?
      • Need all criteria be measured in order to be judged fairly?

3. Are monetary data less relevant in times of changing prices?
   (a) Should price-adjusted or nonmonetary quantitative measures (or some combination of both) be used?
      • As supplements or complements?
   (b) Should the effects of inflation in both host and home countries be isolated?
      • If not, how can the results of circumstance be separated from those of accomplishment?
      • If so, are exchange rates realistic mirrors of relative price levels?
      • Can double-counting be minimized, if not avoided?
   (c) Should the beneficial aspects of inflation also be recognized?

4. Should ratio analyses look beyond the ratios themselves and focus upon trends?

5. Can appropriate forms of responsibility accounting be applied to most activities?
   (a) How are traceability and variability to be reckoned?
   (b) How are efficiency and effectiveness to be defined?
      • What measures and standards are to be developed?

6. Can budgets be tailored to fit the particular circumstances of various activities?
   (a) Should subsequent variances be related to changes in markets and environments?
   (b) What exchange rates should be used in preparation?
      • In ex post facto comparisons?
      • Where differences are generated, should they be analyzed to isolate amounts due to: (1) errors in prediction and (2) local inflation?

7. Should current exchange rates be used to retain the essence of foreign statements?

8. To assist outsiders to make realistic evaluations, should reported exchange "differences" be segregated into:
   (a) Conversion (real) and translation (paper) amounts?
   (b) Short- and long-term unrealized segments?
   (c) Major currency components?

Figure 8-4. Measurement Questions.

---

1. Does the organization structure suggest a framework for systems and objectives of performance evaluations?
   (a) How are the objectives to be made known and understood?

---

2. Since their purposes often conflict, how should tax, financial, and managerial reportings be differentiated in content and frequency?

---

3. How should multiple criteria be weighted?
   (a) Should the factors to be identified and the tolerances established vary with the subsidiaries and their circumstances?
   (b) If direct comparability is not realistic, what alternatives are available?

---

4. Are intercorporate allocations worthwhile?
   (a) How should they be reflected in user evaluations?
   (b) Should they be treated as common costs?
   - Are allocations poor substitutes for effective evaluations of the support centers concerned?

---

5. Should different methods of transfer pricing be employed for different purposes?
   (a) Would more cost detail in transfer prices enhance decision making at all levels or merely promote bickering?
   (b) Would dual transfer prices (in local and parent currencies) be desirable? Practical?

---

6. How should budgets be constructed?
   (a) Is the "bottom-up" approach feasible?
   - What guidelines and other data not available locally should be sent to subsidiaries?
   (b) Would the "top-down" method be easier?
   - How much fine-tuning should subsidiaries be permitted?
   (c) What guidelines for exception reportings should be set?

---

7. What time frames should be used for evaluations?
   (a) Are interim (informal) as well as annual (formal) evaluations beneficial?
   (b) Should timings of formal evaluations of long-term projects be made to coincide with expected returns?
   (c) Would staggered evaluation periods, locations, and teams spread the workloads?

---

8. What communication process should be used?
   (a) How can valuable two-way communication be enhanced?
   (b) Can local managers be convinced that the headquarters listens as well as directs?

Figure 8-5. Implementational Problems.

Finally, the abilities to: (1) trace inputs and outputs to activities, and (2) estimate the ways in which costs respond to changes in activity, will be recognized as the very foundations upon which accountability is based. Of course, if factors cannot be traced conveniently, neither can they be measured for purposes of ongoing control, whether in standard costs, flexible budgets, or in performance evaluations. Eventual ex post facto measures established in the marketplace may be found to be the only reliable measures. If, however, some semblance of coordination (if not control) is desired, then the questions of measurements and standards must be addressed—and applied as far down the organizational structure as is considered to be practicable.

Implementational Problems

The last threshold involves putting the decisions made to work—getting the right information to the right people, at the right time, and at the least cost.

The problems shown in Figure 8-5 include several conceptual issues that tend to surface only after most of the revaluation has been completed. Reconsiderations of the usefulness of certain practices—notably intercorporation allocations and other transfer-pricing mechanisms—are usually not motivated until evaluators become aware of the *real* problems that are created.

Quite often it will be found that too many numbers are being shuffled about under the guise of control. It may prove to be logical and beneficial to insist that common support services be evaluated and justified on their own merits, standing alone. It may also be recognized that even the most ingenious transfer-pricing "systems" can only serve a limited number of masters and purposes. Trade-offs among strategic, control, and evaluation purposes that cannot be eliminated should at least be recognized.

Considerations of timing and communication may do much to assure that coordinative management achieves its real potential—serving the best interests of the corporation, its management team, and its other interested stakeholders.

9
Realistic Evaluations

Once top managements are convinced that evaluations should focus upon realities (domestic and international), an environment conducive to self-study and improvement will have been created.

The process suggested below is as relevant for the review of existing practices as it is for the consideration of new systems. The time and attention necessary will vary only in degree.

A COMMON-SENSE APPROACH

In the jargon of operations researchers, the following process might be considered a modified systems approach. Common sense seems to be a better modifier; it is clearer and less pretentious. Both terms mean the same thing—simply standing back and making an orderly examination of a complex issue.

The following steps would help assure that all important aspects are considered:

- Determine the objectives of units and their segments.
- Define the roles of units, managers, and personnel.
- Establish criteria to measure performances.
- Determine standards to evaluate performances.
- Select the timing of evaluations.
- Determine the methods for communicating the results.
- Implement the system.

Fair warning should be given that the initial steps will tend to be the most difficult and tedious. They are also critical thresholds.

Determining Objectives

Objectives can be determined by asking why a unit was (or is to be) established.

What strategic purposes are to be served? Purposes of overseas investments may agree or differ with those of domestic operations. The top ten reasons cited[1] for foreign investments have been to:

1. Maintain or increase market share
2. Overcome protectionism or shipping costs
3. Meet competition
4. Host-country pressures
5. Greater sales prospects
6. Availability of materials or components
7. Reduce wage costs
8. Improve profits
9. Follow important customers
10. Host-country inducements.

Other reasons may also surface: to protect technologies; to preempt competitor entry; to acquire market footholds; to create new life cycles for tired domestic products; to enhance domestic economies of scale; to maintain or create vertical integration; or to protect or divert earnings generated elsewhere.

The above and similar probings will help sort out and identify the major purposes of each unit and the general results expected. Usually the results may be subdivided into short, medium, and long range, with each supported by appropriate strategies.

The purposes of each unit should be further refined by considering: environmental conditions, inherent strengths and weaknesses, and management perceptions of opportunities and risks. These considerations will: place each unit into context; help delineate product and/or service outputs; indicate how the outputs will be consumed or marketed; and determine the natures of the contributions expected (Figure 9-1).

The above considerations are similar in many respects to those typically employed in the annual planning process. Consequently, revaluations of the objectives of established activities can coincide

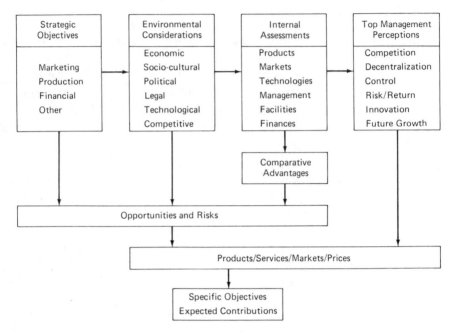

Figure 9-1. Determining Objectives of Units and Segments.

with regular annual review, planning, and budgeting programs. The primary differences, however, are: (1) initial determinations and revaluations of objectives must be made from the top down, and (2) a zero-base approach or attitude should be employed. The two latter approaches will do much to assure that the goals to be pursued are appropriate and desirable, as well as make certain that the necessary resources will be made available. (Guidelines for subsequent budget preparations will be useful by-products.)

Defining Roles of Activities

The roles of segments of a complex enterprise will be determined by the organizational structure which, in turn, will be affected by strategies and objectives—none of which remain static in growing companies.

The following is a typical scenario of change. Most industrial companies develop within a *functional* framework because of the operating *efficiency* afforded. Growth creates complexities. Plants begin to produce multiple products to be distributed, consumed, or sold in a variety of markets. New products and plants are added. Compatible products become more manageable when grouped into lines. Organization by *product* divisions becomes desirable for the *effectiveness* or synergism attainable.

Stresses for changes in structure from functional to product divisions create three dilemmas:

- The necessity of a *balanced* trade-off between efficiency and effectiveness.
- The desirability of similar restructuring of overseas operations from international to product divisions.
- The effects of any additional interdependencies upon performance evaluations of divisions and managers.

Hindsight indicates that the *domestic* operating results of most complex companies have been improved by management along the lines of product divisions. Conversely, there is a growing amount of evidence and opinion (as mentioned earlier) that product divisions have not been beneficial where applied to *international* operations. Evidently, tactical responses to market needs have proven to be less effective when diffused by multiple environments.

The effects on performance evaluations have been dependent upon the abilities of companies to make further restructurings of operations and/or attitudes. A particular domestic manufacturing plant may have been associated with one or a few products or lines marketed domestically. In those cases, a relatively freestanding division may have been identified in which objectives, results, and resources employed could be related.

Where clean-cut demarcations could not be established with domestic operations, the interdependencies that remained created real problems of control and evaluation. In the international realm, it is safe to speculate that strategic objectives will continue to prevail, if not increase in relative importance. For both dilemmas there are no easy solutions. Only reasonable compromises can be suggested for consideration.

Role definition relates the objectives determined with activities and with functions that are reasonably controllable by activity managers and subordinate personnel. This is the milieu of responsibility accounting.

Each unit and important segment thereof should be classified as the type of responsibility center that is compatible with its primary objective and the factors controllable at that level. Multiple objectives will mean multiple roles and the eventual need for multiple performance criteria with some reasonable rank ordering or weighting.

True profit centers should be similar to *independent businesses* in miniature, financed by a parent. They should possess certain freedoms, mentioned earlier, and repeated below for convenience:

- The unit must have the freedom to produce or purchase its inputs where and when it chooses. (Decisions regarding capital expenditures, usually above a modest specified amount, are reserved for higher headquarters.)
- The unit must be free to market its outputs externally (to outside customers) where it chooses, or within a specified territory. To respond to the marketplace, the unit must also control selling price and other marketing aspects.

Internal transfers, coordinated functions, inabilities to relate inputs and outputs with activities, and other interdependencies may rule out all but a few units as true profit centers. For example, perhaps only international divisions (or product divisions, in some cases) will qualify as profit centers. The subordinate units may well be assortments of centers having lesser objectives, authorities, and controls.

Investment centers should evidence the freedoms mentioned above as well as exercise control over investment decisions and financings. In some cases, net incomes may only be related with the identifiable assets of nonintegrated and large divisions—perhaps only with the corporate entity as a whole. As a result, the control and evaluation mechanisms afforded by investment-center concepts may only serve macro-purposes.

Provisions of support services will identify expense and service centers. Where resource extraction, manufacturing, or assembly is involved, appropriate cost centers should be designated since control of costs will be important, regardless of where outputs will be distributed or marketed. Most marketing units will fit the roles of revenue centers.

Role definitions *can* be carried down to the level of a single machine or person. They *should* be applied to every activity over which control and evaluation are considered to be important.

(Before addressing the next step, it should be emphasized that the foregoing applies to *internal* role definitions. Overseas subsidiaries are legal entities within their host countries and, as such, will be considered profit-producing and tax-paying businesses by local governments. The conflicts that are often introduced by different *external* roles of units will be addressed a bit later.)

Establishing Criteria and Measurements

Half the battle will have been won when it is recognized that suitable measurements can be selected. A suitable measurement will be one that measures what it purports to measure, appears to be reasonable, and does not mislead.

Measurements will vary with, and depend upon, the nature of the activities to be measured. Selected examples of normal performance criteria are shown in Figure 9-2. A wide variety of other classes, plans, and units may also need to be employed (See Chapter 5). Eclectic approaches will preclude expressions of the measures in a common denominator. It will also follow that the measurements will not be additive. An integrated whole, in which micro-units, taken together, will signify macro-results, will not be possible. (Management accountants have been challenged to devise such a system. Success, however, does not appear to be in the offing.[2])

An integrated system would enable productivity (the bottom line *physical* measure) to be related with profits (the bottom line *financial* measure). Given a mix of products, only a very blunt relationship (such as total sales divided by total costs) is possible today.

Ideal systems would not necessarily help managers manage. The more comprehensive a measure is, the more useful it may appear *to an evaluator.* On the other hand, comprehensive measures are often of little value as instruments of control for the managers concerned. Macro-goals, such as profits, are usually managed by shepherding the component parts. Here is where help is needed and can be furnished by practical measures of the identifiable segments.

MEASURES	RESPONSIBLE MANAGERS
Return on Equity Earnings per Share Corporate Image	Chief Executive Officer and Board of Directors
Working Capital Current Ratio Debt-equity Ratio	Chief Financial Officer
Sales Market Shares Inventory Levels Receivable Levels Divisional Contributions Royalties Licensing Fees	Division Executives
Sales Market Shares Product Contributions Sales Mixes Distribution and Marketing Expenses	Product Managers
Plant Utilizations Production Schedules Volume Variances Idle Plant Costs	Plant, Division/Product Managers
Manufacturing Costs Recoveries of Capital Employed	Plant Managers
New Products Research, Development, and Patent Expenses Product Safety and Environmental Criteria	Research and Technology Support Managers

Figure 9-2. Examples of Normal Performance Criteria for a Multidivision, Multiproduct Industrial Company.

Inputs and outputs should be directly *traceable* to units. This will preclude most routine allocations of costs and expenses for purposes of *management control and performance evaluation.*

Even certain items that are directly traceable to a unit may not be *controllable* by its managers; their own salaries are an example. Consequently, noncontrollable items should be identified and excluded from evaluation reports. (Where multipurpose reports are planned to serve successive authority levels, noncontrollable items should be reflected separately and not permitted to compromise the validity and realism of the evaluations at any level. Contrary to popular opinions and practices, inclusions of noncontrollable data have little real information or other relevant value.)

Interdependencies will require recognition of one troublesome form of cost allocation—transfer prices. Where units produce for other units as well as market for their own accounts, temptations to attach arbitrary profits to the interunit transfers must be resisted. More methods of performance evaluation are invalidated at this juncture than perhaps anywhere else. The contributions of internal transfers—as well as other aspects of synergism—can be recognized by other more appropriate means to be suggested later. Profit should be defined as accruing only as the result of a bona fide sale to an unrelated entity.

Naturally, external financial reportings of foreign subsidiaries (as legal entities) will be expected to reflect reasonable profits. *Parallel* and *dual* systems of transfer prices will become necessary. Each will serve different purposes and should not be confused.

For external reports, transfer prices should be defensible as reasonable approximations of "arm's length" criteria. (In this respect, foreign governments do not tend to be as picayune as the U.S. Internal Revenue Service,[3] so long as companies do not become too greedy.)

For internal management purposes, transfer prices can employ any realistic base, and be expressed in parent or local currencies, alone or in combination. As a general rule, internal transfers should be based upon standard manufacturing costs plus a reasonable charge to cover the costs of capital employed. The inclusion of capital costs may well be the only realistic alternative in those situations where a given plant produces outputs for several different divisions in addition to its own. The relationships of assets employed to divisions would not be feasible. (It would also follow that the divisions served could *not* be evaluated by any criteria related to assets employed.) Recognition of capital costs in transfer prices in such cases would: (1) prevent responsibilities for the assets employed from being ignored; (2) enable responsible market pricings of the outputs transferred; and (3) enhance realistic evaluations of all the interdependent products and divisions.

Whether or not opportunity costs should be considered in addition will depend upon specific situations and plant utilizations. Regardless of the pricing formula selected for an activity, the component parts of the transfer prices should be *detailed* in transfer documents so that: (1) rational decisions can be made by transferees, and (2) amounts in excess of cost can be identified and eliminated from inventories for consolidated external reportings.

For many companies, internal transfers may be handled best in terms of the parent currency, regardless of the locations involved. Overseas refinements, such as the "dollar indexing" used by Honeywell (see Chapter 7), can accommodate fluctuating exchange rates, minimize distortions upon financial evaluations, and enable more realistic pricing considerations by transferees. For some companies, similar indexing approaches to domestic transfer (as well as final market) prices may be the most practicable means of combating inflation and the increasing costs of capital.

Measures of efficiency and effectiveness will call for different approaches.

Effectiveness (doing the right something) must address inputs (such as sales orders) and outputs (products and services). Physical measures (in units) and qualitative measures (such as sales mixes or product qualities) will be necessary—and can be devised.

Efficiency (doing something right) usually lends itself to monetary measurement. Here again, it will be useful to construct qualitative checks and balances to discourage cost reductions that denigrate the acceptability of outputs.

An appropriate unit of measure can be devised for every objective, activity, or thing. Quantitative measures are desirable since they are the most convenient—but *not* because they are the most realistic. Some very important aspects can only be assessed qualitatively and appropriate means must be designed.

Money measures are necessary but hardly sufficient. Since money has become a defective common denominator, domestically and internationally, other quantitative measures must be accorded greater attention. Appropriate emphasis upon quantities in terms of units will enhance discriminations between the results of accomplishment and those of circumstance.

Unfortunately, circumstances will generally dictate that internal accountings by foreign activities be made in terms of local and parent currencies. The former are needed for statutory reportings and should follow local accounting and tax rules. The latter serve to facilitate integrated management. Both will prove to have value.

Determining Standards

Just as most activities are performed better if they are measured, the results have little real meaning unless they can be compared with benchmarks.

Reasonably attainable standards should be determined for each measurement selected. Most activities will be subject to multiple measures, some of which may require possible trade-offs to be recognized in the development of standards. Enlisting the participation of local managers and other supervisory personnel may not only produce more realistic standards, but facilitate their acceptance as well.

For all manufacturing operations, standard cost systems have proved their usefulness and will likely already be in place. Consideration may be given to regularly scheduled adjustments of important input costs by the use of specific and/or general price indexes. Concurrent revisions in transfer and selling prices may also be considered, conditions and competition permitting.

Standard costing methods represent budgets for units of product. Similar approaches—flexible budgets—should be considered for application to all other important activities. To do so, the *variability* of inputs with changes in levels of activity will need to be estimated. Together, standard costs and flexible budgets represent the most realistic and adaptable performance criteria and *primary standards* yet invented.

Budgets can be tailored to fit the particular roles and circumstances of units and their segmented activities. The results projected can be examined for reasonableness from both the subsidiary and corporate viewpoints. At scheduled intervals, actual results can be compared with the approved budgets, after necessary adjustments to reflect the inputs allowable at the output levels actually achieved.

Secondary standards are often useful as supplements to assess important factors not routinely addressed within the budgets (market shares, new products, plant utilizations, and the like).

Predetermined ranges of reasonable variances will enable managements to focus upon any important exceptions. Variance analyses, supplemented by relevant nonmonetary data, can provide evaluators with a better understanding of operations and enable them to make more realistic assessments of the contributions of activities and managers.

Some companies may find it desirable for overseas activities to submit dual budget proposals, side by side. One would be in foreign currencies and in accordance with local accounting and tax rules. The other would be in terms of the parent currency and accounting standards. The exchange rates projected and the operating assumptions upon which the budgets were prepared would also be essential.

Whether approved budgets are considered to be contracts or subject to revisions will depend upon top management's perceptions of the relative costs and benefits. Revisions cost valuable time and money, yet they minimize "surprises." In the final analysis, only the magnitudes of the budget variances (and the depths of explanation) will be affected.

Selecting Times and Time Periods

Two timing considerations will surface—the frequencies at which evaluations are to be made and the time frames or periods of operation to be examined.

Frequencies have internal and external determinants. Naturally, for activities controllable at subordinate levels of management, activity reportings serve as early-warning devices. They tend to be detailed and made as frequently as daily or weekly.

Today, activity reports of units usually follow the pattern of financial reporting adopted by the parent companies. Not too many years ago communications, and concerns for confidentiality, were such that "monthly" overseas reports were generally processed out-of-cycle. Even reasonably complete quarterly reports called for staggered closings and a good bit of expediting. The general pattern now calls for interim reviews, either monthly or quarterly, complemented by extensive, formal annual evaluations. Paradoxically, advances in communications technologies have generated concerns of "information overload" and cost reduction. Since more information is not necessarily better, some companies have limited monthly reports to selected key data, augmented by flash reports as necessary. The volatilities of environments and risks of particular overseas operations may determine reporting frequencies as much as anything else.

The time spans of operations covered, particularly in annual reviews, should be made compatible with their natures, their particular segments, their objectives, and the aspirations of the people concerned. More about this will be mentioned a bit later.

Implementing and Communicating

Procedural aspects and the communication process are interrelated to the extent that they can be covered together.

In order to make the system operational, top management commitment to improve existing methods is essential. An appropriate staff should be selected and charged with developing a suggested plan. The activity levels (and their components) to be evaluated should be identified, as well as the measurement techniques and reporting procedures that are most compatible.

The information required on a regular basis should be identified by area, numbers, and items. The kind of information (static or over a period of time) should also be specified. (The staff should be informed, at the outset, that interdependencies will most likely require that some compromises be made in order to select the best available information.)

Extensive overseas operations may call for staggered annual reviews. In addition to timing, the locations may also be varied among on-site, regional, and parent locations, as well as between regional or corporate review boards. Valuable educational benefits may accrue as well as sharings of workloads. Similarly, interim, informal "staff visits" provide for interchanges of information, problems, and expectations—as well as enhance empathy and breadth of outlook.

Two-way communication should be *the* objective. Local managers need be assured that headquarters listens as well as directs. As yet, no communication devices have proven to be better than hands-on involvement and participation by the parties concerned.

ACTIVITY EVALUATIONS

Evaluations of all activities are similar in that retrospective and prospective assessments should be made.

All evaluations of activity reports are essentially *retrospective* and attempt to determine whether or not activities are generating sufficient benefits given the resources invested in them.

Wherever practical, *prospective* evaluations of activities should also be made to decide whether existing levels of resources employed should be maintained, altered, or redeployed elsewhere.

Activity evaluations will differ in terms of scope, depth, variables examined, and magnitude of tolerable variance from expectation.

Dependent Activities

Activities that provide support services and functions have become essential.

Complex enterprises seem to function as effectively as word- and data-processing centers permit. Production facilities depend upon preventive maintenance and responsive repairs. Marketing outlets (revenue centers) add new customers and economies of scale.

With the possible exception of revenue centers, regular performance evaluations of dependent activities tend to be begun only after real cost or control problems arise.

Expense and Service Centers. Primary efficiency evaluations of the less complex dependent activities will tend to be financial. Expense and service centers should be assessed on their relative abilities to:

- Produce services and other contributions of acceptable quantity and quality,
- Within the constraints imposed by approved budgets, adjusted to reflect the inputs allowable at the actual levels of activity.

Ancillary financial assessments of the efficiencies of some larger expense and service centers may be practicable insofar as trends of activity/expense relationships are concerned.

Effectiveness generally will lend itself best to nonmonetary quantitative measures in units and related with plans, trends, or other relevant variables. An illustration of expense center reporting on budget and key item performances is shown in Figure 9-3.

Qualitative evaluations are often important, and may seem to be difficult, yet should be made concurrently. The best approach may well be the regular solicitation of *user* opinions of the services received.

(As an aside, yet an important one, the planned performance data in the key-item section of Figure 9-3 should represent the self-imposed goals of a corporate-wide system of management by objectives.)

I. Budget Performance

Expenses	Current Month				Year-to-Date			
	Flexible Budget	Actual Amounts	Variances		Flexible Budget	Actual Amounts	Variances	
			$	%			$	%
Controllable: Variable (list) Fixed (list)								
Non-controllable: (list)								
Totals								

II. Key Item Report

Item	Performance		% Variance From	
	Actual	Planned	Prior Year	Plan
Utilization of Department				
Turnaround Times: — Reports — Letters — Memos				
Cost Per Page: — Reports — Letters — Memos				
Personnel: — Grade 3 — Grade 4 — Grade 5				
Equipment: — Downtime (hours) — New Units Required				

Figure 9-3. Examples of Expense Center Activity Reports.

Revenue Centers. Efficiency assessments of revenue centers should also begin with activity reports based upon flexible budgets, supplemented by appropriate key information.

As is the case with other centers, flexible budgets relate actual expenses incurred with amounts allowable at the actual level of operation. The variances identified tend to be more realistic.

Evaluations of revenues should address amounts in terms of both money and units. Variances from budgeted revenues should be broken down into volume and price components. The latter would be essential whether or not the revenue center was authorized to establish and alter selling prices. Price variances would be isolated for inclusion in reports of the activity or activities responsible for selling-price administration.

Supporting segmentations by product line, geographic area, customer category, and similar classifications should prove to be desirable.

If revenue center activity reports also address expected contributions (revenues minus cost of goods sold as well as expenses), then the changing natures of sales mixes also require identification. Since neither costs nor qualities of products are normally controllable by revenue centers, sales-mix data would be memo information for subsequent inclusion in activity reports at the appropriate levels of control.

Other selected key information to be included might be: backlog orders, days of inventories and receivables (if appropriate), market shares, and other activity indicators. An example of an activity report for a revenue center is shown in Figure 9-4.

Quite often, key trends in sales and expenses, segmented in various fashions, can be monitored readily by the use of graphic presentations.

Production Cost Centers.   As mentioned, standard cost systems will usually be in place. Where they are not in use, they certainly should be given consideration since reasonably attainable standards represent the best methods of controlling and evaluating production efficiency and effectiveness.

Well-designed systems will segment and direct control reports to the appropriate supervisors and managers. All too frequently plant managers have been forced to wade through piles of printouts or else use comprehensive reports that really do not permit responsive actions.

The most satisfactory solutions have been the design and use of: (1) tactical reports that focus upon key performance numbers or amounts, and (2) computer-generated graphics[4] that highlight trends as well as the key operating indicators themselves.

The method of presentation is not all that relevant and will depend upon the support services available. What is important is recognition of the value of key management indicators and devoting the resources and attention needed to develop them.

Realism also calls for recognition that some of the variances reported may involve shared responsibilities. Variance analyses will identify such instances. Examples are:

Budget Performance

Item	Current Month				Year-to-Date			
	Flexible Budget	Actual Amounts	Variances		Flexible Budget	Actual Amounts	Variances	
			$	%			$	%
Revenues								
Expenses: Controllable: — Distribution — Marketing								
Noncontrollable								
Total Expenses								
Key Data:								
Contribution								
Variances: Volume Price Mix								
Sales/Exp. Ratio								

II. Sales Analyses (By Product, Area, Customer Segments, etc.)

Item	Amount or Number		Variances		Amount or Number		Variances	
	Plan	Actual	$/#	%	Plan	Actual	$/#	%
Sales–dollars								
Sales–units								
Market Share								
Sales/Representative								

Figure 9-4. Activity Report—Revenue Center.

- Idle plant capacity will usually represent a combination of three elements:
  (1) Excess capacity (practical capacity minus sales budget)— may be due to several causes.
  (2) Sales shortfall (production based on budgeted sales minus orders received)—marketing failure to meet plans.
  (3) Idle capacity (production based on orders received minus actual production)—plant inefficiency, poor production scheduling, etc.
- Materials usage variances may reflect inferior products procured by the purchasing department (and may negate favorable price variances attributed to purchasing).

- Labor efficiency and related variable overhead variances may have been the result of rush orders, special requests from marketing, or other factors outside the purview of plant management.

Reasonably attainable standard costs, augmented by self-determined standard values for key operating indicators, will identify controllable items and their benchmarks. A responsive monitoring system will enhance responsive control. Together, the systems not only can help evaluate efficiency and effectiveness, but can do much to *encourage* them as well, particularly when keyed to appropriate reward mechanisms.

Profitability Centers

Profit and investment centers are sufficiently similar that their evaluations can be addressed jointly.

Financial Evaluations. The context of this section is senior management and the board of directors. Custom has dictated that the primary, retrospective, financial evaluations of profitability centers will be based upon macro-data, rarely carried below the level of the operating company and division or product line as applicable. Prospective (budget) evaluations are customarily made concurrently and in the same relative context, along with detailed presentations of major problems and/or prospects.

Over time, profit (or income) has been segmented and labeled in several fashions to serve particular purposes. The labels shown in Figure 9-5 are illustrative since terminology has not been standardized. Both the contribution and conventional approaches arrive at identical measures of profitability and permit the use of whatever ultimate standard is preferred.

The contribution approach offers several advantages over the conventional system:

- The data base lends itself to upward consolidation more readily.
- The methods are compatible with direct (variable) costing applications for added management control.
- Identification of results controllable at various levels assists management control and evaluation.

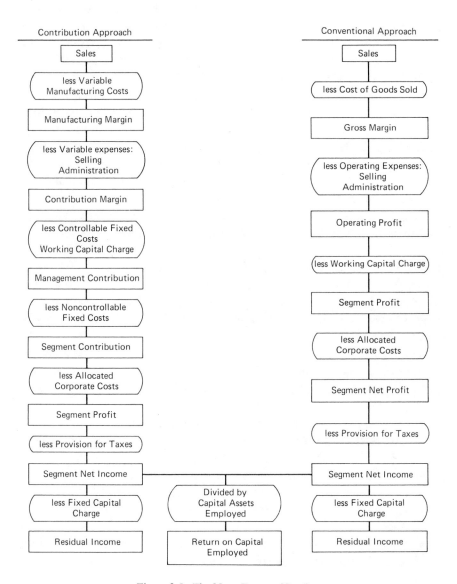

Figure 9-5. The Many Facets of Profit.

The disadvantages are the additional costs associated with the changeover and ongoing operation of contribution reporting. Moreover, the operations of many companies may be so interdependent that reasonable relationships of assets employed with activities are simply impracticable. Consequently, the primary financial evaluations of profitability centers will tend to be as situational as anything else.

The format of an activity report on the conventional basis that could be adapted for use with profit and investment centers is shown in Figure 9-6. Naturally, similar reports should be prepared for each of the identifiable segments of profit and investment centers.

Prospective financial evaluations usually consist of reviews and approvals of proposed budget projections. Any disinvestment decisions will also be prospective (in that they will examine present values of future cash flows), but are outside the scope of this work.

Strategic and Tactical Evaluations. To close the loop on activity evaluations, so to speak, requires reassessments of the objectives depicted in Figure 9-1. Standing back and looking at where a company is, where it wants to be, and how to get from here to there is basically what is involved.

The results of this process are useful in supplementing the financial evaluation process mentioned above. Moreover, no better tools have yet been devised to:

- Interrelate short-, medium-, and long-term goals.
- Assure that the time frames of evaluations conform with project expectations and the phasing in/out of products or activities.
- Make in-depth comparisons with major competitors.
- Place overseas objectives into appropriate context.
- Recognize the synergisms that financial evaluations usually diffuse or ignore.
- Recognize the contributions of intercompany transactions eliminated in financial reports.

The above considerations should be made a major team effort. Inputs and the expertise of all functional, product, and international management should be integrated. The outputs should represent:

- The core of a system of management by objectives or results.

	Current Month			Year-to-Date		
	Actual	Plan	Var. %	Actual	Plan	Var. %
Net Sales						
Cost of Goods Sold						
Gross Margin						
Distribution						
Marketing						
Administration						
Total DMA						
Operating Profit						
Working Capital Charge						
Segment Profit						
Corporate Allocation						
Segment Profit Before Taxes						
Income Taxes						
Segment Net Income						
% of Sales:						
Gross Margin						
Total DMA						
Segment Profit						
Capital Employed						
% ROC						

Graphic Supplements:
- % of Sales: Gross Margin/DMA/Segment Profit
- % of Sales: Return on Capital/Cost of Capital

Figure 9-6. Profitability Reports—Conventional Format (Amounts in $ Millions).

- The foundation to support the allocations of resources in proposed budget submissions or revisions.
- A realistic set of criteria and standards to complement or supplement (as appropriate) the financial evaluations of activities and managers.

The benefits of synergisms and intracompany transactions will prove to be difficult but not impossible. Synergisms will be identifiable and can be related in reasonable fashions with activities.

Treatments of intracompany transactions will require the use of activity reports prior to their restatement and/or translation for consolidation purposes. The mere presence of intracompany transactions would call for the recognition of shared contributions. How the contributions will be derived will depend upon the transfer pricing employed. In many cases, sharings of final revenues or profits can be apportioned on some basis, such as cost or value added. Such considerations not only add realism to evaluations but enable the existing interdependencies to be revaluated as well.

This stage would also be appropriate to assure that foreign-currency considerations are properly reflected during financial reviews. Real (conversion) gains/losses should be separated from translation differences where financial reviews are to be made in dollar terms. How exposures are to be considered and managed will depend upon the many variables mentioned earlier (Chapter 4).

Similar examinations should be made to determine the effects, both beneficial and detrimental, of domestic inflation upon the company and its segments. Analyses should, of course, enable the firm to comply with the FASB requirements but should be expanded as necessary to enable the real effects of changing prices to be *understood*. Only then can they be managed on a day-to-day basis, as well as explained internally and externally.

Important ancillary benefits will accrue from the above efforts. Relevant items, data, and trends will be identified for inclusion in the annual report of the corporation.

EVALUATIONS OF MANAGERS

As has been developed, managers (and all personnel, for that matter) should be evaluated based upon their contributions—the results of actions for which they are responsible, and which they have taken in the best interests of the company.

Evaluations should focus upon the roles and objectives of each manager. Usually, multiple roles and objectives will be found, including profit generations. The management levels, situations, and environments will help determine the relative emphases to be placed upon assessments of efficiency and effectiveness.

Key criteria and standards should address controllability and reasonable attainability. Flexible budgets will often represent the only form of financial evaluation that satisfies the requisites and can be tailored to fit and recognize almost all circumstances. Upon approval, the budgets represent reasonable standards against which actual results can be compared (after the variable budget inputs have been adjusted to amounts allowable at the actual level of activity). Review processes of most large enterprises are adequate to minimize budget optimism and "sandbagging."

A multipurpose investment center report (Figure 9-7) can often be constructed to serve as a *guide* for budget preparations, as well as the *starting point* for a variety of activity and managerial evaluation systems. Naturally, most of the special adjustments and allowances for interdependencies, synergisms, and strategic objectives recommended for activity evaluations also apply here.

One final observation should be made concerning the bonus components based upon financial performances of managers. Some companies believe that a standard rate should be applied to all managers at a given level within domestic and/or international areas. The validity of such practices depends upon the equalities of purpose, challenge, and opportunity. Rarely will such equalities exist.

Self-imposed goals of an effective MBO system are also valuable tools. All sorts of objectives and standards can be accommodated: efficiency, effectiveness, quantitative, qualitative. Medium- and long-term goals can be addressed in manageable stages. To be effective, however, MBO inputs must be accorded proper emphasis. Most successful applications have been institutionalized and inputs have become weighted factors in determining salary and bonus increments.

With reasonable interest, consideration, and care, realistic managerial evaluations can be constructed that will motivate, recognize, and reward accomplishment.

Sales & Transfers:	
External sales	$ 900
Intercompany transfers	450
Total	$1,350
less: Variable expenses	550
Division Contribution Margin	$ 800
less: Controllable fixed costs	200
Management Contribution	$ 600
less: Noncontrollable direct costs	100
Division Contribution	$ 500
less: Allocated corporate costs	80
Division Profit	$ 420
less: Provision for taxes	80
Division Net Income	$ 340
less: Capital charge	248
Residual Income	$ 92

Assets employed:

Controllable by manager	$1,250	
Total investment in division	$2,480	

Return on investment:

For evaluation of manager	($600 ÷ $1,250)	48%
For evaluation of division	($500 ÷ $2,480)	20.16%

Residual income:

For evaluation of manager	[$600 − (.10 × $1,250)]	$475
For evaluation of division performance	($500 − $248)	$252
For comparison with corporate decision		
to make original investment		$ 92

Figure 9-7. Example of a Multipurpose Investment Center Report (in thousands).

CORPORATE CONSIDERATIONS

Regardless of what is written here or suggested by other outsiders, corporate executives must select those evaluation methods they believe are best suited for their companies and situations. They must decide whether or not their present methods:

- Encourage reasonably congruent decisions on the part of responsible managers.
- Assist the acceptance and internalization of corporate objectives by managers.

- Motivate and guide managers to keep their corporate family competitive tomorrow as well as today.
- Recognize and reward competence.

Few, if any, executives will be entirely satisified or even comfortable with their judgments of the above aspects. Complex companies do not remain static. Neither does competition nor the environment.

Unfortunately, few solutions will have been furnished here. Some realizations, perhaps, will have been assisted.

All that has gone before will have been worthwhile if it is recognized that no *single* criterion can replace a comprehensive system of realistic budgeting and evaluation tailored to the unique characteristics of the individual activities and their managers. Objectivity, while expedient and desirable, will be useful only to a point. Thereafter, a reasonable blend of objectivity and judgment will become necessary. Seasoned executives will have acquired the expertise and temperamental empathy needed to complement blunt analyses.

Complex organizations have prospered with coordinative management. Coordinative management is a collaborative enterprise. So should be the process that evaluates its participants. Such a realistic process will do much to assure that the whole continues to represent more than the sum of its parts.

NOTES

1. Adapted from: "Tax Reform—Foreign Income," *Journal of Accountancy,* November 1975, Exhibit I, p. 40.

2. Donald J. Wait, "Productivity Measurement: A Management Accounting Challenge," *Management Accounting,* May 1980, pp. 24–30. A blue-ribbon committee (currently composed of Mr. Wait, of General Electric, and representatives from 3M Co., A.O. Smith Corp., Burlington Northern, Arthur Andersen, academia, and the NAA) is continuing a three-year effort to measure and improve productivity.

3. In most cases, advance rulings from the IRS can take forever, raise more issues than they solve, and only serve to attract attention. Very few challenges have been or will be made under Sections 482 (transfer prices) or 861 (geographic source-of-income rules).

4. Robert L. Janson, "Graphic Indicators of Operations," *Harvard Business Review,* November-December 1980, pp. 164–170.

10
Future Change

The opinions sprinkled liberally throughout this book, as well as some of the reported practices, have been offered to encourage considered change.

Change will come. Unidimensional financial accounting data have become obsolete measures. Continued reliance upon them may not only mislead but may prove to be counterproductive as well.

Circumstances and technologies have enabled managerial accounting to come of age. Appreciation and use of its devices are overdue.

BUSINESS CLIMATES

Changes in world business climates generate challenges waiting to be converted into opportunities. The international scorecard of the performances of U.S.-based MNEs indicates that unanswered challenges are beginning to counterbalance, if not outweigh, those converted.

Many American chief executives (some self-described as "hard-nosed") take pride in their accomplishments and the performances of their companies. It would be unnatural if these executives would not "smart" under criticism from outsiders, no matter how constructive and well-intentioned. Yet, the viewpoints of interested outsiders are sometimes broader and even more hard-nosed.

Past adventures and successes in an evolving, interdependent world economy may have been as much the result of the absence of effective competition as of competence. There is cause for concern that success has bred complacency. American MNEs may have regressed to the business philosophies prevalent in the 1920s. Controls over price and production may have regained supremacy over serving the needs of the world marketplace.

The delicate but effective balance between control and coordination may have tipped. Evidence, opinion, and hindsight indicate that short-term emphases have been ill-advised. *Rentier* philosophy—focused upon cash cows and current profits—has dissipated the entrepreneurial spirit. Competitive myopia has also been reflected in a number of mirrors. Steel industry giants have refused to invest in updated plants. The auto oligopoly was confident that it could continue to convince consumers to accept energy-obsoleted products rather than retool to meet the apparent requirements of the times. Others forgot the marketing concept. Parochial home-country product emphases and organizations were permitted to displace the eclectic market-sensitive benefits of international divisions.

In the final analysis, the productive and competitive sustenance of important American industries has been consumed—not by unfair competition, over-regulation, or inflation, as so often alleged, but by myopic internal attitudes fostered by complacency and obsession with the "bottom line."

No one kept a record of opportunity costs. Concerns surfaced only when markets were threatened or surrendered.

Paradoxically, those same industries that prospered by espousing capitalism, free enterprise, and competition, now, in various states of self-inflicted deterioration, plea for government assistance.

If, as some observers believe, multinational enterprises have two choices today—contract or grow into "transnational networks"—then the initiative must come from within.

CHANGES IN ATTITUDES

Many favorable changes in attitude and emphasis are already apparent. More are in the offing.

Habits that have become safe harbors are not changed easily, particularly where some degrees of risk are involved. Chief executives appear to be concerned—and understandably so—whether the effects of significant trade-offs among current earnings, dividends, and future growth would be understood and accepted by stockholders and the financial community. Philosophical discussions of the relative efficiencies of financial markets are one thing. Risking the financial futures of one's company and self are quite another.

The interest of the Conference Board has been evidenced by a sponsored study of the adequacy of the external reportings of 218

U.S.-based MNEs. The results of the study indicated that, while improvements had been made in recent years, only about half the information needed was being provided—and the areas considered to be satisfactory also tended to be of secondary importance.[1]

Fortunately, a consensus is emerging that leaders in the financial community (as well as in business) are receptive to changes in external reporting practices.[2] The only skepticism concerns the pace of change.

The trend of the future is perceived to call for de-emphasis upon antiquated macro-measures (such as earnings per share) and more attention directed toward multiple indicators (such as components and sources of earnings, responses to the effects of inflation, etc.). This welcome change in attitude is considered to be a positive development because "it means that the interaction of the performance of a corporation with the world outside of management and stockholders has now taken a priority over traditional stewardship accountability."[3] On the other hand, the changes in attitudes may reflect the belated recognition that modern enterprises have a diverse group of interested stakeholders —not only stockholders—to whom they should account for performances in a variety of areas.

Welcome changes in the attitudes of the FASB may also be appearing over the horizon. Historically, the communication systems of the FASB have been similar to those attributed to U.S.-based MNEs—effectively one-way. Although the FASB has usually solicited outside comments regarding changes proposed in financial reports, they have indicated more of a tendency to direct than listen.

The personal opinions of FASB staff and task force members, at least, indicate a welcome concern that matters of "economic substance" be reported more effectively and explained.[4] Serious considerations are being given to methods that will transfer emphases from *any single earnings figure* to more meaningful disaggregations. By so doing, it is believed that the financial community will tolerate fluctuations in earnings if they can understand the "underlying economic factors affecting operations, and management's stategy in dealing with these factors."[5]

External obsessions with unidimensional measures of corporate performance may have been self-imposed by the companies themselves. Aversion to *disclosure and explanation* of unusual economic events and changes may have precluded reportings of past performances from being understood.

A new form of earnings statement (along the lines of internal activity reports suggested in this book) has been recommended for consideration (Figure 10-1). It is doubtful that managements will be willing to risk the potential competitive disadvantages of such a report even in consolidated format. Nonetheless, managements will be given the necessary opportunities to weigh the benefits and associated risks of more realistic reportings, whether within the financial statements themselves or in supplementary sections of annual reports. It would seem that the disaggregations needed to be of value would tend to favor supplementary disclosures, perhaps in conjunction with the segmented information required by *FASB-14*.

The challenge has been issued. Management has the information and must determine whether it should be shared.

Better information may help users to assess future earnings and cash flows, and it may also help business to report more meaningful measures of performance. With reduced user emphasis on the bottom line and possibly a changed bottom line, management may communicate more effectively the record of company performance with which it should be judged.[6]

TECHNOLOGICAL ASSISTS

Internally, responsibility accounting practices will need to be broadened in base to accommodate the day-to-day needs of management, to generate result-sensitive performance evaluations, and to communicate the results effectively to a variety of concerned stakeholders.

Computer graphics (or business graphics) have already begun to assist multinational managements in the regular monitorings of dispersed activities. Test results of general management applications of computer graphics by a score or more large MNEs presage a boom in graphics terminals—if not the creation of a new, specialized industry.[7] Speed, low cost, accuracy, resolution (in eight colors), flexibility (as early-warning and reporting devices), understandability, and impact are the reported advantages. The next step will experiment with the feasibility of hands-on use of graphic terminals by middle managers via linked networks. The ultimate success of these and similar applications of distributed data processing will probably depend upon the

EARNINGS STATEMENT
(MILLIONS)

	1978	1977
Net Retail Sales	$1,310	$1,104
Cost of Retail Sales	823	692
Gross Margin	487	412
Operating Expenses tending to vary with the level of ongoing operations:		
Selling, general and administrative	31	24
Buying and occupancy	25	19
Rental	10	7
Other	5	4
Total	71	54
Contribution Margin	416	358
Operating Expenses incurred to administer and support operations:		
Depreciation and amortization	18	16
Rental	10	7
Buying & occupancy	57	50
Selling, general and administrative	208	178
Other	8	8
Total	301	259
Operating Earnings	115	99
Nonoperating Items:		
Store start-up costs	8	7
Estimated loss on disposal of certain operations	6	–
Estimated loss on closing department store	2	–
Merger fees	1	–
Settlement of litigation	1	–
Adjustments of past estimates	(1)	–
Total	17	7
Earnings Before Results of Financing Activities and Income Taxes	98	92
Results of Financing Activities:		
Carrying charges–net of associated expenses	(2)	(1)
Interest expense	(7)	(7)
Total	(9)	(8)
Earnings before Income Taxes	89	84
Income Taxes:		
Current	42	37
Deferred	2	6
Total	44	43
Net Earnings	$ 45	$ 41
Net Earnings Per Share	$ 1.90	$ 1.75

Source: Alfred M. King and Charles J. Evers, "Reported Earnings Procedures–Ready for a Review," *Financial Executive,* November 1979, p. 21. Reprinted by permission.

Figure 10-1. Earnings Statement–A Prospective Approach.

invention of software or other means to enable managers to use the tools without being programmers.

Satellite communications should further speed the flows and upgrade the qualities of vital information.

Technical advances such as the examples cited should enable managers to obtain, analyze, and understand a larger quantity of data and in greater depth without the feared paralysis of analysis. The valuable time saved should enable increased attention to be given to the real management problems that will persist as well as the new ones that will continue to surface.

Unless international resolve can restore a semblance of order among international money-changers and arrest, then cure, the disease of global inflation, monetary distortions will continue to create illusions in all types of performance reportings.

Interim assistance is being offered by a growing number of the larger banks, such as Morgan Guaranty and Chase Manhattan. These banks are interested in designing and providing international performance management services for companies, particularly those attempting to operate within hyperinflationary economies.

Ultimately, rampant inflation may be recognized as the only *real* threat to capitalism, freedom of enterprise, and an interdependent world community. If left unchecked, inflation will solve most of the dilemmas mentioned by eliminating them. Government regulations will prescribe what performances are to be reported and how they will be evaluated.

INTERNATIONALISM

Assuming that collective national reason will prevail, history may record the 1980s as merely one of the turbulent, adolescent stages of internationalism.

Not long ago, an inimitable colleague made an otherwise ordinary dinner memorable by presenting an ingenious parody (not altogether with tongue in cheek) that depicted the seven ages in the ongoing development of the accounting profession.[8] His idea was borrowed from "The Seven Ages of Man," a small verse he credited to "that distinguished nonaccountant, William Shakespeare." The ages cited were those of: innocence, improvisation, uniformity, inflation, intervention, integration, and innovation.

Reflection upon a twice-borrowed idea might place today somewhere between inflation and intervention. However, if optimism may be permitted to further alter literary license, it would appear that liberal applications of innovative ideas today might help reduce the traumas of intervention and achieve the promises of an interdependent world community.

Wittingly or not, multinational enterprises have been charged with major responsibilities in world affairs. They have also been afforded the opportunity to exercise effective influence over the manner in which their performances will be judged. It may well be that changes in external performance measures will enable executives of multinational enterprises to concentrate more upon their real roles—managing the resources that the world society has entrusted to their care.

It may also follow that more realistic external measurements will permeate and influence internal performance evaluations. The process will have come full circle, providing tangible benefits for all concerned.

NOTES

1. *Reporting Transnational Business Operations* (New York: The Conference Board, 1980). For a synopsis, see: "News Report: International," *Journal of Accountancy,* September 1980, pp. 18, 20.

2. "Study Finds Receptivity to Change in Corporate Financial Reporting," in: *Status Report,* No. 102, June 12, 1980, issued by the FASB. The results of interviews of 400 business and financial leaders by Louis Harris & Associates were summarized. The poll was commissioned by the Financial Accounting Foundation, the sponsor of the FASB.

3. Ibid.

4. Alfred M. King and Charles J. Evers, "Reported Earnings Procedures—Ready for a Review," *Financial Executive,* November 1979, pp. 14–21.

5. Ibid., p. 15.

6. Ibid., p. 21.

7. "The Spurt in Computer Graphics," *Business Week,* June 16, 1980, pp. 104, 106.

8. Athol S. Carrington, "Accounting Standards and the Profession—Seven Ages of Development," in: V.K. Zimmerman (ed.), *The Multinational Corporation: Accounting and Social Implications* (Urbana, Ill.: University of Illinois, Center for International Education and Research in Accounting, Department of Accountancy, 1977), pp. 41–46.

Appendix A
The 3M Company—
A Current Update

In Chapter 7, a brief synopsis of the management review process employed by the 3M Company in 1969 was furnished. The process required a considerable amount of top management involvement and was described as "comprehensive and innovative."

Curiosity naturally motivated the desire to determine whether or not the same extent of personal interaction of top management could be maintained in the face of growth over more than a decade. International operations grew indeed, from 30 overseas subsidiaries in 3 world areas (in 1969) to 70 such companies within 4 regions (in 1981).

What follows is a description of the system used by the 3M Company to review its international operations today. Except for the insertion of a few section headings — and some end comments — the procedures are exactly as described by Mr. H.B. Klenk, Controller, International Operations, to whom this author is especially grateful.

EXPLANATION OF 3M'S INTERNATIONAL
MANAGEMENT REPORTING AND REVIEW PROCESS

Today, 3M has 70 subsidiary companies outside the United States. Each of these companies operates as a legal entity under the laws of the country in which it is situated and has a Board of Directors to direct and run the business. However, in order to provide effective staff support to these 70 companies, 3M has divided the world outside the United States into four areas: the European area, the Latin American area, the Australia/Asia/Canada area, and the Africa/Middle East/Eastern Europe area. Each area has an Area Vice President, who is based at the company headquarters in St. Paul.

To keep these Area Vice Presidents and other head office management and support staff informed of the progress of each company and of its total international operations, the company has developed a comprehensive financial and operations reporting and review system. The system is audited regularly to make sure that the information provided by the subsidiaries is still applicable and needed.

DEVELOPING COMMITMENTS

Each year, each company prepares, for the immediate year ahead, a detailed forecast of sales and profits, the balance sheet position, employee count, capital expenditures, etc. These forecasts are prepared for each quarter of the year. In addition, a five-year forecast is prepared in broader terms than the annual forecast. It is intended to give a 5-year outlook for sales, profits, the balance sheet, etc.

The format for the information contained in the forecasts has been developed and refined over a number of years by the St. Paul head-office staff to ensure that pertinent, meaningful information is available to both subsidiary and head-office management. In effect, these forecasts are the business plans of each segment of the subsidiary company which have been totalled to give the overall subsidiary forecast.

Before the subsidiary company forecasts are accepted as part of the overall corporate plan, they are subjected to two reviews. The first review is by the Area Vice President and the Area Controller, who visit each subsidiary and working as a team, assist the Managing Director and his management group to refine their objectives and plans in preparation for the second review, which is the Annual Corporate Review.

Preliminary Reviews

During the preliminary review, the Area Vice President and Area Controller look at the profit and loss history of the company by product line. They determine the reasons for operating results being better or worse than were forecast a year ago. They examine trends of raw materials, labor and overhead costs.

The forecast for the coming year is examined critically to ensure that it is based on a good knowledge of current market conditions, and those that can be expected to prevail relative to the local economic situation, competition, product performance, and similar factors. Ways and means of improving profit performance are sought by looking at product pricing, advertising and promotion costs, the sales produced per salesperson, productivity improvements in the factory or administrative areas, etc.

On return to the head office, the Area Controller prepares an overview or briefing book from the information obtained during the course of the preliminary review. These books are given to members of the corporate review team before departure to the corporate review meetings.

The overview books contain the following information:

- Consolidated P&Ls for the Area. The P&Ls show:
    - (i) The previous year's actual results
    - (ii) The current year's forecast

(iii) The current year's estimated results

(iv) The next year's forecast.

- The effect of the *FASB-8* accounting adjustments on the area's profit.
- Historical and forecast translation rates.
- For each company, a one page summary of operating results and indexes for the past 4 years, together with the results for the first three quarters of the current year. The information includes:

    (i) Sales, sales growth and profits

   (ii) Cash, debt and fixed asset additions

  (iii) Tax rates

  (iv) Dividend payouts

   (v) Accounts receivable ratios

  (vi) IMC index of inventories

 (vii) Current ratio and debt/equity ratio

(viii) Asset turnover ratio

  (ix) Ratio of the return on assets

   (x) Brief comments on current borrowing rates, etc.

- For each country in which the company operates, a one page "Economic Profile" (prepared by International Economic Service) giving a brief commentary on:

    (i) General economic situation

   (ii) Gross National Product

  (iii) Consumer prices

  (iv) Industrial production

   (v) Labor and wages.

Annual On-Site Corporate Reviews

Early in the year the dates for the Area Corporate Reviews are fixed and the review teams appointed. The Latin American, Australian/Asian, and African area reviews usually take place at the same time, while the European area review takes place about two months later. The review teams are made up of senior corporate executives. A number of executives who travel to Latin America, Australia/Asia, or Africa, also go to the European reviews.

About three days prior to departure for the area reviews, the corporate review team assembles for a verbal briefing by the Area Controller. At this briefing, the Area Controller reviews the results of the area as a whole, and highlights any significant conditions or happenings in an individual country. The briefing is not only intended to give the review team general information on the area, but also to provide an opportunity for members of the review team to ask questions of the Area Vice President or the Area Controller about any points that may have arisen from study of the overview book.

In addition to the area overview books prepared at the head office, each company compiles a company report book, which is made available to each member of the review team the day before that company's review meeting takes place. The report book contains charts and forms (designed in St. Paul) and is a great help to the review team, enabling it to know what to look for and where it may be found. The book contains, inter alia, the following documents showing historical, current, and forecast information on a comparative basis:

    (i) Profit and loss statements
   (ii) Balance sheets and cash source-and-usage statements
  (iii) Product line sales, costs, and profits
  (iv) Capital expenditures
   (v) Inventory and accounts receivable analyses.

Local Management Presentations. At the review, the Managing Director and his Financial Director present verbally and visually, the overall position of the total company, while the managers of each division are expected to report on the results for the products for which they are responsible.

The Managing Director shows a chart that sets out the actual and forecast sales and profits over the past ten years. (This chart is known as the "Credibility Chart," and is considered to be important because it helps to bring realism to the forecasting.) He then conveys the general economic situation prevailing in the country in which he operates, together with his forecast of future economic trends. He also reports on any companywide matters, such as the objectives that he has set for the company, sales incentive programs, recruitment drives, corporate publicity campaigns, among others.

The Financial Manager reports on the total company income statement and balance sheet—including the position on accounts receivable, inventories, borrowing, dividend payout, capital spending, etc.

Each division manager is expected to report on the past and forecasted performance of his division, particularly in relation to sales and profits. In doing this, he comments on the following:

    (i) Sales growth analyzed by volume and price
   (ii) Market size, share and trend
  (iii) Sales programs—the success or otherwise of past and current programs and those programs that will be implemented to achieve the forecast.
  (iv) New product introductions
   (v) Salesmens' and sales cost controls
  (vi) Advertising and promotion programs
 (vii) Product quality, service and pricing—in relation to competition.

The reports of the division managers are the key reports because, in effect, they represent formal commitments to corporate management to produce the sales and profits that have been forecasted.

Interchange and Consensus. During the course of the presentations, members of the corporate review team ask questions, make comments, and may suggest that consideration be given to the changing of plans. Generally, about one third of the time that is taken for the review is spent on questions, answers, and comments. This procedure has a number of benefits. Subsidiary managers are given an opportunity to explain their plans to corporate management and to make their commitments in terms of sales and profits. Foreign personnel are assured that the individual subsidiary companies and their people are not forgotten outposts of a corporate empire, but that corporate management is interested in them, that they are a vital part of the organization, and are contributing to its success as a whole. It also provides an opportunity for the corporate senior executives to meet with the people in the subsidiaries, to get to know each other better, and to offer help and advice both during and after the review sessions.

After the subsidiary review is completed and accepted by the corporate review team, the forecasts are finalized and a forecast information package containing the following information is mailed to St. Paul:

- Sales — Domestic, export and intercompany for each month
- Condensed income statements for each quarter
- Balance sheets for each quarter
- Capital expenditures
- Miscellaneous information such as: intercompany receivables and payables, details of investments, and taxes.

Much of the detail that was presented at the review is not included, since the Area Controller will have on file in St. Paul, his copy of each company's report book.

The information contained in the forecast package is used in St. Paul for two purposes. First, consolidated totals for each area and for international operations as a whole are developed (the total is included in the overall corporate plan). Second, the data will be used (month by month, quarter by quarter) to compare actual results with those forecasted, in order that the head office staff may monitor the progress that each company is making towards meeting its objectives.

REPORTING PROGRESS

The continuous reporting system of actual operating results requires the subsidiary companies to send to the International Operations Office in St. Paul: 18 monthly reports, 8 reports prepared on a quarterly basis, and 6 reports (excluding the forecast package) that are prepared on an annual basis.

To speed the consolidation of the information and the flow of data from the subsidiaries to the head office, 3M has developed (and is continuing to develop) a communications network. Much of the information, particularly from the larger subsidiary companies situated in Europe, is transmitted by subsidiary computer output, through a central switching center in London or in Brussels, directly into a computer in St. Paul.

Regular Reports

The majority of the reports that come into St. Paul from the subsidiary companies are consolidated. The reports usually show (for each country with area subtotals) the current actual performance compared with that forecasted as well as with the results of the prior period.

The first report sent each month by the subsidiary companies is a preliminary "Sales Flash." This report states that amount of the subsidiary's previous month's sales, and is sent on the 3rd working day. On the 8th working day, an "Operations Flash" is transmitted to St. Paul. This report shows the subsidiary's total sales and profits, together with the balance of inventory on hand at the end of month. On the 9th working day, a listing of sales by product is sent. By the 10th working day, this information has been received, translated from local currencies to U.S. dollars, *FASB-8* adjustments have been calculated, and a consolidated sales and profit report is in the hands of head office management.

Over the next several working days, each subsidiary mails or transmits to St. Paul the following reports:

- Condensed income statement
- Balance sheet
- Managing Director's Report—a letter of one or two pages in length in which is set out the highlights of the economic and political situation in the country, together with salient points on operating results. The purpose of the letter is to keep area management current on the situation in any country. If there are operational problems, head office staff specialists can be assigned to furnish assistance.
- Product line P&L information
- Various other reports such as intracompany sales, royalties, and inventory balances.

Reports prepared on a quarterly basis include:

- Balance sheet forecasts
- Analyses of inventories
- Accounts receivable—age analyses.

Behind every report produced in St. Paul from the information provided by each subsidiary there is a real purpose. It is not reporting for reporting's sake.

Staff Assistance

The 3M Company maintains an international support staff in St. Paul and in Brussels. This staff is comprised of specialists who cover every aspect of the business from product development through manufacturing, marketing, selling, and distribution. Administrative, financial, and tax assistance are also provided.

The staff travels to each of the 70 subsidiary companies to assist local management in the development of their business. Aided by the outputs of the International Operations' reporting and information system, staff members can visit a subsidiary with a good, general prior knowledge of that subsidiary's performance. Consequently, the support staff can apply more of its available time overseas to the benefit of the subsidiaries and the corporation as a whole.

COMMENTS AND OPINIONS

The capstone of the 3M evaluation process continues to be the on-site annual review. Extensive top management participation has also continued even though the magnitude of international operations has increased from 30 to 70 overseas subsidiary companies over the last decade.

It is evident that the degree of hands-on involvement of International Operations' management enables the 3M Company to understand and help fine-tune overseas operations much better than any form of product-line organization ever could. Even more important, perhaps, is the philosophy of management implied. Coordinative management has been selected rather than management-by-conflict.

The lesson to be learned seems to be that results can be achieved by recognizing that people work *with* managers rather than *for* them.

Appendix B
Monsanto Company—
Management By Results

Coordinative management of interdependent units produces synergism. It also obscures the contributions of individual units and their managers.

There is well-earned satisfaction attached to the realization that, at year end, the achievements of related activities working together are greater than the sum of their individual results. Frustrations arise, however, in attempts to relate the synergistic surplus with the component activities.

Realistic evaluations usually will depend upon the ability of top management to identify and separate important factors from the mundane. The Monsanto Company has developed a management style that emphasizes comparisons of planned and actual results.

MONSANTO COMPANY IN PERSPECTIVE

The world headquarters of Monsanto are located in Saint Louis, Missouri where the company was founded in 1901. From its beginnings with saccharin and aspirin, Monsanto has grown to be the fourth largest firm in the U.S. chemical industry. Worldwide sales in 1980 were $6.6 billion.

Today, Monsanto produces an assortment of chemicals and related products in a worldwide network of more than 180 plants and research centers located in 20 nations. Products are marketed, directly or through affiliates, in more than 120 countries. In terms of people, Monsanto represents some 64,000 employees and 86,000 common shareholders.

Organizational Structure

Monsanto's organizational structure has evolved by adapting to the changing demands of business environments and technologies. As of January 1981, the evolution was still in process. Figure B-1 reflects the corporate structure existing at the beginning of 1981 as well as some international restructuring under consideration at that time.

Basically, Monsanto consists of five operating companies, a majority-owned subsidiary, and an international operation. Each operating company is composed

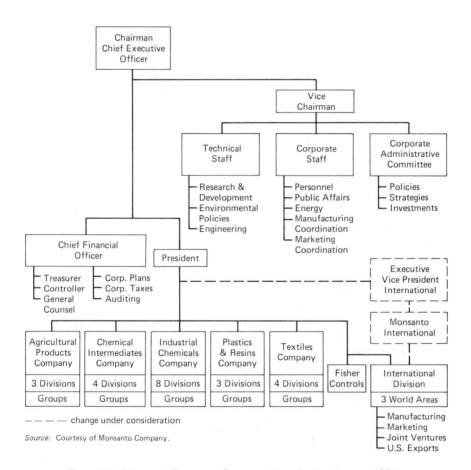

Figure B-1. Monsanto Company, Corporate Organization, January 1981.

of from three to eight divisions representing compatible product groups. The most complex division involves over 2000 products.

RESPONSIBILITY ACCOUNTING

A modified *matrix* system of management has been devised to achieve efficiency and effectiveness and to accommodate the interdependencies that are inherent as well as created. The latter results from strategic actions and from the new resources, products, and industries created by technological advances.

Interdependencies

Significant interdependencies exist within as well as among the operating companies.

The five U.S. operating companies (each headed by a Vice President) and the managers of their component divisions have worldwide profit responsibility. Two of the companies (Chemical Intermediates and Industrial Chemicals) serve as primary suppliers of their sister companies. All such intercompany transfers are made on a "market basis."

Within each domestic company, sophisticated standard cost systems are used to control manufacturing costs and enable gross profit to be computed by product. However, manufacturing plants within each company responsibility center usually produce products for several divisional responsibility centers. Consequently, plant assets can be related with companies, but cannot be readily identified with the component divisions.

Outside the United States, additional interdependencies result from the activities of an International Division, segmented into three world-areas: Europe/Africa, Canada/Latin America, and Asia/Pacific. The managers of the International Division and the three regions also have profit responsibility for operations in their areas: processing and/or marketing intermediate and finished products exported from U.S. units; on-site manufacturing and selling by majority and wholly-owned subsidiaries; and managing seven or more joint ventures. (Several joint ventures are sizeable businesses: one is the largest of its kind in Brazil; another the seventh largest in Japan.) Transfers among the three world-areas, as well as U.S. exports, are recorded at "market basis." Profitability of international operations is reported in total, by overseas entity, and by domestic operating company and division for U.S. exports.

(International operations have outgrown any stepchild status that may have existed at one time. All countries of major market importance for Monsanto outperformed the United States in economic growth in 1979. Exports from U.S. plants increased 31% during 1979. Also, sales outside the United States, including exports, topped the $2 billion mark in 1979 and accounted for 38% of Monsanto's consolidated sales. For 1980, foreign sales were $2.24 billion and represented 34% of the Company's total. In short, worldwide opportunities are increasing at a faster pace than in the United States. These greater rewards are accompanied by somewhat greater risks in unfamiliar markets. As a result, Monsanto International is scheduled to become a sixth operating company to be headed by an Executive Vice President. Changes in the relationships between the International and other operating companies are not known at this writing, but will surely result.)

Another dilemma of interdependency concerns the management of marketing, administration, and technical resources. Not only have these expenses become significant ($900 million per year) but their annual rate of increase (15%) has exceeded that of sales (9%). The annual planning of these resources has been conducted by 44 strategic planning units that cross divisional but not operating company lines. Planning has been done off-line (not tied in with reportings) and there has been no effective accountability required of the planning units or the divisions.

Finally, the company has wanted to encourage managers to incorporate the effects of changing price-levels in their day-to-day decisions without costly redesigns of existing systems.

PRACTICAL SOLUTIONS

By 1974, a new top-down form of management approach was institutionalized (Figure B-2). The process identified and defined both short and long-term objectives as well as provided a framework within which they could be achieved.

Corporate objectives and policy guidelines were set by top management. Based upon these statements, the senior operating managers developed more explicit statements (or "direction papers") of strategies to be pursued. The above materials were then translated by the operating companies into "long-range plans" supported by specific statements of tactics and strategies (or "operational plans"). The next step required individual managers to identify the specific results they must produce to support the operating plans. The end results were comprehensive annual budgets that stipulated the outputs desired and the inputs necessary to achieve them.

The process summarized above shrouds several innovations that were designed to accommodate desirable interdependencies while minimizing their effects upon controls and performance evaluations.

Concepts of Income

Since assets could be related with operating companies but not divisions, different concepts of income were necessary.

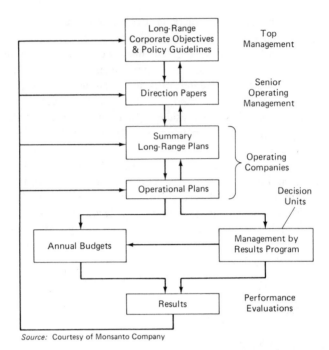

Source: Courtesy of Monsanto Company

Figure B-2. Monsanto Company: Cybernetic Style
of Management and Performance Evaluation.

Since 1975, profitabilities of divisions and business groups have been evaluated officially by their "performance income":

Sales	$
Cost of Goods Sold	_____
Gross Profit	$
less MAT Expenses:	
Marketing $	
Administration	
Technology	_____
Operating Profit	$
plus: Other Income & Credits	
less: Working Capital Charge	_____
Performance Income	$ _____

Evaluations of operating companies were carried to net income (performance income minus corporate overhead allocations and provisions for taxes). Also, return on capital (ROC) was computed (net income plus the after-tax working capital charge added back, divided by the capital employed). Similar ROC calculations are made experimentally for divisions but are not part of their official evaluations.

Management By Results

A key element in Monsanto's management style is the "Management by Results" program instituted in 1975.

A variant form of management by objectives, the MBR program enables each manager or decision unit to establish specific results that are to be achieved to support operating plans. The number of results may be one or two or perhaps half a dozen. In type, the results may vary from specific goals for earnings-per-share or return-on-equity to productivity improvement, cost reduction, or meeting safety/environmental standards.

The availability of external standards is also very helpful in establishing realistic results. Monsanto prepares for internal use an annual "competitive report" that relates the company's performance in a variety of segmented areas with its "Big Seven" competitors in the industry.

Since the results specified by decision units are subjected to the stringent reviews of the budget process, MBR goals represent realistic benchmarks for subsequent evaluations of the actual results achieved.

Priority Resource Budgeting

Sophisticated standard cost systems assured that costs of plant assets consumed were attached to the products produced, even though specific assets were not traceable to particular divisions. The "missing link" in cost control concerned the marketing, administrative, and technical (MAT) expenses mentioned earlier, as well as factory indirect expenses (FIE).

In 1978, a modified form of zero-based budgeting was tailored to fit the company's needs. The new system—Priority Resource Budgeting (PRB)—was introduced in 1979 to serve two purposes: (1) to hold total expenses consistent with budgeted operating results, and (2) to assure that available resources were allocated in support of strategic plans.

According to Monsanto's PRB manual, decision units were identified as "the smallest meaningful group of people and/or other resources devoted to achieving a common, significant business purpose." The manager of each decision unit (typically 5 to 15 people with a $150,000 to $400,000 annual budget) defined its purpose and the minimum or "threshold level" of resources (people and money) needed to remain viable. Resource increments needed to accomplish additional results (established by the MBR program) were then specified, justified, and ranked in their perceived order of importance.

Changes in rankings may occur during the defenses and reviews held at the director, division, and operating company levels. The final budget that emerges will have: (1) identified results desired, (2) related the resources needed to accomplish them, and (3) ranked activities above and below the "funding line" so that any future changes necessary are also facilitated.

(A case concerning PRB was developed in 1979 by the Harvard Business School with the cooperation of Monsanto Company. The case, No. 9-380-048, is entitled "Monsanto Company: the Queeny Division—parts A and B.")

Price-Level Refinements

Consolidated operating results are based upon LIFO inventory methods, while the FIFO basis is employed internally. Prior to 1974, division and company managers had no specific responsibilities for the effects of the LIFO adjustment upon costs of goods sold.

To increase management awareness of the effects of changing prices upon input resources, the LIFO adjustment was made part of the operating results of company managers in 1974. This benefit was acquired with minimal cost and change in procedures. Also, use of an adjustment enabled retention of inventories at recent costs as well as more realistic data on working capital and return on capital employed.

Comprehensive Budget Review

Budget submissions to the corporate review committee by operating companies contain narrative summaries, financial exhibits, and supplemental information.

The narrative summary includes qualitative assessments of business environments, premises, assumptions, and budgeted results. Significant changes from the prior period are also addressed.

Financial exhibits consist of executive summaries supported by detailed analyses of sales, performance incomes, MAT expenses, manning tables, capital employed, and asset management. Sales analyses address changes projected from the prior year by cause: prices, volumes, mixes, product additions/deletions, and the like. Analyses of changes in levels of MAT expenses focus primarily on significant items and those portions of increases caused by inflation. Asset management relates to levels projected for inventories, receivables, and capital expenditures. To minimize effects of changing price levels, indicators such as days supplies of inventories and days sales outstanding for receivables are used in addition to nominal dollar amounts.

Supplemental information highlights start-up expenses of major projects, data concerning changes in key product activities, plant utilization statistics, and major technical commitments (such as R&D).

PERFORMANCE EVALUATIONS

The process of budget construction and review produces realistic benchmarks with which actual results can be compared and assessed.

Performances of activities and individuals are reviewed shortly after the end of the calendar year. Incentive compensation is distributed during March.

Activity Reviews

Performance incomes of operating companies serve as the primary benchmarks. As mentioned earlier, performance income is considered to be readily traceable to and reasonably controllable by operating companies.

Activity reviews are made at the corporate level. Presentations consist of comprehensive comparisons of planned and actual results. Since only a minor portion of the Company's products are sold to end users, the estimated and actual market conditions in the industries served represent important barometers. Also, while quarterly updatings of operating plans are made, the variances from the original budgets are addressed in annual reviews.

Usually, evaluations of divisions and product groups are tied to the performance incomes of their respective companies. Not only does the modified matrix form of management obscure divisional boundaries, but the numbers and compositions of the product groups themselves are somewhat fluid because of technological and strategic change.

International operations are examined in total, by world area, by overseas entity, and by the export activities of domestic operating companies. The many interdependencies that exist mandate that more attention be given to the results of the component parts rather than the whole.

Managerial Performances

Evaluations of managers of all decision units consist of two parts.

A portion of incentive compensation is based upon the performance income posted by the operating company to which the manager is assigned. This serves to encourage decision makers to keep the best interests of their operating companies in mind as well as those of the unit or division in which they function. Also, individuals are not penalized as readily for temporary downturns of their product groups.

The second portion of the incentive program is determined by the manager's level of achievement reflected by his or her MBR program. Evaluations of MBR progress are made from the bottom up in much the same fashion as the goals were established originally. This assures that results are evaluated by next-line supervisors as well as at successive levels.

Contributions of managers of overseas activities are evaluated primarily by MBR due to the multiple roles performed.

Corporate Performance

The Competitive Report prepared annually compares Monsanto's performance with that of its "Big Seven" competitors in the industry.

The report contains extensive, detailed analyses that help place the company's past results into the most appropriate context, indicate areas of leadership as well as concern, and guide the preparation of future strategic and operating plans.

Management will readily admit that the system is not perfect and seems to be in a state of continuous refinement. Yet, given the interdependencies to be coped with, the process is both comprehensive and realistic.

Appendix C
Emerson Electric—
Disciplined Growth

Discipline implies orderliness and efficiency. Both attributes are characteristic of Emerson Electric Company. The traits permeate manufacturing processes, management philosophies, and corporate strategies.

EMERSON IN PERSPECTIVE

Emerson Electric Company was organized in Missouri in 1890. Disciplined growth has enabled Emerson to evolve from a relatively inconspicuous manufacturer of electric motors and fans prior to World War II into a $3 billion diversified multinational enterprise in 1980.

The company is engaged in over 200 product lines that may be grouped in three industry segments: commercial and industrial components and systems sold principally to original equipment manufacturers; consumer products (electric fixtures, residential products, and tools) sold primarily to distributors; and government and defense products and systems.

As of September 30, 1980, Emerson operated 146 manufacturing plants worldwide, with 41 of these outside the United States in 12 foreign countries. International operations represented 155 overseas locations encompassing 29 divisions in 36 countries. During 1980, international sales were $778 million, including $270 million in U.S. exports, and represented 25.4% of consolidated sales. Emerson Electric Company consists of more than 29,000 shareholders and 53,000 employees.

Organizational Structure

Emerson's corporate structure (Figure C-1) is relatively flat, and is as much the product of evolution as design.

Operationally, Emerson consists of 45 "nearly autonomous" divisions. As acquisitions were made over time in search of diversification and external growth, many of the larger units were retained and operated as somewhat independent businesses.

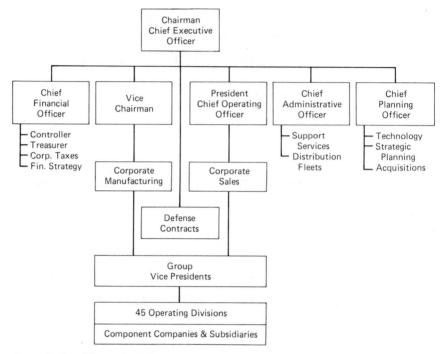

Source: Courtesy of Emerson Electric Company

Figure C-1. Emerson Electric Company, Corporate Structure, February 1981.

The corporate staff is "lean" by design. The "Office of the Chief Executive" is composed of six persons: the Chairman, Vice Chairman, President, and three Vice Presidents. Each executive also has a relatively small staff that enables (as well as requires) a great deal of hands-on management.

RESPONSIBILITY ACCOUNTING

Since Emerson's acquisitions have been aimed at balanced diversification, the company has been able to maintain relatively clean lines of demarcation between operating divisions.

Each division is regarded as a separate business. Divisions maintain their own capital structures and separate financial statements. Uniform internal accounting and reporting procedures are prescribed by the parent. Systems are detailed and comprehensive. As a result, return on capital can be computed for each of the 45 divisions as well as their operating company components.

The small size of the corporate staff forces operating decisions to be made at the responsible operating level. Interdependencies have not been of any material consequence, at least to date, and interunit transfers that are elected to be made are processed at "negotiated" prices. The customary corporate support services are furnished, including self-insurance and centralized banking. (The latter service enables divisions to borrow from or lend to the parent company at established interest rates.)

At the operating level, Emerson has earned the reputation of a "quality low-cost producer." Sophisticated standard cost systems, revised at the beginning of each fiscal year, serve as the foundation for responsibility accountings. These systems are buttressed by effective programs of cost reduction and productivity improvement.

Controls are further enhanced by the relatively low economies of scale enjoyed by most of the operating units. Volumes of subsidiary companies vary from $6 million to $350 million. Of the 146 manufacturing plants, only 6 have 1,000 employees, and the average is 350 employees per plant.

In short, Emerson's system of management focuses upon planning and controlling growth and profitability at the division level.

THE MANAGEMENT PROCESS

Emerson's management process is based upon tough but attainable targets, intensive planning mechanisms, extensive performance reviews, and compensation for results.

The above devices, in combination, have enabled a blending of short-, medium-, and long-range goals that has produced disciplined growth.

Target Devices

Strategic five-year plans provide specific objectives for the company as a whole which each division must address.

Specifics of the five-year plan ended September 30, 1980 are summarized below as examples.

- To achieve a 15% average annual compound growth rate in sales, net earnings, and earnings per share. (Five-year annually compounded growth rates achieved were reported as 16.9%, 17.5%, and 17.0%, respectively.)
- To obtain internal growth of $200 million in sales during fiscal 1980 from new products developed and introduced since 1975. (Amount reported was $256 million, or 8.3% of sales in 1980, and consisted of more than 300 new product programs.)

  To encourage technical innovation at the division level, Emerson developed a "Strategic Investment Program" that helps cushion the shock on divisional short-term operating results. Basically, the parent will fund the start-up costs of approved programs and charge them to the divisions over a period of time greater than that estimated for product introductions. All new product investments are subjected to present value (discounted cash flow) reviews prior to approval.
- To generate $500 million in international sales by 1980. (Actual sales of $693 million were reported, representing an annual growth rate of 23%, and accounting for 23% of total 1980 sales.)
- To add, by acquisitions, new product lines. (An average of three such acquisitions per year was reported.)
- To maintain the "controlled commitment" to defense and government business. (Actual sales reported were 8%, well within the 10% maximum commitment.)
- To diversify, by acquisitions, within electrical product lines to assure that no product or customer accounts for more than 10% of total sales, nor any domestic industry sector for more than 15%. (The 1980 annual report indicates that, while the constraints were not exceeded, three product lines had reached the limits imposed.)

Two additional goals were established regarding management development and financial position that, although important, are not germane here.

The 1980-1985 plan encompasses the same items although specifics were made available only for: (1) continuance of the 15% annual growth rate; (2) a doubling of total sales (to $6 billion) by the end of 1985; (3) a doubling of investment in growth programs; and (4) a fiscal 1981 cost-reduction target of $117 million.

Planning Devices

The principal planning device is known as the "Data Base" and is the product of a comprehensive and intensive budgeting process.

Each May a packet of budgeting materials is sent to each of the 45 divisions together with the necessary instructions for completion. The parent also provides economic and inflation forecasts, as well as currency forecasts for Brazil and Mexico. The divisions are also furnished data regarding: allocated items (such as insurance); the interest rate that will apply to intracompany borrowings; the base tax rates to be used; and the dividend payout required (currently 60% of the prior year's net income).

The completed packets are received by the parent headquarters in July, and include the following data, among others, for each division:

1. Consolidated results for the current year, the prior year, and the four quarters of the budget year.
2. Segmented results, over the same time periods, as follows:
    a. Geographically — domestic operations; exports, to affiliates and out-siders; and total overseas operations.
    b. By product line — sales and gross margins. Breakouts of historical and projected changes due to: real growth (in volumes), price in-creases, cost increases, cost reduction programs, new products, ex-ports, and international business.
    c. By entity within each division — sales, margins, operating profits, pretax incomes, and returns on capital employed.
    d. Relationships of sales and headcounts by quarter.
    e. Ten year trends (five historical, five projected) in costs of goods sold and returns on capital.

Upon receipt in July of the above input data, the corporate staff is broken out into task groups, each charged with analyzing a particular function or objec-tive. The staff units prepare their own five-year forecasts for each division as well as compute the "worth" of each division as multiples of total capital em-ployed. (Currently, a "good" return on divisional capital is considered to be more than 20 percent.)

Within the last ten years, greater attention has been given the international operations of each entity within the divisions. As mentioned earlier, transfer prices are "negotiated" as a general rule. Foreign currency translations are made at the fixed rates existing on each September 30th (for internal purposes) and in accordance with *FASB-8* (for external reporting only). Also, foreign operating results are computed using U.S. generally accepted accounting principles. (At this writing, the most troublesome void existing in the management and control process concerned how local inflation could best be coped with and reported.)

Each division and component company must address all the specific targets established by the corporation: growth rates, productivity increases, cost reductions, new product introductions, and international operations. For example, units are not required to have international programs — perhaps domestic growth is all that can be handled — but the target topic must at least be addressed.

(It should also be mentioned that, given the increased importance of international operations and the lean corporate staffing, some internal restructurings of the corporate organization are being considered.)

By the end of September, the above process culminates in the budgets for the ensuing year. To minimize surprises, expectations are updated monthly by each division, but the approved budgets represent the official benchmarks to be met.

Control Devices

The principal control device is the "President's Operating Report" that is prepared monthly by each division and submitted to the parent.

The report is an analytical tool by which the divisions reflect prescribed key operating and financial data within a uniform format. This report is the focal point of monthly divisional board meetings and also serves as the vehicle by which expectations may be updated. Each report must be signed by the president and chief financial officer of the division.

At the corporate level, the reports are analyzed by the Controller's staff. A form of management-by-exception is employed by which the divisions are ranked according to their respective achievements toward their multiple targeted goals.

A second important control device is the internal audit program. Emerson's goal in this area calls for internal reviews of 30 percent of the total corporation each year. A lesser amount is acceptable only when constraints are imposed by unusual levels of acquisition activities.

Also, lock-box systems are used to facilitate cash management. Capital expenditure requests in excess of $75,000 require corporate approval and are subjected to present value analyses.

PERFORMANCE EVALUATIONS

The level of hands-on participation of the corporate staff described in the management process is also reflected in the review process.

Activity Reviews

Monthly board meetings of the 45 divisions are attended by at least one member of the corporate staff. In addition to the regular financial reports, a prescribed summary — called "Situation at a Glance" — is used to highlight important relationships and ratios.

During the mid-month of each quarter, the President's Council, composed of corporate executives, conducts a week-long review of programs and strategies, essentially from the short-term point of view.

Annual reviews of the 45 divisions are performed over a two-week period at the corporate headquarters. Past performances are evaluated based upon the benchmarks established by the budgeting process. Future expectations are assessed by means of internal and external (survey) opinions of the abilities of activities to serve their respective growth niches.

Management Performances

Executive performance appraisals and extra compensation amounts are based upon criteria that parallel closely those concerning their respective divisions.

Currently, additional compensation is based upon results and is determined by performances in five areas:

- One-half is based upon a matrix that relates achievements in sales and in margins. The matrix recognizes possible trade-offs between the two goals that may be elective or circumstantial.
- Twenty percent is determined by asset management, particularly in terms of inventory turns and day's sales outstanding.
- Ten percent is based upon *each* of three areas: New product introductions, trade union relationships, and written personal objectives.

Responsibilities for the effects of foreign currency differences are shared. Transaction gains/losses accrue to division executives since they are reasonably controllable at that level. Translation exposures, as well as the decisions to hedge the exposures or not, are corporate responsibilities (vested in the Treasurer).

Emerson's concept of compensating for results is aimed at congruence of corporate, division, company, and management goals. Moreover, particular efforts are made to minimize conflicts between short- and long-term objectives.

Corporate Performance

Annual corporate planning conferences relate goals and achievements and, each fifth year, establish new five-year targets.

To date, Emerson has planned for and achieved disciplined growth by: (1) effective cost reduction and control, (2) broadening its product base, and (3) by selective diversification.

The latter point in particular — a feature that could be termed "disciplined diversification" — has produced management as well as economic benefits. Economies of scale and interdependencies have been kept at minimum levels. Relatively clear cut lines of demarcation between and among units have been retained. Management structures have been kept lean and flat, enabling (as well as requiring) significant amounts of hands-on attention and time of corporate executives.

Company executives have described Emerson's position as one in which "we don't have any big areas on which we can rely for growth, but we don't have any big problems either."

Should future growth depend less upon external diversifications and more upon internal synergisms and interdependencies, the existing management structures and processes would likely require corresponding adjustments.

General Bibliography

American Accounting Association. "Report of the Committee on International Accounting." *The Accounting Review, Supplement to Vol. 1973*, pp. 120–167.

Armstrong, Marshall S. "The Politics of Establishing Accounting Standards." *Journal of Accountancy*, February 1977, pp. 76–79.

Benke, Ralph L., Jr., and Edwards, James Don. *Transfer Pricing: Techniques and Uses*. New York: National Association of Accountants, June 1980.

Blake, George B. "Graphic Shorthand as an Aid to Managers." *Harvard Business Review*, March-April 1978, pp. 6–8, 12.

Brown, Alvin. *Organization of Industry*. Englewood Cliffs, N.J.: Prentice-Hall, 1947.

Bursk, Edward C., Dearden, John, Hawkins, David F., and Longstreet, Victor M. *Financial Control of Multinational Operations*. New York: Financial Executives Research Foundation, 1971.

Carrington, Athol S. "Accounting Standards and the Profession—Seven Ages of Development." In: V.K. Zimmerman, ed. *The Multinational Corporation: Accounting and Social Implications*. Urbana, Ill.: Center for International Education and Research in Accounting, Department of Accountancy, University of Illinois, 1977, pp. 41–46.

Cattela, R.C. Spinosa. "An Introduction into Current Cost Accounting and its Application Within Philips." In: *Notable Contributions to the Periodical International Accounting Literature–1975-78*. Sarasota, Fla.: American Accounting Association, 1979, pp. 102–117.

Chandler, Alfred D., Jr. "Management Decentralization: An Historical Analysis." *Business History Review*, Vol. XXX, June 1956, pp. 111–174.

Committee on International Accounting, American Accounting Association. "Report of the Committee on International Accounting." *The Accounting Review, Supplement to Vol. 1973*, pp. 120–167.

Committee on Social Measurement, American Institute of Certified Public Accountants. *The Measurement of Corporate Social Performance*. New York: AICPA, 1977.

Dearden, John. "Appraising Profit Center Managers." *Harvard Business Review*, May-June 1968, pp. 80–86.

____. "The Case Against ROI Control." *Harvard Business Review*, May-June 1969, pp. 124–135.

____. "Limits on Decentralized Profit Responsibility." *Harvard Business Review*, July-August 1962, pp. 81–89.

____. "Problem in Decentralized Financial Control." *Harvard Business Review*, May-June 1961, pp. 72–80.

____. "Problem in Decentralized Profit Responsibility." *Harvard Business Review*, July–August 1962, pp. 79–86.

____. " 'Time-Span' in Management Control." *Financial Executive*, August 1968, pp. 23–30.

Denosowicz, Randolph L. "A Corporate Viewpoint: An Interview with Walter Wriston, Chairman of Citicorp." *Columbia Journal of World Business*, Fall 1977, pp. 125–128.

Dietemann, Gerard J. "Evaluating Multinational Performance under FAS No. 8." *Management Accounting*, May 1980, pp. 49–55.

Drucker, Peter F. "Behind Japan's Success." *Harvard Business Review*, January–February 1981, pp. 83–90.

____. "Managing for Tomorrow." *Industry Week*, April 14, 1980, pp. 54–57, passim.

____. *Managing in Turbulent Times*. New York: Harper & Row, 1980.

Evans, Thomas G., Folks, William R., Jr., and Jilling, Michael. *The Impact of Statement of Financial Accounting Standards No. 8 on the Foreign Exchange Risk Management Practices of American Multinationals: An Economic Impact Study*. Stamford, Conn.: FASB, 1979.

Ewell, Charles M., Jr. "Measuring Managerial Effectiveness in the Hospital: It Can be Done." *Arthur Young Journal*, Summer–Autumn 1978, pp. 24–32.

Ferrara, William L. "Accounting for Performance Evaluation and Decision Making." *Management Accounting*, December 1976, pp. 13–19.

Financial Accounting Standards Board. *Conceptual Framework for Financial Accounting and Reporting*. Discussion Memorandum. Stamford, Conn.: December 2, 1976.

____. *Financial Reporting in Units of General Purchasing Power*. Exposure Draft. December 31, 1974.

____. *Foreign Currency Translation*. Exposure Draft. August 28, 1980.

____. *Statement of Financial Accounting Standards No. 8*. "Accounting for the Translation of Foreign Currency Transactions and Foreign Currency Financial Statements." October 1975.

____. *Statement of Financial Accounting Standards No. 14*. "Financial Reporting for Segments of a Business Enterprise." December 1976.

____. *Statement of Financial Accounting Standards No. 33*. "Financial Reporting and Changing Prices." September 1979.

Fujita, Yukio. "Internal Performance Evaluation in Japanese Multinational Companies." *Collected Papers*, American Accounting Association, Annual Meeting, August 21-25, 1979, pp. 41–44.

Garda, J.A. "The Measurement of Financial Data in Evaluating Overseas Managerial Efficiency." *International Journal of Accounting*, Fall 1976, pp. 13–17.

Goetz, Billy E. "Transfer Prices: An Exercise in Relevancy and Goal Congruence." *Accounting Review,* July 1967, pp. 435–440.

Goudeket, A. "An Application of Replacement Value Theory." *Journal of Accountancy,* July 1960, pp. 37–47.

____. "How Inflation is Being Recognized in Financial Statements in the Netherlands." *Journal of Accountancy,* October 1952, pp. 448–452.

Griffin, Paul A., ed. *Proceedings: Financial Reporting and Changing Prices.* Stamford, Conn.: FASB, 1979.

Haimann, Theo and Scott, William G. *Management in the Modern Organization,* 2nd ed. Boston: Houghton Mifflin Company, 1974.

Hayes, Robert H., and Abernathy, William J. "Managing Our Way to Economic Decline." *Harvard Business Review,* July-August 1980, pp. 67–77.

Henderson, Bruce D., and Dearden, John. "New System for Divisional Control." *Harvard Business Review,* September-October 1966, pp. 144–146, 149–152, passim.

Herzberg, Frederick. "One More Time: How Do You Motivate Employees?" *Harvard Business Review,* January-February 1968, pp. 53–62.

Horngren, Charles T. *Cost Accounting: A Managerial Emphasis.* 4th ed. Englewood Cliffs, N.J.: Prentice-Hall, Inc., 1977.

____. *Introduction to Management Accounting,* 4th ed. Englewood Cliffs, N.J.: Prentice-Hall, 1978.

Janson, Robert L. "Graphic Indicators of Operations." *Harvard Business Review,* November-December 1980, pp. 164–170.

Johnson, Johnny R., Rice, Robert R., and Roemmich, Roger A. "Pictures that Lie: the Abuse of Graphs in Annual Reports." *Management Accounting,* October 1980, pp. 50–56.

Keller, I. Wayne. "All Accounting is Management Accounting." *Management Accounting,* November 1976, pp. 13–15.

Kerley, James J. "Statements in Quotes." *Journal of Accountancy,* July 1979, pp. 79–81.

King, Alfred M., and Evers, Charles J. "Reported Earnings Procedures–Ready for A Review." *Financial Executive,* November 1979, pp. 14–21.

Knickerbocker, Frederick T. Address in: "Proceedings: First Annual International Business Conference." Unpublished. Saint Louis, Mo.: Saint Louis University, School of Business and Administration, December 1, 1975.

Leivian, Gregory M. "How to Communicate Financial Data More Effectively." *Management Accounting,* July 1980, pp. 31–34.

Madison, Ronald L. "Responsibility Accounting and Transfer Pricing: Approach with Caution." *Management Accounting,* January 1979, pp. 25–29.

Malmstrom, Duane. "Accommodating Exchange Rate Fluctuations in Intercompany Pricing and Invoicing." *Management Accounting,* September 1977, pp. 24–28.

Mauriel, John J. "Evaluation and Control of Overseas Operations." *Management Accounting,* May 1969, pp. 35–39, 52.

____, and Anthony, Robert N. "Misevaluation of Investment Center Performance." *Harvard Business Review,* March–April 1966, pp. 98–105.

McInnes, J.M. "Financial Control Systems for Multinational Operations: An Empirical Investigation." *Journal of International Business Studies,* Fall 1971, pp. 11–28.

Miller, Elwood L. *Accounting Problems of Multinational Enterprises.* Lexington, Mass.: Lexington Books/D.C. Heath and Company, 1979.

____. *Inflation Accounting.* New York: Van Nostrand Reinhold Company, 1980.

____. "What's Wrong with Price-Level Accounting," *Harvard Business Review,* November–December 1978, pp. 111–118.

Perlmutter, Howard V. "Alternative Futures for the Multinational." *Proceedings.* Second Annual International Business Conference. Saint Louis, Mo.: Saint Louis University, School of Business and Administration, December 16, 1976, pp. 17–25.

____. "The Tortuous Evolution of the Multinational Corporation." *Columbia Journal of World Business,* January–February 1969, pp. 9–18.

Persen, William, and Lessig, Van. *Evaluating the Financial Performance of Overseas Operations.* New York: Financial Executives Research Foundation, 1979.

Planning, Managing, and Measuring the Business. New York: Controllership Foundation, 1955.

Professional Management in General Electric. New York: General Electric Company, 1954.

Pyhrr, Peter A. "Zero-base Budgeting." *Harvard Business Review,* November–December 1970, pp. 111–121.

Rappaport, Alfred. "Effects of Changing Prices on Management Decision Making and Performance Evaluation." In Paul A. Griffin, ed. *Proceedings: Financial Reporting and Changing Prices.* Stamford, Conn.: FASB, 1979, pp. 37–44.

Reece, James S., and Cool, William R. "Measuring Investment Center Performance." *Harvard Business Review,* May–June 1978, pp. 28–30, 34, passim.

Reporting Transnational Business Operations. New York: The Conference Board, 1980.

Robbins, Sidney M., and Stobaugh, Robert B. "The Bent Measuring Stick for Foreign Subsidiaries." *Harvard Business Review,* September–October 1973, pp. 80–88.

Securities and Exchange Commission. *Accounting Series Release No. 279.* "Amendments to Annual Report Form, Related Forms, Rules, Regulations and Guides; Integration of Securities Acts Disclosure Systems." Washington, D.C. September 2, 1980.

____. *Accounting Series Release No. 280.* "General Revisions of Regulation S–X." September 2, 1980.

____. *Accounting Series Release No. 281.* "Uniform Instructions as to Financial Statements–Regulation S–X." September 2, 1980.

Shank, John K., Dillard, Jesse F., and Murdock, Richard J. *Assessing the Economic Impact of FASB No. 8.* New York: Financial Executives Research Foundation, 1979.

Shank, John K., and Shamis, Gary S. "Reporting Foreign Currency Adjustments: A Disclosure Perspective." *Journal of Accountancy*, April 1979, pp. 59–65.

Solomons, David. *Divisional Performance: Measurement and Control.* Homewood, Ill.: Richard D. Irwin, Inc., 1968.

___. "The Politicization of Accounting." *Journal of Accountancy*, November 1978, pp. 65–72.

Stata, Ray, and Maidique, Modesto A. "Bonus System for Balanced Strategy." *Harvard Business Review*, November–December 1980, pp. 156–163.

Suzuki, Ryohei. "Worldwide Expansion of U.S. Exports—A Japanese View." *Sloan Management Review*, Spring 1979, pp. 1–4.

Vancil, Richard F. "What Kind of Management Control Do You Need?" *Harvard Business Review*, March-April 1973, pp. 75–86.

Vernon, Raymond. "Gone Are the Cash Cows of Yesteryear." *Harvard Business Review*, November–December 1980, pp. 150–155.

Wait, Donald J. "Productivity Measurement: A Management Accounting Challenge." *Management Accounting*, May 1980, pp. 24–30.

Watt, George C., Hammer, Richard M., and Burge, Marianne. *Accounting for the Multinational Corporation.* New York: Financial Executives Research Foundation, 1977.

Wells, M.C. "Profit Centres, Transfer Prices, and Mysticism." *Abacus*, Vol. 4., No. 2., December 1980, pp. 174–181.

Zenoff, David. "Profitable, Fast Growing, but Still the Stepchild." *Columbia Journal of World Business*, July–August 1967, pp. 51–56.

Index